CAMBRIDGE TEXTS IN THE
HISTORY OF POLITICAL THOUGHT

PLATO
Gorgias, Menexenus, Protagoras

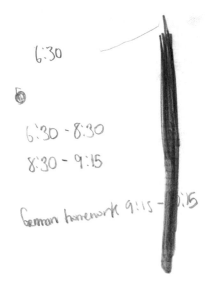

6:30

6:30 - 8:30
8:30 - 9:15

German homework 9:15 - 10:15

CAMBRIDGE TEXTS IN THE HISTORY OF POLITICAL THOUGHT

Series editors

RAYMOND GEUSS
Professor in Philosophy, University of Cambridge

QUENTIN SKINNER
Professor of the Humanities, Queen Mary, University of London

Cambridge Texts in the History of Political Thought is now firmly established as the major student textbook series in political theory. It aims to make available to students all the most important texts in the history of western political thought, from ancient Greece to the early twentieth century. All the familiar classic texts will be included, but the series seeks at the same time to enlarge the conventional canon by incorporating an extensive range of less well-known works, many of them never before available in a modern English edition. Wherever possible, texts are published in complete and unabridged form, and translations are specially commissioned for the series. Each volume contains a critical introduction together with chronologies, biographical sketches, a guide to further reading and any necessary glossaries and textual apparatus. When completed the series will aim to offer an outline of the entire evolution of western political thought.

For a list of titles published in the series, please see end of book

PLATO

Gorgias, Menexenus, Protagoras

EDITED BY
MALCOLM SCHOFIELD

TRANSLATED BY
TOM GRIFFITH

CAMBRIDGE
UNIVERSITY PRESS

CAMBRIDGE
UNIVERSITY PRESS

University Printing House, Cambridge CB2 8BS, United Kingdom

Cambridge University Press is part of the University of Cambridge.

It furthers the University's mission by disseminating knowledge in the pursuit of education, learning and research at the highest international levels of excellence.

www.cambridge.org
Information on this title: www.cambridge.org/9780521546003

© In the translation and editorial matter Cambridge University Press 2010

First published 2010

A catalogue record for this publication is available from the British Library

Library of Congress Cataloguing in Publication data
Plato. [Selections. English. 2009]
Plato : Gorgias, Menexenus, Protagoras / [edited by] Malcolm Schofield;
[translated by] Tom Griffith.
p.   cm. – (Cambridge texts in the history of political thought)
ISBN 978-0-521-83729-3 (hardback)
1. Ethics–Early works to 1800.   2. Political science–Early works to 1800.   3. Rhetoric–
Philosophy–Early works to 1800.   4. Sophists (Greek philosophy)–Early works to
1800.   5. Protagoras.   I. Schofield, Malcolm.   II. Griffith, Tom.   III. Title.
B358.S36   2009
184–dc22   2009028507

ISBN 978-0-521-54600-3 Paperback

Contents

Editorial note	*page*	vi
Introduction		vii
Principal dates		xxxiii
A guide to further reading		xxxvii
Gorgias		1
Dramatis personae		1
Analysis		4
The dialogue		7
Menexenus		115
Dramatis personae		115
Analysis		116
The dialogue		117
Protagoras		137
Dramatis personae		137
Analysis		140
The dialogue		143
Appendix		205
Index		207

Editorial note

The translation (by TG) is made in the case of *Gorgias* from the text in Dodds's edition, and in the case of *Menexenus* and *Protagoras* from Burnet's edition in the Oxford Classical Texts series. The few variations from these adopted here are mentioned in notes at the appropriate points. The notes to the translation (by MS, as with the rest of the editorial matter) have benefited in various ways from TG's scrutiny, and the translations in their final form are the outcome of several rounds of comment from MS and rethinking by TG. Raymond Geuss and Quentin Skinner as series editors made suggestions for improvements to the draft of the introduction, all gratefully implemented. The book is therefore very much a joint production, which owes its origins to a suggestion by Jeremy Mynott, at the time Chief Executive of the Press – to whom also thanks are due.

TG
MS
December 2008

Introduction

The *Gorgias* and the *Protagoras*

The *Protagoras* and the *Gorgias* are not only the longest, but by general agreement the most important among Plato's 'Socratic' dialogues (the quixotic *Menexenus* – on which more later – is another matter). Both present Socrates in argument with leading members of the sophistic movement, questioning the claims to wisdom or expertise that they make. In both Socrates brings the discussion round to his own central preoccupation with living a good life.

But there the resemblances cease. One difference is purely formal. The *Gorgias* (like the *Menexenus*) is written as drama, with parts for Socrates, Gorgias, and various other characters, notably Polus (a follower of Gorgias who has authored a book on rhetoric) and Callicles (apparently a rising young Athenian politician). There are few indications of time or place. For the *Protagoras*, Plato elected for a more complex structure, beginning with a short exchange in direct dramatic form between Socrates and an unnamed companion, which then frames a lengthy report by Socrates, full of circumstantial detail, narrating an early morning visit from a young friend called Hippocrates, and their subsequent encounter with Protagoras and other sophists at the house of the wealthy aristocrat Callias.

The major difference is one of tone. Plato's writing in the *Gorgias* has little of its usual urbanity. The dialogue often strikes readers as a bitter and passionate piece of writing, in fact more bitter and passionate the longer it goes on. It certainly communicates intense intellectual energy with remarkable directness. The *Protagoras*, on the other hand, is composed for much of its duration in a relaxed register of sly comedy. No reader forgets Socrates' rude awakening before dawn, the unfriendly reception he and Hippocrates get from Callias's doorman, the scene that greets them once admitted, or later in the dialogue the elaborate games Socrates plays with a poem of Simonides in apeing sophistic techniques of interpretation. Whereas the *Gorgias* ends with a myth of last judgment, on the last page of the *Protagoras* Socrates imagines the outcome of the discussion teasing him and Protagoras about the contradictions between their respective initial and final positions. Few Platonic dialogues convey so evocatively an intellectual atmosphere: an almost nostalgic sense of the optimistic rationalism of what has sometimes been called the Greek enlightenment, caught at a moment perhaps just before the outbreak of the Peloponnesian War.[1]

Working out why the *Gorgias* and *Protagoras* are so different is an unresolved conundrum of Platonic scholarship. Date of composition might have something to do with it. But for neither dialogue is there any hard evidence about date of composition (with *Menexenus* we are a bit better off). The usual conjecture has been that the *Gorgias* was written later than the *Protagoras*. I think the *Gorgias* is the work of an angry young man, the *Protagoras* the product of more detached middle age.

The sophists

At the beginning of the *Hippias Major* ascribed to Plato, Socrates tells us this about the sophists (282b–c):

> Gorgias, the well-known sophist from Leontini, came here on public business, as an ambassador from his home city – selected because he was the most capable person in Leontini to handle their communal affairs. When he spoke before the *dêmos* [i.e. the popular assembly], people thought he did so extremely well; he made a lot of money by giving demonstrations and associating with the young in private, and left our city in pocket.

Very similar things are then said of Prodicus, especially in relation to a recent visit made to represent Ceos on public business. Subsequently

[1] Although as often Plato is not careful to avoid conflicting chronological implications about the dramatic date: see N.C. Denyer, *Plato: Protagoras* (Cambridge 2008), p.66. For its part, the conversation in the *Gorgias* seems to be envisaged as occurring in the second phase of the Peloponnesian War (for example, Archelaus of Macedon has only fairly recently committed the crimes which brought him to power in 413 BC), but other remarks made in its course have been thought more consistent with an earlier date.

Protagoras – portrayed by both Socrates and Hippias as belonging to a somewhat older generation – is mentioned as having had similar success at making money.

The sophists – in their heyday perhaps in the quarter century 450–425 BC – were public figures of a new kind, given major diplomatic roles by their home cities not because of their aristocratic standing, but on account of their political skills, above all their abilities as speakers. Plato's *Meno* distinguishes them from 'gentlemen' (95a–b). Their success away from their public duties in making money by 'demonstrations' and 'associating with the young' makes them resemble not so much statesmen of previous eras remembered for their wisdom, such as Solon or Pittacus, but a poet like Pindar, remunerated by his royal or aristocratic patrons for the odes he wrote to celebrate their sporting victories at major Panhellenic festivals, or a musician (like Sophocles' teacher Lampros), retained to instruct their children on the *kithara* and in the associated poetic and musical repertoire, evidently regarded as a key element in a sound education (see *Prot.* 326a–b). The sophists' clientele was likewise mostly the aristocracy: as Plato portrays it in the *Protagoras*, the *jeunesse dorée*. Protagoras in the *Protagoras* goes so far as to claim that in previous times poets and musicians and even athletes actually were sophists, 'practitioners of wisdom', but concealed their educational ambitions behind the mask of their craft or practice (*Prot.* 316d–e). No doubt this attempt at assimilation goes too far. But it is significant that in making it Protagoras is effectively claiming for himself a professional pedigree.

The same section of the *Protagoras* makes it clear that being a sophist was a competitive business. Protagoras's teaching will equip a young man for life and politics, whereas a Hippias (he implies) might force on you technical subjects you were glad to have escaped, like astronomy (apparently a favourite with Hippias) and other mathematical disciplines, technical analysis of verse and music, and so forth. This is of course the sales pitch of the first in the field now scenting rivals coming up close behind, and to be taken with several pinches of salt. No doubt it was precisely his polymathic range that would have attracted students to Hippias. Protagoras himself seems to have had wide interests, with critical analysis of the poets prominent in his repertoire. It is attested by Aristotle (*Soph. El.* 14.173b17–22; *Poet.* 19.1456b15–18) that he found mistakes in the very first line of Homer's *Iliad*: use of the imperative mood of the verb 'sing' in addressing the muse (not right for a prayer, only for a command), and its coupling of a feminine adjective with 'wrath' (*mētis*: wrath is something masculine).

This evidently has little connection with the preparation for political activity Protagoras professed to offer. It must have more to do with impressing late adolescents with the application of irreverent ingenuity to something they had been taught when growing up to take as beyond criticism. When Meno says that for Gorgias what matters is making people clever speakers, so that he ridicules sophists who promise to improve them all round (*Men.* 95b–c), this is to be read primarily as Gorgias's way of differentiating himself from the competition. We should not suppose that he was any more single-minded in his interests than they were. The purpose of his philosophical tract *On what is not* (two paraphrases of the work survive) is debatable, but it can have had little to do with training people in rhetoric. In the *Meno* itself Meno claims to have learned from Gorgias views on philosophical topics as diverse as the nature of virtue and the definition of colour.

Is Gorgias legitimately described as a sophist? He is certainly referred to as such in the *Hippias Major* (see p. viii above; *Apol.* 19e–20a probably has the same implication). And if a sophist is someone who undertakes as his profession to impart 'wisdom' for a fee, then application of the label to Gorgias seems entirely apt. But it was called in question by E.R. Dodds, author of the great modern edition of the *Gorgias*. The *Gorgias* itself does of course forge its own formal distinction between sophistry and rhetoric (see 463a–465c), and Gorgias is made to describe himself there as an expert in rhetoric (449a). But there is no independent evidence that he called himself a *rhêtor*, 'orator' (in the dialogue he volunteers it only after Socrates has taken a full page to explain what sort of identification is being looked for); and it is quite likely that the very expression 'rhetoric' is a fourth century coinage. On the other hand, it may be that Gorgias did not claim the title 'sophist' either, as Protagoras evidently did. In conversation with Gorgias's followers Callicles and Meno (*Gorg.* 519c, *Men.* 95b–c), Socrates is made to talk without challenge as though 'sophist' is associated almost by definition with the specific undertaking – from which Gorgias expressly refrained – to 'teach virtue' (in other words, to improve people).

It is otherwise hard to find any significant difference in the general profiles presented to the world by Protagoras and Gorgias. Like other major sophists, both clearly owed their standing to their abilities as performers. In the *Gorgias* Socrates arrives just too late to hear the speech Gorgias delivers. But we can still read his display orations *Encomium of Helen* and *Defence of Palamedes*, both brilliant exercises in theoretically ingenious exculpation, with the *Helen* particularly full of examples of the alliteration and assonance and the highly artificial antitheses which influenced much subsequent Greek oratorical prose. The *Protagoras* does contain a great set piece performance, written by Plato for Protagoras (and presumably in something like his manner), on how it is that most people become civilised even though there are no professional teachers in civilisation. Prodicus was celebrated for his lecture on the choice of Heracles, portrayed as a paradigmatic figure at a crossroads in life who wins the struggle of virtue with vice (see Xenophon, *Memorabilia* 2.1.21–34). The scene became a favourite in Renaissance iconography. From the *Hippias Major* we learn that there were actually contests in oratory of some sort at the Olympic games. Hippias claims never to have been defeated in them. Perhaps Protagoras has these in mind when he talks of 'opponents in argument' in the *Protagoras* (335a; cf. *Helen* 13).

Near the beginning of the *Protagoras* Socrates gives young Hippocrates a warning. Someone who pays a sophist for his teaching is not in the same position as someone who buys food and drink. You can take food and drink home and inspect them before consumption. With a sophist there is no similar opportunity. As soon as you listen, your soul has ingested what you have paid for – whether it is good or bad. On the other hand, it is hard to find anything morally subversive in the claims and arguments Protagoras advances in the dialogue. 'Man is the measure of all things', the famous Protagorean slogan construed as a charter for epistemological and moral relativism in a later Platonic dialogue (*Theaetetus*), makes no appearance and leaves no obvious trace in the *Protagoras*. The *Protagoras* seems to find the sophists more amusing than threatening.

In the *Republic* Socrates acknowledges that most people do think that there are young men who get corrupted by sophists (*Rep.* 6.492a). There is a self-referential resonance in the line he takes himself on the issue: the whims of the Athenian people – in the assembly or in the courts, on huge public juries – do much more damage. When in the *Meno* Anytus (later to figure as one of Socrates' accusers at his trial) claims that sophists plainly bring about the ruin and corruption of those who associate with them (*Men.* 91c), Socrates replies that it is just not credible that someone like Protagoras could have fooled the whole of Greece and got away with making his students more depraved than they were when he took them on – for forty years (*Men.* 91d). Again, there is an obvious subtext. Socrates may not have charged Protagoras's huge fees, but he certainly associated with the young, and might well have looked to the average Athenian as close to being a sophist as made no difference ('Ugh! Sophists!', says Callias's doorkeeper, as he overhears Socrates talking with Hippocrates). The charge of corrupting young people is double-edged. It is what Anytus would file against Socrates for real.

The *Gorgias* on power

Early in the dialogue Socrates puts it to Gorgias that it shouldn't be the practitioner of rhetoric who advises the city on building walls or fitting out harbours or dockyards, but master builders. Gorgias takes this as his cue to 'unfold the power of rhetoric in its entirety'. 'You are aware', he says (455d–e), 'that your dockyards here, and the walls of Athens, and the building of harbours, owe their origin to Themistocles – or in some cases Pericles – and not to the advice of the experts.' Socrates agrees that he heard Pericles himself on the issue of the 'middle' wall. This is a revealing exchange, for several reasons.

First is the contrast with the *Protagoras*. In the *Protagoras* Socrates raises the same point with Protagoras, but in doing so clearly separates out (as doesn't happen in the *Gorgias* passage) technical questions on which expert advice in shipbuilding (for example) is needed and indeed insisted upon by the Athenians, and policy issues on which they think it appropriate to listen to anybody at all (*Prot.* 319b–d). He goes on to mention Pericles, but only as someone who plainly couldn't transmit his own wisdom to his sons. Socrates' object is to give himself a basis for arguing (as he next goes on to do) that the excellence in political judgment Protagoras claims to teach is *not* any sort of teachable skill. In response Protagoras first tells his myth of the origins of civilisation, and then elaborates on it by arguing that the fundamental ethical attributes needed for civilised life (and by implication for democracy) are not specialised skills to be transmitted as such, but generally distributed human propensities that are developed in a whole range of ways by society at large. This turns out to be just the first instalment of the purely theoretical enquiry into the nature of human goodness that will occupy the rest of the dialogue in one way or another. We hear no more about constructing buildings or ships.

Not so in the *Gorgias*. Walls, harbours and dockyards are something to which Socrates will return in talking with Polus (469e), and above all in his conversation with Callicles, when he ends up launching a scathing attack on Themistocles, Pericles, and other Athenian statesmen. These edifices are now treated as the most visible symbols of all that is rotten in Athenian political life, and its concentration not on justice or making the citizens better people, but on popular gratification (see especially 514a–d, 517b–e, 518c–519a). Similarly, in the *Menexenus*'s coolly ironical pastiche of a funeral oration (which Socrates puts in the mouth of Pericles' mistress, the courtesan Aspasia), the rebuilding of the walls and the reacquisition of a fleet in 394–2 BC are represented meretriciously as a final triumph for Athenian political resolve, first epitomised by the great victory over the Persians at Marathon in 490 BC (*Menex.* 245e; cf. 245a).

There is a much more immediate engagement in these dialogues than in the *Protagoras* with politics and with the realities of political power. As Dodds said: 'Men like Callicles did not pay high fees to Gorgias because they enjoyed playing tricks with words, but because they were hungry for power and the new education was "cause of rule over others in one's own city" (452d)'.[2] What gives the *Gorgias* its special edge is Plato's confrontation with the assumptions and aspirations he saw as driving politics, especially the politics of his native Athens (and from the *Menexenus* it is clear that thoughts of contemporary, not just fifth century politics, were nagging in his mind). For that enterprise, it is not the theory of Gorgianic rhetoric as such that is of sole or in the end principal significance, but rhetorical appeal to a mass audience as the principal ingredient in political decision-making. Plato's ultimate target is oratory as actually practised in the Athenian democracy, conceived by its leading practitioners as a form of control (just as Gorgias thought of it), but in truth – so Socrates will argue – ingratiating servility. 'Gorgias' teaching', to quote Dodds again, 'is the seed of which the Calliclean way of life is the poisonous fruit.'[3]

So Gorgias's talk of unfolding the power of rhetoric in fact anticipates the focus of the *Gorgias*'s moral debate. What Socrates will call in question is the very nature of power. The dialogue's key distinction is drawn in his conversation with Polus: is power the ability to do whatever you please (as tyrants and democratic politicians alike assume), or rather to do the good that a rational person will want if they can discern it? Discussion about the distinction and its implications for the evaluation of the life of politics and the life of philosophy, and of the role of justice within them, will be what occupies much of the rest of the *Gorgias*. It culminates in a moral imperative: accept the argument of the dialogue as authoritative, try to win others to it; the alternative is

---

[2] E.R. Dodds, *Plato: Gorgias* (Oxford 1959), p.10.
[3] Dodds, *Plato: Gorgias*, p.15.

worthless (*Gorg.* 526e). Contrast the *Protagoras*, whose final exchanges are the civilities of leave-taking (*Prot.* 361d–362a).

Socrates launches his critique of the conventional notion of power with the paradoxical claim (466d) that 'both orators and tyrants have the least power in their cities' (tyrants and democratic politicians are seen by all parties to the conversation as birds of a feather). The claim turns on what Socrates says next (466e): 'They do virtually nothing of what they will – though they do as they please.' Socrates is prepared to concede that a tyrant or a politician may be able to do whatever he likes: something Callicles will later represent as the freedom of those 'born with a strong enough nature' (484a) if they assert themselves. But they do not necessarily do what they really want – what they will. And if people cannot achieve what they really want, Socrates argues, they do not have much power. In one way or another, this idea will recur again and again in the dialogue.

Some common-sense examples are supplied to provide preliminary clarification of the idea of willing at issue here. In effect Socrates draws a distinction between means and ends. What we will (or at any rate what we will primarily) is the end or rationale for the things we do, not those things themselves: health rather than taking medicine, the reason for going to sea (to get rich), not going to sea itself. And it is because these goals are good that they constitute the rationale for such behaviour – taking medicine, going to sea.

A potential complication rears its head when Socrates goes on to ask (468b): 'So it is in pursuit of the good that we walk, when we do walk, because we *think* it better?' With the parallel question addressed to the behaviour of orators and tyrants we are within sight of the destination to which he is moving. The examples are no longer blandly uncontroversial: 'And do we put to death, if we put to death, and banish, and confiscate property, because we *think* it is better for us to do that than not to do it?' We start to wonder whether 'for the sake of the good' means 'for the sake of what *we think* good'.

Apparently it doesn't. Socrates now quickly gets agreement from Polus that we will something such as putting to death or banishment or confiscation, if and only if putting to death or banishment or confiscation actually *is* beneficial; if it is harmful, it is not something we *really* want – even if we *supposed* we did, and supposed it to be better (468d). And someone who does not do the good he wills doesn't have great power – that is, if we agree with Polus that great power is something good (here the assumption in play seems to be that for power to be something good it would have to deliver something good).

One might put Socrates' view of what it is that we will as follows. It will normally happen that the rationale for our actions is some good (e.g. health), which we ourselves correctly conceive as such; and that good so conceived is primarily what we will. But it may sometimes happen that though we conceive of our actions as achieving by our design some good, we are mistaken. In which case we don't will the outcome they actually achieve. What we will is the real good, not something we merely suppose to be good. Here our will (which is for the good) comes apart from our conception of what the good is. For them to converge we need proper understanding. Understanding is what orators and tyrants lack – but even though their conception of it is wrong, that doesn't mean that they don't will the good at all.

Polus is going to need a lot of convincing that tyrants and orators *are* wrong about what is good or beneficial for them. But it is perfectly understandable that he ends up agreeing rather quickly with Socrates that they would not will what is actually harmful to them. When we go to the doctor, we want our health back, not medicines which will damage us, even if he or we mistakenly conceive them to be conducive to health.

The argument with Callicles

The idea that power is the ability to do just what you please is not silenced in the dialogue forever by Socrates' argument here. Something very like it is reasserted by Callicles, perhaps the most eloquent and passionate of all Socrates' discussion partners in the dialogues, and someone whose view of life has often been justifiably perceived as Nietzschean. Soon after he bursts into the conversation, it becomes clear that the power of the strong to get the better of the weak is what Callicles counts as power – and indeed as natural justice (483b–484c). When at 491e Socrates puts a question – pivotal for the direction the argument then takes – about ruling not just others but oneself, he responds that 'the person who is going to live in the right way should allow his own desires to be as great as possible, without restraining them'. As he sums it up a bit later (492c): 'Luxury, lack of restraint, freedom – given the resources, that is what virtue and happiness are.' In short, power to do what one likes *does* deliver the goods.

Socrates deploys a range of argumentative tactics against Callicles' position. In the initial sequence (492e–499b) the most effective (as Plato represents it) involves getting Callicles to allow that he is equating the good with the pleasurable and the bad with the painful, but then to admit that hedonism is a poor fit with the wisdom and courage Callicles admires in the person who exercises power (497d–499b; cf. 491a–c). For if the good is what makes a person good and the bad a person bad, fools and cowards are going to turn out just as good as anyone else – because they feel as much pleasure. And in Callicles' scheme of things the division between the naturally superior and the naturally inferior is fundamental.

Yet Socrates' success here against Callicles is limited. More immediately, the problem is that it is only in order to allow Socrates' critique to be developed that Callicles agrees to have his position characterised as hedonism: as the equation of the good and the pleasurable (495a–b). Indeed, this is palpably not the way he chose to articulate his view of virtue and happiness when given the opportunity to put it in his own terms (491e–492c). And when he gives up hedonism in response to Socrates' arguments, he asserts that he was never really committed to it in the first place: which rings true enough (499b). He is only really interested in defending a position which emphasises the power to deploy a range of resources and abilities – which clearly for him have a value of their own – in fulfilling desires, and differentiates it from the absence of any such power.

More broadly, there is a radical disjunction between what Socrates sarcastically dubs the 'lower' and the 'higher mysteries' (497c) in the bad-tempered exchange that interrupts the previous stretch of question and answer dialectic (495a–497d). Callicles represents a conception of what it is for argument to be intelligent and accordingly truly persuasive that is incommensurable with Socrates'. He thinks his grand talk about nature and freedom and the strong can dispense with the slow, precise, particular steps that make up Socratic conversation. For Socrates they are all-important; for Callicles they are 'clever stuff', 'drivel', 'little footling questions' (497a–c). Interestingly Gorgias intervenes at this point, making it clear that he wants the discussion completed (cf. 506a–b), and indicating that Callicles must allow Socrates to test him as he wishes. Presumably Plato is signalling a breach of reasonable norms of debate on Callicles' part. We are reminded of the contrast at the very outset of the dialogue between 'demonstration' and 'discussion' (447b–c – where Callicles reports Gorgias as willing to answer whatever questions people want to put to him).

Callicles does not really engage again with Socrates until questions of power are reintroduced into the discussion (from 509b), particularly in relation to tyranny and more generally the political sphere. He responds with enthusiasm to the thought that to have the power to avoid being wronged by others you must either be a tyrant or a friend of whatever regime is in being (510a–b). This response sets up Socrates' final assault on Callicles' position. Preserving one's life at any cost, he suggests, is something a 'real man' (he echoes Callicles' own language: 483a) should forget about. The alternative – for a politician expert in rhetoric operating in a democracy – is surely more unattractive. It can only be assimilation to the values and ethos of the *dêmos* (513a–c). That is why Themistocles, Pericles and the rest have not tried to make the citizens better people, but only looked for ways of indulging their desires – practising rhetoric as sycophancy. This lengthy critique of Athenian politics is cast not in the form of question and answer interrogation, but as a rather magnificent piece of rhetoric (see especially 517b–519d).

Socrates' critique is represented as both a success and a failure. Callicles is made to end up agreeing reluctantly that politics as he conceives it is what Socrates calls flattery or sycophancy. In other words, in the end he accepts the paradox that the exercise of supreme power in a democracy requires you to become the *servant* of the people (521a–b). Or as Socrates had said in his very first words to Callicles (at 481d): 'You have no power to oppose them.' On the other hand, Callicles does not draw the Socratic conclusion that the only basis for a true politics (502e–503b, 513d–e, 521d) lies elsewhere. The ultimate sticking point for him is Socrates' central ethical claim in the dialogue: that doing wrong is worse for the person who commits it than having wrong done to them – with its concomitant, that avoiding punishment for wrongdoing is worse than being punished.

Callicles concedes that *if* these claims were true, then being powerless to avert the harm involved would be a disgrace (508d–509c). But he isn't and can't be convinced that such theses are true (e.g. 510e–511b), or that Socrates really appreciates how nasty the world actually is (e.g. 521b–c; cf. 486a–c). The *Crito*'s Socrates had insisted that one should never do wrong or injure anyone in return for injury. And there he had commented (*Crito* 49d): 'There is no common ground between those who hold this view and those who do not, but they inevitably despise each other when they see each other's way of thinking about it.'

Modern readers of the *Gorgias* have also resisted Socrates' argument (made in the conversation with Polus) that doing injustice is more harmful than suffering it (474c–475e). In making that argument Socrates never explicitly raises the question: 'Harmful to whom?' One might think the answer: 'Harmful to the community and to general respect for law and order' a more obvious answer than: 'Harmful to the agent', which is how Socrates in fact interprets the conclusion.

Here perhaps lies the central puzzle of the *Gorgias*. Its thesis that wrongdoing is worse than having wrong done to you is fundamental to the dialogue's critique of power politics and of rhetoric as its instrument. Socrates' conviction of the truth of the thesis is represented as underpinning his willingness to face death rather than demean himself by resort to sycophancy (521c–522e). He insists to the last (527b):

> Among so many arguments, while the others are proved wrong, this argument alone stands its ground – that we should more beware of acting unjustly than of being treated unjustly, and that more than anything, what a man should practise, both in private life and public life, is not seeming to be good, but being good.

Yet as actually formulated in the conversation with Polus that argument is so obviously questionable. Perhaps this just shows what it is to stake your life on philosophy.

The *Gorgias* and the *Menexenus*

The *Gorgias*'s clearest philosophical and literary affiliations are with the *Apology* (Plato's version of Socrates' speech at his trial) and the *Crito* (where Socrates explains why he must decline an old friend's offer to help him escape the condemned cell). In its way it is as preoccupied with Socrates' life and death as they are. Its delineation of the inevitable conflict between philosophy and the values and forces of politics clearly echoes the *Apology*, likewise its preoccupation with the care and fate of the soul as the proper focus of the examined life. The *Gorgias*'s central moral argument for the proposition that we can do no greater harm to ourselves than commit injustice or try to avoid punishment for it develops a rationale for Socrates' refusal (explained in the *Apology*) to participate in politics ('a person who really fights for justice must lead a private, not a public life, if he is to survive': *Ap.* 32a), and for the *Crito*'s thesis (with the practical consequences Socrates draws from it) that life is not worth living 'with that part of us corrupted that unjust action harms and just action benefits' (*Crito* 47e).

In all these works Socrates takes a clear stand on what he believes in against the world. They do not end in the puzzlement and inconclusiveness characteristic of many other 'Socratic' dialogues, while at the same time they contain no elements of the metaphysics and epistemology of mature Platonic writings such as the *Phaedo* and the *Republic*. It seems likely enough that among other things the *Republic* is an attempt to work out a more deeply considered version of the *Gorgias*'s central argument. That only confirms the impression that the *Gorgias* belongs with the *Apology* and *Crito* in an earlier phase, notwithstanding its inclusion of speculative material such as we get in the passage on geometry and the world order at 507e–508a. We might guess at a date of composition in the late 390s.

There is one other dialogue which has long been perceived as a companion piece to the *Gorgias*: the extraordinary *Menexenus*. If the *Gorgias* analyses rhetoric and attempts to expose its pretensions and contradictions, the *Menexenus* presents a sample rhetorical performance which bears out the diagnosis of sycophancy pronounced in the *Gorgias*. For his sample Plato chooses a funeral oration, at Athens often the occasion for a showpiece assertion of democratic self-identity. In fact he has Socrates pretend that this specimen is partly composed of material originally prepared for Pericles' funeral speech of 431 BC over the Athenian war dead. Thucydides' version of this (2.35–46) is one of the most important moments in his great history of the Peloponnesian War between Athens and Sparta (431–404), designed as a masterly testimony to the liberal ethos of public life and the rationality of political decision-making under Periclean leadership. Socrates claims that Pericles' speech, like the pastiche oration of the *Menexenus*, was actually written by his mistress Aspasia. The subtext is clear: Periclean rhetoric was designed – like his mistress's professional activities – to give its audience one thing above all: pleasure, albeit in style.

Nineteenth-century scholarship doubted the authenticity of the *Menexenus*. But stylistically it is not unPlatonic; and Aristotle twice refers to the work. The oddest of all the dialogue's oddities itself speaks for rather than against authenticity. 'Aspasia' takes the narrative of Athenian military history which occupies the first and longer section of her oration down into the early fourth century (after Socrates' death in 399, of course, and almost certainly after her own, too). It is hard to believe that any forger would have taken such liberties with chronology. It is usually supposed that the latest event 'Aspasia' refers to is the cessation of hostilities achieved by the so-called King's Peace of 387/6, indicating a likely composition date soon afterwards.

Plato was not the only writer of the time to be composing dialogues figuring Socrates. One probable stimulus for the writing of *Menexenus* was the *Aspasia* by Aeschines of Sphettos (now mostly lost). In Aeschines, too, Aspasia was represented as an intellectual in her own right, sharp of tongue and shrewd in public affairs (Lucian *Imagines* 17). Socrates has her interviewing Xenophon and his wife in Socratic style at one point (e.g. Cicero *De Inventione* 1.51–3). What seems likely is that the *Menexenus* seeks to trump the *Aspasia* by making the courtesan not just the apt pupil of Pericles, but herself the composer of his famous funeral oration (as well as the one in the dialogue).

Something else that may have prompted the writing of *Menexenus* was the publication (probably not for actual public delivery) of a funeral oration by the firmly democratic speech-writer Lysias, somewhere near the end of the 390s, like Plato's 'Aspasia' celebrating Athenians who had died in the Corinthian War. In the *Menexenus* there are naturally dominant echoes of Pericles' funeral speech, particularly at the beginning and end of 'Aspasia's' oration, and in the subtleties invested in the treatment of the Athenian political system as aristocracy tempered by democracy (238c–d; cf. Thuc. 2.37.1). But there are striking resemblances with Lysias's, too, as for example the extravagant assessment of the size of the Persian army at Marathon as half a million, a figure not known to any other ancient writer (240a; Lys. 2.21). There are also places where Plato looks as though he may be meaning to question Lysias's account in a different style. A notable case in point is Lysias's extended celebration of the democrats who overthrew the Thirty Tyrants (Lys. 2.61–5). Plato's briefer account compliments the conduct of all parties following the conflict, yet a crucial silence draws attention to democratic perfidy and brutality by dint of simply omitting mention of it (243e–244a).

Plato leaves the reader in no doubt that the oration he writes for 'Aspasia' is satirically conceived. Quite apart from the conceit that she, not Pericles, is the real orator, the opening exchanges between Socrates and the young Menexenus are designed to make the satirical intent crystal clear. Not content with the heavy humour of a Socrates who feels himself growing 'taller, more noble, and more good-looking' whenever he listens to a funeral speech (with the effect lasting for several days), Plato then goes for bathos. He has Socrates dismiss such speeches as invariably ready-made. Every orator will have one prepared for use, and even if improvisation were necessary, they are easy to produce off the cuff.

The speech 'Aspasia' delivers is subtle pastiche, not obvious parody. It takes the usual form of eulogy of Athens and its history, followed by consolation and encouragement for the relatives of those who have died in battle and for the citizens at large. From comparison with other surviving funeral orations, it is apparent that stock tropes of the genre are being deployed throughout. In Plato's variations on those themes will have come some of the bite of the satire – as with the treatment of the restoration of democracy from 403 as compared with Lysias's (mentioned above), or in the extended passage near the beginning on Athenian 'autochthony': their claim to be sons of their own soil, a standard theme developed by Plato more literally and at much greater length than in any other extant funeral speech.

What is most evident to the modern reader is the strikingly partial and chauvinistic character of the historical narrative, a trait common to the genre, here still more exaggerated. Athens is consistently portrayed as heroic saviour and liberator of the Greeks. She shoulders this burden mostly on her own, receives little gratitude for it, and indeed is victimised by other Greek cities. Her control of a large and profitable empire during most of the fifth century, exercised in effect as a form of tyranny (in the words of Thucydides' Pericles: 2.63.2), goes entirely unmentioned. Other uncomfortable truths are similarly suppressed. The disastrous Sicilian expedition of 415–13 is presented as a highly principled – and nearly successful – war of liberation. Defeat at the end of the Peloponnesian War (in 404) is acknowledged, but represented as an act solely of self-destruction: 'Where our enemies are concerned, we remain undefeated to this day' (243d).

This self-deluding strain is sustained in the treatment of renewed Athenian military activity in the 390s. Again the city emerges as heroic saviour of the other Greeks (and even of the old enemy Persia, 'instinctively anti-barbarian' though the Athenians are) – this time against the imperialistic ambitions of the Spartans. Once Spartan aggrandisement has been curbed, the Great King of the Persians starts to fear Athens again, and proposes unacceptable terms for the continuation of the anti-Spartan alliance. Against his expectation there is craven submission on the part of the other Greeks, with Athens alone holding out. However, she emerges from the hostilities with ships, walls and colonies intact.

So 'Aspasia' claims. What all this disguises is that throughout the period in question, the major powers were Persia and Sparta. It was in fact a Persian fleet that the Athenian admiral Conon commanded in 397–393 during a period of naval successes against the Spartans. Conon subsequently persuaded the Persians to hand over a good part of the fleet to Athenian control. It was with Persian financial assistance that the rebuilding of Piraeus and the long walls was completed in 394–391. But it is all too easy to imagine that there were Athenian politicians of the day who were pretending otherwise and trumpeting home-grown Athenian revival. If so, then anger and disgust at the duplicity of their rhetoric will perhaps have been the main reason why Plato decided to write the *Menexenus.*

The exact contours of the disingenuousness in 'Aspasia's' account of the subsequent negotiations with Persia are hard to determine.[4] In 392–391 at least one abortive attempt was made at a peace settlement (perhaps more than one), but on the initiative not of Persia but of Sparta. What is said about the Athenian diplomatic posture would be accurate if the reference is to these negotiations, although if Xenophon is correct (*Hellenica* 4.8.12–15) the other Greek allies also took the same position (Corinth, Argos, the Boeotians). The references to Athenian losses at Corinth and Lechaeum seem to relate to engagements in 394 and 392. All this points to an imagined date for the speech of 391 or 390. Hostilities, however, were not over (as at 245e it is envisaged that they are), even if – as Xenophon reports – large citizen armies were not employed after 392 (*Hellenica* 4.4.14). So if 'Aspasia' is conceived as speaking in 391 or 390, the main self-deceptions are gross enough. The war is *not* over; the negotiations had not been initiated by the Persians, still less from fear of Athens; and Athens' healthier military position is mostly due not to her own spiritedness but to self-interested Persian investment.

Five years later, in 387–386, the Persians *did* initiate negotiations, and an effective settlement (the King's Peace) was achieved, very much on their terms. Despite further military successes against Sparta, by then the Athenian position was weak, even if her negotiating posture – refusal to abandon the Greeks in Asia – remained as 'Aspasia' claims. In 388 the Spartan Teleutias had made an effective raid on the Piraeus, and in 387 ingenious tactics on the part of the Spartan admiral Antalcidas left him (in Xenophon's words) 'master of the sea', i.e. the Aegean (*Hellenica* 5.1.28). If this is the situation obtaining at the imagined date of 'Aspasia's' oration, then Plato must be doing his best to make her try to mask the Athenians' humiliation by recalling military successes now several years past as though they were somehow still fresh. The disjunction between Athens' current political situation as it really was in 386–385 and the story told by 'Aspasia' would have been stark.

---

[4] I am grateful to Robin Osborne, Peter Rhodes and Stephen Todd for discussion and advice on this matter, although responsibility for the summary in the next two paragraphs is mine.

The closing pages of the speech, offering consolation and encouragement, do so rather more expansively than other surviving funeral orations. Some of the language in the opening few sentences (246a–c) carries
Socratic echoes, as does the stress on the need for self-sufficiency a bit
later (247e–248a). We should not infer that Plato is now offering us what
he regards as *good* rhetoric. As the *Gorgias* has argued, Pericles' sort of
rhetoric always aims to ingratiate itself with its audience and give pleasure.
Just as 'Aspasia's' speech attempts to outperform other funeral orations
in its narrative section by offering superior pleasures of self-deception
through the extremes to which it takes historical distortion, so it endeav-
ours to make the pleasures of the consolation it supplies more consoling
and its encouragement more encouraging – adding a few touches of philosophy as needed for the purpose. To repeat, this is not crude parody,
but sophisticated pastiche.

The *Symposium* and the *Protagoras*

The *Protagoras* is among other things an entertainment. It has obvious
affinities with other Socratic dialogues (especially the treatment of courage in the *Laches*), and with the *Meno*, often seen as a dialogue transit-
ional between the early and middle groups, and as taking up as its topic
the question about the nature and consequently the teachability of human
goodness or virtue left hanging at the end of the *Protagoras*. But there are
also some striking connections with the *Symposium*, the supreme entertainment piece in the Platonic corpus.

The most obvious is the overlap in the casts of characters assembled
in Callias's house in the *Protagoras*, to listen to the sophists, and at the
playwright Agathon's party in the *Symposium*, to celebrate Agathon's victory in the dramatic festival. Of the speakers at the party we find (besides
Socrates) Eryximachus and Phaedrus listening to Hippias, and the lovers
Pausanias and Agathon listening to Prodicus (315c–e). The dazzlingly
talented young Alcibiades, ultimately to lead Athens to disaster and
to become a byword for aristocratic corruption, is also there (as in the
Symposium he arrives after all the others). He makes interventions in the
conversation of the *Protagoras* (336b–c, 347b, 348b), and Socrates' erotic
fascination with him (a major theme in the *Symposium*) is the topic which
launches the whole dialogue (309a–b). Among the speakers at Agathon's
party only Aristophanes, the comic dramatist, is absent. But his spirit
hovers over the opening scenes of the *Protagoras*.

There are other parallels. As Socrates in the *Symposium* stands trans-fixed in thought in Agathon's neighbour's porch after the other guests have arrived (*Symp.* 174d–175b), so in the *Protagoras* he and Hippocrates stand in the doorway of Callias's house finishing their discussion (314c). In the *Symposium* the girls who play the reed pipes are sent away so that the men can concentrate on their talk (*Symp.* 176e). In the *Protagoras* Socrates similarly expresses contempt for parties where people cannot generate their own conversation, but pay high prices for girls to play the pipes (347b–e). The *Symposium*'s narrative frames are even more com-plex than the *Protagoras*'s, but here too the outer shell is a conversa-tion between the narrator and an unnamed companion, which similarly enables the creation of the atmosphere of a vanished social and intellec-tual world. At least one computer analysis of the dialogues makes the *Protagoras* and the *Symposium* closer to each other stylistically than to any other dialogues.[5]

If I had to make a literary judgment, I would opt for the verdict that, where the dialogues run parallel, the *Protagoras* is parasitic on the *Symposium*. The reference to Socrates' pursuit of the beautiful Alcibiades which constitutes the friend's opening sally in the *Protagoras* seems designed to remind us of the *Symposium* rather than to intro-duce any theme integral to the dialogue itself. Gathering together all the speakers at Agathon's party except Aristophanes looks like a device for emphasising his implicit presence in the comedy of the opening scenes. In every case the inclusion of the topic or speaker in the *Symposium* is integral to the development of its plot, whereas in the *Protagoras* it is mostly circumstantial detail that could as well be omitted or substituted. Nothing from the point of view of plot would be lost, for example, if some other pair than Agathon and Pausanias were listening to Prodicus. The remarks Socrates makes later about girls playing music or dancing at a gathering certainly make a good point, but they are strictly surplus to the actual requirements of the conversational tactic he decides to employ at that point in the discussion.

My guess accordingly would be that the *Protagoras* was written sub-sequent to the *Symposium*, probably in the late 380s.[6] It will be said that the *Symposium* is a middle period dialogue. But its inclusion in a middle

---

[5] See G.R. Ledger, *Re-counting Plato* (Oxford 1989).
[6] The composition of the *Symposium* is usually taken to postdate the year 385, on account of the apparent reference at *Symp.* 192e to the Spartans' dismemberment of the Arcadian capital Mantinea.

period group is based not on stylistic criteria, but on philosophical assessment. Even then it is only the speech Socrates says he heard from Diotima, with its explanation of how someone may ascend through *erôs* to a vision of the Form of the Beautiful, that marks it out as 'middle period' – not any development in Socrates' own style of argument or in the theses he himself proposes. As often with relative date of composition of Platonic dialogues, there isn't on examination any solid reason for thinking the *Symposium* could not predate the *Protagoras*.

The *Protagoras* against the sophists

If the *Symposium* is written in such a way as to try to convince us of the 'authenticity' of its Socrates, of its representation of the long extinct aristocratic milieu in which he often included himself, and (ultimately) of the truth about Socratic *erôs*, what are we to make of the *Protagoras*'s use of the same cast of characters, the same kind of milieu, and some of the same thematic elements? Repetition is never just repetition. What the *Protagoras* gives the reader – to begin with, at least – is a burlesque version. Indeed the very idea of staging an assemblage of sophists may have been inspired by a comedy. Aristophanes's elder contemporary Eupolis had written a play called *Sycophants*, which included Protagoras among its characters; and since it referred to Callias's recently coming into an inheritance, it might even have been set in his house (Athenaeus, *Deipnosophistae* 5.218c).

A defining moment in the dialogue is the encounter with Callias's doorkeeper ('Ugh! Sophists!'), taken with its immediate sequel. Negotiating your way past a surly and recalcitrant doorkeeper is a trope of Aristophanic comedy, and the comic register thereby established is sustained and richly developed by the portrayal of the leading sophists: to whom we are now introduced (314c–316a). The focus is on the various physical postures of intellectual authority they strike (aided and abetted by their acolytes). Its amusement value is enhanced by recognition that some of the acolytes are figures familiar to us from a completely different setting in the *Symposium*. It is all too believable, but in its exaggeration unbelievable. That sense of contradiction is reinforced by Socrates' representation of the scene (when he gets to Hippias and Prodicus) as a mock descent into Hades, conveyed by allusions to Book 11 of the *Odyssey*. Prodicus and Hippias remain one-dimensional caricatures throughout the dialogue, constructed like all caricatures to capture one highly simplified

perception or (in this case) cultural memory: Prodicus the linguistic ped-
ant, Hippias the vacuous and self-important all-purpose intellectual.

What information Plato had about Protagoras may be doubted.
Presumably he could read some of his writings, and there were doubtless Athenians still alive in Plato's early manhood who could remember
him or something about him. But I suspect he was able to invent the
Protagoras of his dialogue with a fairly free hand, while at the same time
maintaining an illusion of 'authenticity'. The Protagoras he creates is no
comic stereotype (Plato's writing starts to move into a different register once discussion with him begins), but a figure of considerable intellectual complexity, more so than any of Socrates' interlocutors in other
dialogues. It is as though Protagoras and his idea of wisdom (*sophia*) are
being projected on to the screen of the *Protagoras* as the best the sophistic
movement could produce.

Nonetheless Plato's Protagoras is an intellectually evasive character.
And the critique of his views and his intellectual style constituted by
the main body of the dialogue is less than straightforward. The identity
and rationale of its successive explicit components are clear enough. At
the same time its overall direction has a more implicit trajectory that I
shall now try to trace. The subtext to Socrates' demonstration of the
unclarity of Protagoras's thinking about human goodness is the implication that he never quite decided where he stood in what the *Gorgias*
presents as the choice between philosophy and politics, or what in the
Protagoras's own terms might be described as the posture of the sophist or intellectual towards 'the many' – popular belief and culture, and
the democratic environment in which he had to function (in Athens, at
least). For John Stuart Mill this was a central preoccupation of Plato's
oeuvre as a whole: the confrontation between philosophy and what he
called 'commonplace' – 'the acceptance of traditional opinions and current sentiments as an ultimate fact'.[7]

A keynote is struck at the outset with Protagoras's introduction of
himself as someone whose guiding principle is caution (316c–317c). Any
foreigner who associates with young people is liable to be regarded with
resentment and hostility, so he has adopted the policy of talking to them
in the presence of others. And, he says, he takes other precautions, too
(though it is left to us to guess what these might be). It will transpire

[7] Mill, *Collected Works*, Vol. XI, p.403.

that chief among them (at any rate on a visit to democratic Athens) is a refusal to expand on his claim to teach wisdom in the management of domestic and political affairs (318e–319a) – and indeed to bring about daily improvement in those who spend time with him (318a) – in any way that might brand him as anti-democratic. For when Socrates challenges the claim by arguing that experience of the way politics is conducted and politicians behave at Athens (and, he implies, elsewhere) indicates that such wisdom *cannot* be taught (319a–320c), Protagoras's impressive and impressively sustained reply dodges the main issue.

Protagoras first tells a myth about Epimetheus and Prometheus (320c–322d), and then offers an interpretation of the lesson it suggests about moral and political education (322d–328a). The speech is in effect the most penetrating theoretical defence of democracy to survive in Greek literature. Its strength lies in its strategy of rooting democracy in the basic conditions that have to be satisfied if there are to be communities of any size and complexity at all. The social virtue necessary for the existence of a political system is the social virtue sufficient for active participation in citizenship. What *must* be universally distributed to satisfy the existence condition is for that very reason universally *available* for purposes of integrating people into the political body. It follows that if it is to be taught as knowledge, non-specialist conceptions of both teaching and knowledge have to be developed to account for that. We might describe these as performative: teaching is effected mostly by a range of basic methods universally employed for influencing *behaviour*, and what someone educated in this way knows is *how to behave*.

What the speech omits entirely is discussion of the particular intellectual skills or accomplishments which Protagoras will foster in those members of the aristocratic élite – like the young Hippocrates – who come to study with him out of ambition for major roles in politics. All he will now claim for himself is that he is 'better than other people at helping to turn out fine, upstanding citizens', well worth his fee (328a–b). He is silent now on 'good judgment' or 'excellence in deliberation' (*euboulia*), which had been the focus of his initial manifesto. The qualities he does mention are justice, prudence, piety. Wisdom – what Hippocrates wants from him – only re-enters the discussion when Socrates starts to press Protagoras on the unity of goodness (329b–330a). 'There are plenty of people', Protagoras says (now sounding a note with which Callicles would have been sympathetic, and which is struck even more loudly at 349d), 'who are courageous but unjust. Or just but not wise.' Socrates seizes on this at once: so courage and wisdom are parts of goodness too?' The reply: 'Wisdom is the most important of the parts.' Moreover, we might say, wisdom is the attribute democracy has the most difficulty in accommodating within its intellectual and institutional framework – which might have something to do with why Protagoras is made to say nothing about it in his reply to Socrates' observations about what one might infer from democratic practice.

Socrates' intellectualist argument

We have reached the point in the dialogue where Socrates shifts the discussion from the origins, presuppositions and mechanisms of civilisation to logic. 'Just one small additional question', he says (329b) – a Socratic trademark phrase, recognisable as the expression of a properly philosophical desire for clarity and precision. It launches the sequence of strenuous argumentation about human goodness and its parts (if parts are what it has) that will occupy much of the rest of the dialogue. In fact it turns into a small battery of questions, at the end of which Protagoras has given it as his view that the different attributes he has mentioned are not all different names for one and the same thing, but *parts* of one thing (human goodness), which have different functions and characteristics, and which do not necessarily belong together: people may have different combinations among them (329c–330b). In response Socrates will produce a series of considerations that question the existence or nature or degree of difference between the attributes (330b–334c, 349a–351b, 351b–360e).

At the end of the dialogue 'the outcome of the discussion' is allowed a say (361a–c). It takes Protagoras as having attempted in his long speech to make human goodness something other than knowledge. Socrates, on the other hand, it construes as wanting to demonstrate that 'the whole thing' is knowledge, or that 'all things are knowledge – justice and prudence and courage'. This is very much a retrospective reading of the discussion. Its account of Socrates' strategy would be hard to substantiate on the basis of his first round of argument (at 330e–333e), which does not focus on knowledge at all. Instead it privileges the long and complex final argument (running from 351b–360e), and in particular the strategic importance of the passage at 352a–e. Here Socrates indicates that in his view knowledge is what directs and rules a person if he possesses it, so that 'he will never be overpowered by anything which will make him act

differently from the way knowledge tells him to act' (352c): a classic statement of at least one form of Socratic 'intellectualism'.

'Knowledge' (*epistémē*) is Socratic, not Protagorean, vocabulary.
Nonetheless Socrates has begun the passage with an invitation to
Protagoras to 'lay bare another part of your mind for me' (352a) – does
he go along with the contrary view commonly held about knowledge
(what 'the many' think) or not? Protagoras is made to take the point. He
advertises himself as a sophist (once more it is his own position in society which informs his response). So he would be 'embarrassed not to
maintain that of all things human, *wisdom* (*sophia*) and knowledge are the
most powerful'. He *does* lay bare his mind, and allows that the wisdom he
undertakes to impart has to be a form of knowledge, for which he must
make high claims.

So Socrates has succeeded at last in flushing Protagoras out from the
caution and evasiveness that permeated his initial self-introduction and
subsequently his long speech. The implications are now pressed home
(352d–353a). 'The greater part of humanity' has a different opinion,
Socrates points out. 'People say a lot of things which are incorrect', is the
response. And when Socrates asks for help in trying to persuade them
otherwise, Plato makes Protagoras say: 'Why should we examine the
opinion of the majority – people who say the first thing that comes into
their heads.' In other words, if you pressed someone like Protagoras really
hard, he would have been unable to mask the contradiction between his
lucrative profession – teaching wisdom to an élite – and his calculated
articulation of views that falsely suggest a sympathy with the way ordinary people view things.

The ingenious argument Socrates now develops is articulated in the
form (used elsewhere by Plato) of an imaginary conversation. It is conducted between 'the many', on the one side, and Socrates and Protagoras
in concert, on the other – for in virtue of his newly expressed commitment
to the power of knowledge Protagoras can be conscripted to the Socratic
cause. The argument aims to demonstrate the untenability of the popular
view that people sometimes know what is best, but refuse to do it (353c–
357e). Unfortunately it has no agreed interpretation. The main bone of
contention is Socrates' abrupt and initially puzzling introduction into the
discussion of the issue of hedonism (351b–e), and his subsequent use of the
hedonistic premise that the good and the pleasurable are identical. If 'being
overcome by pleasure' is equivalent to 'being overcome by good', the sort
of explanation commonly offered for thinking that despite knowing what

is best, people don't do it, will not work. You would have the absurd result that someone who knows what is best (most pleasurable in the long run, all things considered) deliberately chooses what is – presumably – a lesser good when he could have had what he knows to be a greater.

Hedonism is what the argument relies on. But does Plato (1a) really mean to represent hedonism as Socrates' own ethical position? Or (1b) is his Socrates only assuming its truth opportunistically, to manoeuvre 'the many' into having to agree to what he himself really is committed to: the intellectualist thesis that a person who has knowledge of good and bad cannot fail to act in accordance with it? Or is it even (2) wrong to think that *Socrates* is in any sense assuming the truth of hedonism? Is the point rather that *popular opinion* can be shown to be based on hedonistic assumptions, and so to have no way of avoiding the intellectualist consequence?

I would myself settle for option (1b). The Socrates of the *Protagoras* engages in a good deal of opportunism to unsettle or outflank his interlocutors at various points in the dialogue, not least in his extended parody of sophistic literary interpretation at 339e–347a. Nonetheless what is indisputably true is that the argument concludes by insisting against the majority that *they* have now agreed that (357d) 'it is lack of knowledge that causes people to make wrong choices about pleasures and pains – good things and bad things, in other words'. They do not actually believe that the reason is ignorance, however, says Socrates. And with tongue firmly in cheek, he adds that because of that, they make the disastrous mistake of not paying the sophists to teach them or their children the requisite knowledge. It is hard to avoid an impression of playfulness at this point. But it is playfulness with an edge to it. What Socrates says to 'the many' is what Protagoras – given his newly declared commitment to the power of knowledge – *ought* to say to them, instead of the anodyne and mock-modest words he uttered at the end of his long speech, about having more talent than others at 'helping to turn out fine, upstanding citizens' (328b).

When Protagoras queried whether it was necessary to examine the opinion of the majority, Socrates replied that it has a bearing on the question of the relation of courage to the other parts of goodness (353a–b). The dialogue's final three pages of argument now do apply to this issue the conclusions just drawn about knowledge, pleasure and the good (358a–360e). Socrates turns away from the view of the majority, establishes at the outset that Protagoras, Hippias, and Prodicus all now agree that hedonism is true, and proceeds to show that, given the psychology of choice and action worked out in the proof that knowledge cannot be rendered ineffective by pleasure, cowardice must be nothing but ignorance, and courage knowledge of what is or is not to be feared.

This argument has something about it that disturbs the reader, if not quite in the same sort of way as the argument used in the *Gorgias* to get Polus to agree that committing injustice is worse than having it done to you (474c–475e). The thesis that knowledge is at the core of courage, like every moral attribute, is the destination to which the dialogue's entire train of thought has been tending (as 'the outcome of the discussion' will shortly confirm). But the idea that the cowardly act as they do out of ignorance of what is pleasant (derived without any further elaboration from the truth of hedonism) is provocatively counter-intuitive. Isn't courage pre-eminently a matter of refusing to take the pleasurable option?

Of course, Socrates could have reminded the sophists that short-term pleasure (avoiding the enemy weaponry) is different from the long-term pleasure that someone who voluntarily undergoes anything painful (surgery or military service have been earlier examples) is hoping to secure by that means (354a–c). But he doesn't. He wants to skewer Protagoras with paradox. Perhaps once again the point is that Socrates and his interlocutors – the sophists in this case – have found themselves having to follow the argument where it leads, albeit with Protagoras protesting not unreasonably at Socrates' determination to win at all costs.

Retrospect and prospect

The three dialogues contained in this volume are written each in an entirely different register from the other two. This introduction has attempted to bring out the extraordinary versatility of an author who can exploit the dialogue form in such varied ways for his philosophical purposes. One constant is the combativeness of Plato's Socrates. His ideal is cooperative conversation in pursuit of the truth. But he conducts his conversations within the context of an intensely competitive oral performance culture. Even as he questions the values inherent in the idea and practice of intellectual performance espoused by a Gorgias or a Pericles or a Protagoras, Plato makes him deploy the very techniques of orators and sophists himself – with evident relish – in his efforts to subvert rhetoric and sophistry, whether in pastiche (as in the *Menexenus* and *Protagoras*) or in deadly earnest (as in the *Gorgias*).

So the reader is left wondering whether the realm of dispassionate rational enquiry in which Socrates thinks true philosophy needs to be conducted can ever exist, or whether philosophy must always be at odds with the political and cultural values of the world in which it actually finds itself. This is a question the *Gorgias* itself already asks (in the debate between Socrates and Callicles). Plato would make that same question a major focus of the longest and most important dialogue of his maturity as a philosopher and a writer, the *Republic*.

Principal dates

550   Cyrus the Great, king of Persia, becomes king of the Medes.
546   Cyrus captures Sardis, capital of Lydia.
539   Babylon falls to Cyrus.
525–522   Persian conquest of Egypt.
514   Darius extends Persian rule into Europe, and campaigns north of the Danube against the Scythians.
498–493   Revolt of the Asiatic Greeks against Persia.
490   Darius's expeditionary force against the Greeks is defeated at the battle of Marathon, where Miltiades persuades the Athenians to confront the invaders.
480   The Greeks win a decisive naval victory against the Persian fleet at Salamis, after previous activity off Artemisium (on the north coast of Euboea).
479   Defeat of the Persian army by the Spartans and Athenians at the battle of Plataea in Boeotia.
470s   The Athenians rebuild the 'long walls' between Piraeus and the city, under the prompting of Themistocles, chief architect of the victory at Salamis.
477   Foundation of the Delian league of Aegean cities under Athenian leadership.
477–463   Miltiades' son, Cimon, commands most of the league's naval operations during this period, with a notable victory over the Persians at the mouth of the river Eurymedon (in modern southern Turkey) in 469.

459	The Athenians engage in renewed military activity against the Persians, with successes particularly in Cyprus and Egypt (where the campaign is sustained for a six year period, unsuccessfully in the final outcome).
459–458	The Athenians win victories over her main commercial rivals, Aegina and Corinth, as the first Peloponnesian War (461–446) gets under way.
457	The Athenians fight the Spartans and their allies at Tanagra and (in a decisive victory) at Oenophyta in Boeotia.
450s	Ascendancy of Pericles in Athenian politics begins, to continue to his death in 429.
454	The treasury of the Delian league is transferred to Athens.
447–433	Construction of the Parthenon.
446–445	Athens and Sparta conclude a thirty years' peace.
431–421	Peloponnesian War (first phase: the 'Archidamian' War).
431	Pericles' funeral speech over the Athenian war dead.
430	Athens is struck by plague.
429	Death of Pericles.
425	The Athenians achieve a notable military success on Sphacteria, an island protecting the bay of Pylos in the western Peloponnese.
421	Peace of Nicias concludes the first phase of the Peloponnesian War.
415–413	The Athenian expedition to Sicily.
412	The Spartans make a treaty with the Great King of Persia.
411	An oligarchic revolution installs the brief domination of the 'Four Hundred' in Athens.
411	The Athenian fleet proclaims its allegiance to democracy, and wins a naval battle against the Peloponnesians at Cynossema in the Bosphorus.
410	The Peloponnesian fleet is annihilated at Cyzicus, on the southern shore of the Black Sea.
406	The Athenians succeed in lifting the Spartan blockade of Mytilene on Lesbos at the battle of Arginusae, but fail to pick up their own dead and wounded.
404–403	Following final defeat in the Peloponnesian War, Athens is governed by the 'Thirty Tyrants', under the leadership of Plato's relative Critias. The long walls are dismantled.

403	Civil war leads to the defeat of the Thirty; an amnesty between the warring parties is agreed.
399	Trial and death of Socrates.
397–393	The Athenian admiral, Conon, commands the Persian fleet, and achieves dominance over the Spartans in the Aegean.
395–386	The 'Corinthian War': a complex sequence of hostilities between Sparta and other mainland Greek states.
394–391	Rebuilding of the long walls at Athens with Persian financial assistance.
394	Battle of the Nemea River near Corinth.
392–391	Sparta initiates two successive conferences, in an unsuccessful attempt to achieve a peace settlement with Persia and the other major Greek cities.
387–386	The 'King's Peace', which brings a conclusion to hostilities at a low point in Athenian military fortunes, on terms dictated by the Great King, but more agreeable to Sparta than the other Greek states.

A guide to further reading

General background

For the broad historical context, a good general introduction to ancient Greece is *The Oxford History of Greece and the Hellenistic World*, ed. J. Boardman, J. Griffin, and O. Murray (Oxford University Press 2001). For a more detailed but accessible historical account of the fifth and fourth centuries BC, see P.J. Rhodes, *A History of the Classical Greek World 478–323 BC* (Malden, MA/Oxford/Carlton, Victoria: Blackwell 2006). N.G.L. Hammond, *The Classical Age of Greece* (London: Weidenfeld and Nicolson 1975), remains a supremely readable account. Two important general studies of the intellectual world of the Greeks are K.J. Dover, *Greek Popular Morality in the Time of Plato and Aristotle* (Oxford: Blackwell 1974; repr. Indianapolis: Hackett 1994), and G.E.R. Lloyd, *The Revolutions of Wisdom: Studies in the Claims and Practice of Ancient Greek Science* (Berkeley, CA: University of California Press 1987). The third edition of *The Oxford Classical Dictionary*, ed. S. Hornblower and A. Spawforth (Oxford and New York: Oxford University Press 1996), is the fullest and most convenient single volume general reference work. Two useful further resources are the *Encyclopedia of Classical Philosophy*, ed. D. Zeyl (Westgate, CT: Greenwood Press 1997), and D. Nails, *The People of Plato* (Indianapolis and Cambridge, MA: Hackett 2002), a biographical dictionary of all participants in Platonic dialogues, sometimes distinctly idiosyncratic in judgment.

The Platonic dialogue

There is a convenient and reliable one volume collection of all Plato's dialogues in English translation: *Plato, Complete Works*, ed. J.M. Cooper (Indianapolis and Cambridge, MA: Hackett 1997), which contains an excellent introduction on the main issues to be faced in interpreting Plato. The most recent multi-authored companions to Plato's oeuvre are *A Companion to Plato*, ed. H. Benson (Oxford: Blackwell 2006) and *The Oxford Handbook of Plato*, ed. G. Fine (New York: Oxford University Press 2008), both with helpful bibliographical information. W.K.C. Guthrie, *A History of Greek Philosophy*, Vol.IV: *The Man and his Dialogues, Earlier Period* (Cambridge University Press 1975), is a judicious and highly readable single author survey of the group of dialogues to which our trio belong. For Plato as political philosopher, see M. Schofield, *Plato: Political Philosophy* (Oxford University Press 2006).

In recent scholarship there has been a great deal of debate about the basis for dating Plato's dialogues, and about the distinct but related issue of evidence for developments in Plato's philosophy. The two major recent studies are: G.R. Ledger, *Re-counting Plato* (Oxford: Clarendon Press 1989), and L. Brandwood, *The Chronology of Plato's Dialogues* (Cambridge University Press 1990). Useful briefer treatments are by L. Brandwood, 'Stylometry and chronology', in *The Cambridge Companion to Plato*, ed. R. Kraut (Cambridge University Press), pp. 90–120, and C.H. Kahn, 'On Platonic chronology', in *New Perspectives on Plato, Modern and Ancient*, ed. J. Annas and C. Rowe (Washington, DC: Center for Hellenic Studies 2002), pp. 93–127, a collaborative volume which tackles also developmental questions and debates Plato's use of the dialogue form, another topic much discussed in recent years. On this last topic one particularly influential article has been M. Frede, 'Plato's arguments and the dialogue form', *Oxford Studies in Ancient Philosophy*, suppl. vol. (1992) pp. 201–19, and an important book A.W. Nightingale, *Genres in Dialogue: Plato and the Construct of Philosophy* (Cambridge University Press 1995).

Two sharply contrasting views of Plato's presentation of Socrates in the early dialogues are by G. Vlastos, *Socrates: Ironist and Moral Philosopher* (Cambridge University Press 1991), which takes his aim – unlike works such as the *Phaedo* or *Republic* – to be that of presenting the thought of the historical Socrates; and by C.H. Kahn, *Plato and the Socratic Dialogue: the Philosophical Use of a Literary Form* (Cambridge University Press 1996), which argues that Plato's Socrates is from the beginning a literary construct

Plato generated and developed for his own philosophical purposes. C.J. Rowe, *Plato and the Art of Philosophical Writing* (Cambridge University Press 2007) presents a third view again: Plato's own philosophy is indeed what is being developed, but it remains through and through Socratic, with the dialogues his chosen means of converting readers to Socrates' radical perspective on life. See also A. Nehamas, *The Virtues of Authenticity: Essays on Plato and Socrates* (Princeton University Press 1998). An older classic work, one of the 'few indestructibles', as Guthrie called it, which warms to Socrates more than to Plato, is G. Grote, *Plato and the Other Companions of Socrates*, 3 vols. (London: John Murray 1865).

Socrates and the sophists

The full treatment in W.K.C. Guthrie, *A History of Greek Philosophy*, Vol.III, Part I: *The World of the Sophists*, Part II: *Socrates* (Cambridge University Press 1969), is the most helpful and informative overview. On Socrates there is a sparkling introduction by C.C.W. Taylor, *Socrates: A Very Short Introduction* (Oxford University Press 1998). Another stimulating study is C.D.C. Reeve, *Socrates in the Apology* (Indianapolis and Cambridge, MA: Hackett 1989). A good collection of articles remains *The Philosophy of Socrates*, ed. G. Vlastos (Garden City, NY: Doubleday Anchor 1971). See also G. Vlastos, *Socratic Studies* (Cambridge University Press 1994), which reprints among other papers his important essay 'The Socratic elenchus', first published in *Oxford Studies in Ancient Philosophy* (1983) pp. 27–58.

For the sophists, see further G.B. Kerferd, *The Sophistic Movement* (Cambridge University Press 1981), which presents them as in aspiration systematic philosophers, and organises its material thematically. Four interesting articles on the sophists are: E.L. Harrison, 'Was Gorgias a sophist?', *Phoenix* 18 (1964) pp. 183–92; D.L. Blank, 'Socrates versus Sophists on payment for teaching', *Classical Antiquity* 4 (1988) pp. 1–49; R. Bett, 'The Sophists and relativism', *Phronesis* 34 (1989) pp. 139–69; and A. Ford, 'Sophists without rhetoric: the arts of speech in fifth-century Athens', in *Education in Greek and Roman Antiquity*, ed. Y.L. Too (Leiden/Boston/Koln: Brill 2001), pp. 85–109.

The nature of the rise of rhetoric as an intellectual practice in classical Greece is controversial. The standard account is G.A. Kennedy, *The Art of Persuasion in Greece* (Princeton University Press 1963). More recent studies have argued that its development and theorisation as a technical practice is probably a phenomenon of the early fourth century: see T. Cole, *The Origins of Rhetoric in Ancient Greece* (Baltimore and London: Johns Hopkins University Press 1991), and E. Schiappa, *The Beginnings of Rhetorical Theory in Classical Greece* (Yale University Press: New Haven and London 1999). H. Yunis, *Taming Democracy: Models of Political Rhetoric in Classical Athens* (Ithaca, NY and London: Cornell University Press 1996) studies rhetoric in its political context: Chapters 5 and 6 are devoted to the *Gorgias*.

The *Gorgias*

E.R. Dodds, *Plato: Gorgias* (Oxford: Clarendon Press 1959) is one of the great modern editions of a classical Greek text. Its introduction (like the appendix on Callicles and Nietzsche) could still hardly be bettered. The commentary provides lucid summaries of each section of argument, together with an overview of the problems it presents or the issues raised in that section. Both are thoroughly accessible to readers who may not wish or be able to consult the detailed discussion of particular Greek expressions that follows. The extensive notes to T.H. Irwin (trans.), *Plato: Gorgias* (Oxford: Clarendon Press 1979) supply a detailed philosophical analysis and critique of the arguments of the dialogue. C.H. Kahn, 'On the relative date of the *Gorgias* and the *Protagoras*', *Oxford Studies in Ancient Philosophy* 6 (1988) pp. 69–102, defends the view of the relative chronology of the two dialogues adopted in this volume. Chapter 4 of J. Ober, *Political Dissent in Democratic Athens: Intellectual Critics of Popular Rule* (Princeton University Press 1998) situates the *Gorgias* in its political context. See also an interesting essay by J.P. Euben, 'Democracy and political theory', in *Athenian Political Thought and the Reconstruction of American Democracy*, ed. J.P. Euben, J.P. Wallach, and J. Ober (Ithaca, NY and London: Cornell University Press 1994), pp. 198–226. The character of the Socratic argumentation in the dialogue and of Polus's and Callicles' resistance to it has been the subject of a good deal of recent discussion. C.H. Kahn, 'Drama and dialectic in Plato's *Gorgias*', *Oxford Studies in Ancient Philosophy* 1 (1983) pp. 75–121, explores what are diagnosed as 'personal and logical elements' in the confrontation. R. McKim, 'Shame and truth in Plato's *Gorgias*', in *Platonic Writings, Platonic Readings*, ed. C.L. Griswold (New York and London: Routledge 1988), pp. 34–48, sees shaming rather than logic as Socrates' decisive weapon, particularly against Polus. Studies that concentrate more on the ineffectiveness of Socratic dialectic in the dialogue are D. Scott, 'Platonic pessimism and moral education', *Oxford Studies in Ancient Philosophy* 17 (1999) pp. 15–36, and R. Woolf, 'Callicles and Socrates: Psychic (dis)harmony in the *Gorgias*', *Oxford Studies in Ancient Philosophy* 18 (2000) pp. 1–40. The truth claims Socrates makes at *Gorgias* 505e–509c are examined by C. Gill, 'Form and outcome of arguments in Plato's *Gorgias*', in *Gorgias-Menon; selected Papers from the Seventh Symposium Platonicum*, ed. M. Erler and L. Brisson (Sankt Augustin: Academia Verlag 2007), pp. 62–5.

A major study which focuses on Socrates' critiques of Gorgias and Callicles, interesting particularly for its distinction between Socratic and Calliclean psychology, is J.M. Cooper, 'Socrates and Plato in Plato's *Gorgias*', in his *Reason and Emotion: Essays on Ancient Moral Psychology and Ethical Theory* (Princeton University Press 1999), pp. 29–75. On Gorgias and Plato's Gorgias see N. Notomi, 'Plato's critique of Gorgias: power, the other, and truth', in *Gorgias-Menon; Selected Papers from the Seventh Symposium Platonicum*, ed. M. Erler and L. Brisson (Sankt Augustin: Academia Verlag 2007), pp. 57–61; and more fully Chapters 1 to 3 of R. Wardy, *The Birth of Rhetoric: Gorgias, Plato and their Successors* (London and New York: Routledge 1996). The pivotal argument about the nature of power in the Polus conversation is the subject of two important articles: T. Penner, 'Desire and power in Socrates: the argument of *Gorgias* 466a–468e that orators and tyrants have no power in the city', *Apeiron* 24 (1991) pp. 147–202; H. Segvic, 'No one errs willingly: the meaning of Socratic intellectualism', *Oxford Studies in Ancient Philosophy* 19 (2000) pp. 1–45, which also discusses the treatment of the power of knowledge in the *Protagoras*. The argument which forces Polus to concede that doing injustice is more harmful than having it done to you is the subject of G. Vlastos, 'Was Polus refuted?', *American Journal of Philology* 88 (1967) pp. 454–60.

Callicles' view of justice is set in its sophistic context by D.J. Furley, 'Antiphon's case against justice', in his *Cosmic Problems* (Cambridge University Press 1989), pp. 66–76 (as by Guthrie and Kerferd in their books on the sophists listed above). On Callicles' hedonism (and its relationship with the hedonism developed in the *Protagoras*) the most helpful study remains J.C.B. Gosling and C.C.W. Taylor, *The Greeks on Pleasure* (Oxford: Clarendon Press 1982), Chapter 4. On his love of the people see R. Kamtekar, 'The profession of friendship: Callicles, democratic politics, and rhetorical education in Plato's *Gorgias*', *Ancient*

Philosophy 25 (2005) pp. 319–39. The final myth is the subject of a far-reaching study, exploring material in the Polus and Callicles conversations also, by D. Sedley, 'Myth, punishment and politics in the *Gorgias*', in *Plato's Myths*, ed. C. Partenie (Cambridge University Press 2009), pp. 51–76.

The *Menexenus*

The Budé edition of L. Méridier (Greek text with facing French translation) has a full and highly informative introduction, which discusses with excellent judgment all the main aspects of the dialogue and the issues it raises. It is available in *Platon: Oeuvres Complètes*, V.1: *Ion, Ménexène, Euthydème* (Paris: Société d'Édition 'Les Belles Lettres' 1931). The secondary literature is relatively disappointing, but there is a major historical and literary study of the Athenian funeral oration, which situates the dialogue in its political context: N. Loraux, *The Invention of Athens: The Funeral Oration in the Classical City* (Princeton University Press 1986). A briefer but excellent account of the same topic, focusing on the *Menexenus* as an implicit commentary on the genre, is R. Thomas, *Oral Tradition and Written Record in Classical Athens* (Cambridge University Press 1989), Chapter 4. There is an older study, still well worth consulting, by C.H. Kahn, 'Plato's funeral oration: the motive of the *Menexenus*', *Classical Philology* 58 (1963) pp. 220–34. A useful recent discussion is Chapter 7 of S.S. Monoson, *Plato's Democratic Entanglements: Athenian Politics and the Practice of Philosophy* (Princeton University Press 2000). M.M. Henry, *Prisoner of history: Aspasia of Miletus and her biographical tradition* (New York: Oxford University Press 1995) is an interesting read.

The *Protagoras*

For a full and detailed philosophical commentary on the *Protagoras* there is an excellent resource in C.C.W. Taylor (trans.), *Plato: Protagoras* (Oxford: Clarendon Press 1976; rev. edn. 1991). The Greek text is edited with introduction and extensive notes by N.C. Denyer, *Plato: Protagoras* (Cambridge University Press 2008). The most helpful and stimulating philosophical assessment of the dialogue as a whole remains the long introduction by G. Vlastos to a revision of Benjamin Jowett's translation by M. Ostwald: *Plato: Protagoras* (Indianapolis and New York:

Bobbs-Merrill 1956). My own discussion of the dialogue here is particularly indebted to the introduction by M. Frede in S. Lombardo and K. Bell (trans.), *Plato: Protagoras* (Indianapolis and Cambridge, MA: Hackett 1992). Protagoras's 'great speech' is discussed by Guthrie and Kerferd in their books on the sophists. For a more recent treatment, with a useful review of the scholarly literature, see W.J. Prior, 'Protagoras's great speech and Plato's defense of Athenian democracy', in *Presocratic Philosophy: Essays in Honor of Alexander Mourelatos*, ed. V. Caston and D.W. Graham (Aldershot: Ashgate 2002), pp. 313–27.

A lucid critical overview of the Socratic arguments of the *Protagoras*, as a progression from the 'merely dialectical' to the 'demonstrative or didactic', is provided by J. Allen, 'Dialectic and virtue in Plato's *Protagoras*', in *The Virtuous Life in Greek Ethics*, ed. B. Reis (Cambridge University Press 2006), pp. 6–31. The Socratic thesis of the unity of virtue has been much debated in recent scholarship, beginning with an article by G. Vlastos, 'The unity of the virtues in the *Protagoras*', *Review of Metaphysics* 25 (1971–2) pp. 415–58, reprinted in his *Platonic Studies* (Princeton University Press 1981 (2nd edn)), pp. 221–65, with a vigorous reply by T. Penner, 'The unity of virtue', *Philosophical Review* 82 (1973) pp. 35–68, reprinted in *Essays on the Philosophy of* Socrates, ed. H.H. Benson (New York and Oxford: Oxford University Press 1992), pp. 162–84, and in *Plato 2: Ethics, Politics, Religion, and the Soul*, ed. G. Fine (Oxford University Press 1999), pp. 78–104. The most recent major study, reviewing previous literature, is D. O'Brien, 'Socrates and Protagoras', *Oxford Studies in Ancient Philosophy* 24 (2003) pp. 59–131. On the Simonides' poem episode and the subsequent remarks on musical entertainment, see D. Frede, 'The impossibility of perfection: Socrates' criticism of Simonides' poem in the *Protagoras*', *Review of Metaphysics* 39 (1985–6) pp. 713–53.

The vexed question of Socrates' stance on hedonism has likewise been frequently discussed. The view that he should not be interpreted as himself subscribing to hedonism in the *Protagoras* is argued (for example) by D. Zeyl, 'Socrates and hedonism: *Protagoras* 351b–358d', *Phronesis* 25 (1980) pp. 250–69. A contrary view is taken by M.C. Nussbaum, *The Fragility of Goodness* (Cambridge University Press 1986), Chapter 4. C.C.W. Taylor suggests that Plato deliberately left the matter indeterminate: 'The hedonism of the *Protagoras* reconsidered', in *Plato's Protagoras: Proceedings of the Third Symposium Platonicum Pragense* (Prague: Oikoumenê 2003), pp. 148–64. On Socrates' no less frequently analysed argument that knowledge cannot be overcome by pleasure, see besides Segvic's article (listed under *Gorgias* above) the recent contributions of R. Woolf, 'Consistency and akrasia in Plato's *Protagoras*', *Phronesis* 47 (2002) pp. 224–52, and D. Wolfsdorf, 'The ridiculousness of being overcome by pleasure: *Protagoras* 352b1–358d4', *Oxford Studies in Ancient Philosophy* 31 (2006) pp. 113–36.

Gorgias

Dramatis personae

Dates of birth and death given below are conjectural, except for Socrates.

CALLICLES His boyfriend Demos, son of Plato's stepfather Pyrilampes, was in Dodds's words (*Plato: Gorgias*, p.261, relying here primarily on Aristophanes' *Wasps* 98) 'a leading beauty about 422'. On usual assumptions about relative ages of lover and beloved, we might infer that Callicles was probably in his mid to late twenties at the same point in time. Although his ambition to succeed in politics makes Socrates describe him as lover of the Athenian demos (punning on Demos), this behaviour must be interpreted as opportunistic on Callicles' part. The views Plato attributes to him are anything but democratic. And it is probably significant that of the friends of Callicles mentioned at 487c, one at least – Andron – is known to have been a member of the short-lived oligarchic regime of the Four Hundred in 411, and the other two probably to be identified with Athenians known from other evidence to have been wealthy men. There is no trace of Callicles in history outside the *Gorgias*. It seems likely that for whatever reason his ambitions were unfulfilled.

CHAEREPHON (467–401) One of Socrates' oldest and closest friends, and a well-known figure in the Athens of the Peloponnesian War, frequently the topic of jokes on the comic stage, perhaps in part because of his demonic energy (*Apology* 21a, *Charmides* 153b).

Aristophanes treats him as Socrates' partner in running the bogus philosophical school portrayed in the *Clouds* of 423 BC. Plato's *Apology* tells us that it is he who consults the Delphic oracle and is told that there is nobody wiser than Socrates. Chaerephon went into exile with other democrats when the regime of the Thirty seized political control in Athens in 404, and was among those who returned under the leadership of Thrasybulus the following year. But by the time of Socrates' trial (399) he was dead.

GORGIAS (485–380) In 427 led a delegation to Athens from his home city of Leontini in Sicily to enlist support against its neighbour Syracuse. His speech on that occasion is said to have dazzled the Athenians with what was to them its novel use of balancing antitheses, assonance, and rhyming endings. These and other artifices are apparent in his surviving display orations, especially *Defence of Palamedes* and *Encomium of Helen*, and were hugely influential on writers as diverse as Agathon (who is made to speak Gorgianic prose at its most relentless at *Symposium* 197c–e), Thucydides, Lysias, and Isocrates. The *Gorgias* is clearly reacting against Gorgias's basic conception of the art of speech as 'incantatory power' enchanting, persuading, and transporting the soul by its 'bewitchment' (*Helen* 10). The fictitious second visit to Athens that the dialogue stages, perhaps fifteen or so years on from 427, imagines what might be the logical sequel to the first – as an occasion not for enchantment, but for vigorous disagreement.

POLUS A professional teacher of rhetoric, like his idol Gorgias from Sicily, though in his case from the city of Acragas (modern Agrigento). He is portrayed in the *Gorgias* as thoroughly convinced that rhetoric is the key to power, although there is no strong suggestion that he had political ambitions for himself. Polus is a young man: Socrates puns on his name – he behaves like the colt (*pôlos*) that he is (463e). However, he is spoken of as already the author of a handbook on rhetoric (462b), and the speech to Chaerephon about the basis of the arts and sciences that Plato gives him at 448c is obviously designed to give a flavour of what the book was like. Elsewhere Socrates quotes some of his technical vocabulary: 'reduplication', 'sententiousness', 'imagery' (*Phaedrus* 267b–c). Whether Polus's book would really have been available for Socrates to read in (say) 410 BC, or alternatively a fourth century production, is impossible to know, given Plato's insouciance in matters of chronological consistency.

SOCRATES (469–369) The *Gorgias*'s Socrates resembles the Socrates of the *Apology* and the *Crito* in holding firm views about the philosophical life (to which his passionate commitment is explicit), and about what it requires of us, especially in regard to justice and injustice. In its way, the *Gorgias* is as much preoccupied with his trial and death as are those earlier works. On the other hand, as the sophistic intellectual style seems to rub off on Socrates himself in the *Protagoras*, so too does the rhetorical style of his interlocutors in the *Gorgias*. Although Socrates here deprecates the use of long speeches instead of proper conversation, Plato makes him quite self-consciously adopt this mode of argument himself, and in fact there is a great deal of sustained Socratic rhetoric of various sorts (including allegory and myth) in the later stages of the dialogue.

Analysis

447a–e – The initial encounter
447c–461b – Conversation with Gorgias
- *447c–449c:* Gorgias's art: rhetoric
- *449c–451a:* Defining rhetoric: speech
- *451a–453a:* Defining rhetoric: persuasion and power
- *453a–455a:* Defining rhetoric: the function of persuasion
- *455a–457c:* Defining rhetoric: its universal scope and moral status
- *457c–458e:* Interlude: the nature of philosophical discussion
- *458e–459c:* Examining rhetoric: persuading without knowledge
- *459c–461b:* Examining rhetoric: knowledge of justice and injustice, and its consequences for rhetoric

461b–481b – Conversation with Polus
- *461b–463a:* Socrates on rhetoric: an unscientific technique for producing pleasure – sycophancy
- *463b–466a:* Socrates on rhetoric: classification of forms of sycophancy
- *466a–468e:* Socrates on power: why orators and tyrants have little power
- *468e–470e:* Socrates on power: why justice is key to securing benefit and happiness
- *471a–472c:* Interlude: rhetorical and dialectical refutation
- *472d–476a:* Proof that doing injustice is worse than suffering it
- *476a–479e:* Proof that escaping punishment is worse than being punished
- *480a–481b:* Socrates on rhetoric: its proper use is to expose crimes of friends and ensure enemies are not punished

481b–527c – Conversation with Callicles
- *481b–482c:* Philosophy vs rhetoric: Socrates' challenge to Callicles
- *482c–484c:* Callicles on power
- *484c–486d:* Rhetoric vs philosophy: Callicles' reply to Socrates
- *486d–488b:* Interlude: Socrates on the real question, of how to live one's life
- *488b–491d:* Examining Callicles' thesis: who are the better and superior?
- *491d–492e:* Callicles on the power to satisfy one's desire
- *492e–494e:* Socrates' critique (i): the leaky jar analogy

- *495a–497d:* Socrates' critique (ii): proof that because pleasure and pain can coexist, hedonism is false
- *497d–499b:* Socrates' critique (iii): proof that courage and wisdom would be devalued if hedonism is true
- *499b–500a:* Callicles abandons hedonism
- *500a–503d:* Distinguishing good from bad rhetoric: critique of rhetoric as sycophancy
- *503d–505b:* Distinguishing good from bad rhetoric: order and justice and restraint in the soul
- *505b–506c:* Interlude: Callicles withdraws from the conversation
- *506c–509a:* Socrates recapitulates and develops his thesis that happiness comes from restraint and justice
- *509b–c:* Power: Callicles agrees that inability to avert what harms us most is most shameful
- *509c–511a:* Power: friendship with tyrants or the current regime
- *511a–513c:* Rhetoric: if self-preservation is the goal, sycophancy is the only option for the orator
- *513c–515b:* Politics: the real test of a politician is, has he made the citizens better?
- *515b–519a:* Politics: the test is failed by Themistocles, Pericles, and other celebrated Athenian policians
- *519b–520e:* Politics: the analogy between politicians and sophists
- *521a–522e:* Politics: Socrates is the only true politician in Athens, incapable of saving his life by sycophancy
- *523a–524a:* The myth: narrative
- *524a–525d:* The myth: the way punishment benefits the soul
- *525c–527a:* The myth: prospects for politicians and philosophers
- *527a–e:* Resumé of the entire argument of the dialogue

Gorgias

CALLICLES: You're in nice time, Socrates. For a war or battle, as the 447
saying goes.

SOCRATES: Does that mean we're too late? Have we missed the feast, as
they say?

CALLICLES: Yes, and what a feast of culture it was! Gorgias has just
been putting on a wonderfully varied demonstration for us.

SOCRATES: Not my fault, Callicles. Blame Chaerephon here. He kept us
hanging around in the agora.[1]

CHAEREPHON: Don't worry, Socrates. Let me also be the one to put b
things right. Gorgias is a friend of mine. He'll put on a demonstration for
us – now, if you like, or, if you prefer, some other time.

CALLICLES: Is that it, Chaerephon? Does Socrates want to hear Gorgias?

CHAEREPHON: That's exactly what we are here for.

CALLICLES: Well, any time you care to come here to my house. Gorgias
is staying with me. He'll put on a demonstration for you.

SOCRATES: Thank you, Callicles. But would he prepared to have a
discussion with us? I want to learn from him what the power of the
man's art is, and what it is he promises and teaches. The other stuff c
– the demonstration – well, he can put that on another time, as you
suggest.

CALLICLES: Nothing like asking the man himself, Socrates. Indeed, that
was one feature of his demonstration. He's just been telling the people
indoors to ask whatever question any of them wanted, and saying he
would answer all questions.[2]

SOCRATES: That's a good suggestion. Ask him, Chaerephon.

CHAEREPHON: Ask him what?

SOCRATES: What he is.   d

CHAEREPHON: What do you mean?

---

[1] The agora was the main public space at or near the centre of an ancient Greek city, where
people would congregate and talk, and where a good deal of commercial exchange took
place. Hanging about in the agora is characteristic of the demotic component of Socrates'
lifestyle.

[2] Socrates and Chaerephon have evidently made for a gymnasium or other public building
where a lecture by Gorgias has been advertised. They appear to have met Callicles emerging, ahead of Gorgias (and no doubt others of the company), perhaps in the portico of
the building. But Gorgias has by now come out himself, and is free enough of immediate
company for Chaerephon to be able to put a question to him without any preamble.

SOCRATES: Well, suppose he were in fact a maker of shoes, the reply he'd give, I imagine, would be that he was a leather cutter. Or do you not see what I'm getting at?

CHAEREPHON: No, I do see. I'll ask him. Tell me, Gorgias, is Callicles here telling the truth when he says you promise to answer whatever question anyone asks you?

448 GORGIAS: Yes, Chaerephon, he is telling the truth. That is indeed exactly the promise I was making just now. And I can tell you that it's many years now since anybody asked me anything new.

CHAEREPHON: In that case, Gorgias, I'm sure you'll have no trouble answering.

GORGIAS: By all means put it to the test, Chaerephon.

POLUS: For heaven's sake, Chaerephon. Why not ask me, if it's all the same to you? Gorgias has just been explaining all sorts of things. He's really had enough, in my view.

CHAEREPHON: What, Polus? You think you can answer better than Gorgias?

b POLUS: Does that matter, if my answer's good enough for you?

CHAEREPHON: Not in the least. If that's what you want, you answer.

POLUS: Ask away.

CHAEREPHON: Very well, here goes. If Gorgias were in fact an expert in the science[3] in which his brother Herodicus is an expert, what would be the right thing for us to call him? Wouldn't we call him the same thing we call Herodicus?[4]

POLUS: We certainly would.

CHAEREPHON: In which case, we wouldn't go far wrong in calling him a doctor.

POLUS: Indeed.

CHAEREPHON: And if he were an expert in the art practised by Aristophon the son of Aglaophon, or his brother, what would be the correct thing for us to call him?

---

[3] 'Science' here translates Greek *technē*, from which English 'technical', 'technique', 'technology' derive. Sometimes 'art' or 'art and/or science' is more appropriate. 'Craft' or 'skill' (but see 462c below) might on occasion be a workable rendering. Polus's thesis that 'experience is what makes science' (in Aristotle's formulation: *Metaph.* 1.1, 981a3–5) may have been inspired by ideas of the Presocratic Anaxagoras: see further notes on 462c, 465d.

[4] This Herodicus is not to be confused with the more famous physician of the same name (mentioned at *Protagoras* 316e). Gorgias reintroduces his brother into the conversation later on (456a–b). Aristophon's more famous brother was the painter Polygnotus, an associate of the Athenian politician Cimon.

8

POLUS: A painter, obviously.   c

CHAEREPHON: As it is, however, since he is – well, what art or science *is* he an expert in? What *would* be the right thing for us to call him?

POLUS: Chaerephon, there are many arts and sciences among men. They have been discovered experimentally, through experiences. Experience makes our life advance scientifically, lack of experience haphazardly. Among all these arts and sciences, some people are involved in one, some in another, but the best are the preserve of the best people, of whom Gorgias here is one, and the art he is involved in the finest there is.[5]

SOCRATES: Well, that's quite a way with words Polus seems to have d developed, Gorgias. For what it's worth. But he's not keeping his promise to Chaerephon.

GORGIAS: How exactly is he not keeping it, Socrates?

SOCRATES: I don't think he's even begun to answer the question that was asked.

GORGIAS: *You* ask him then, if you prefer.

SOCRATES: Not if you're willing to answer yourself. I'd much rather ask you. It's quite obvious, even from the little he has said, that Polus has had more practice at what is known as rhetoric than at discussing things.

POLUS: Why, Socrates?   e

SOCRATES: Because, Polus, Chaerephon asked you what art or science Gorgias was expert in, and you make a speech in praise of his art – as if someone were criticising it – but you didn't answer the question '*what* is it?'

POLUS: Yes, I did. Didn't I say it was the finest?

SOCRATES: That's certainly what you said. But nobody asked what Gorgias' art was like; they asked what it was, and what we should be calling Gorgias. Think of the examples Chaerephon offered you earlier, and the excellent, brief answers you gave him, and in the same way now tell us what Gorgias' art is, and what we should be calling him. Or better, 449 tell us yourself, Gorgias, what we should call you, and on the strength of expertise in what art?

GORGIAS: The art of rhetoric, Socrates.

---

[5] Polus's reply to Chaerephon is couched in a highly artificial rhetorical style modelled on Gorgias's own (as attested in his surviving display speeches, such as *Encomium of Helen*), in sharp contrast to the informal conversational Greek all speakers have employed up to this point. Socrates regards it as inappropriate for 'discussing things' (compare his contrast at 447b–c between 'demonstration' and 'discussion', *dialegesthai*).

SOCRATES: In which case we should call you an orator?

GORGIAS: Yes. And a good one, Socrates, if you want to call me what, in Homer's phrase, 'I make it my boast' to be.

SOCRATES: Yes, that's what I want.

GORGIAS: Then call me that.

b SOCRATES: And are we to say you have the ability to turn others into good orators as well?

GORGIAS: That is exactly what I claim – not just here today, but in other places I've been to as well.[6]

SOCRATES: Well then, Gorgias, would you be prepared to go on with the kind of discussion we are having at the moment – now asking a question, now answering one – and put off to another time the kind of lengthy disquisition Polus made a start on? Be true to your promise, and be prepared to give a short answer to what is being asked.

GORGIAS: There are some answers, Socrates, which necessarily call for c a lengthy explanation. All the same, I will try to answer as concisely as possible. That is another of my claims, actually, that no-one can match me for conciseness of speech.[7]

SOCRATES: Well, that's certainly what we need, Gorgias. Please give us a demonstration of exactly that – of speaking concisely. Speaking at length can wait for another time.

GORGIAS: I will do that. And you will agree that you have never heard so concise a speaker.

SOCRATES: Let's make a start, then. You say you're an expert in the art d of rhetoric, and that in addition to that you can turn someone else into an orator as well. Now, this rhetoric – what kind of thing is it actually concerned with? For example, the art of weaving is concerned with the production of clothes, isn't it?

GORGIAS: Yes.

SOCRATES: And the art of music with the making of tunes?

GORGIAS: Yes.

SOCRATES: My word, Gorgias, I do like your answers. They are the shortest anyone could possibly give.

GORGIAS: Yes, Socrates, I think I'm making a pretty good job of it.

SOCRATES: And you're right. So come on, give me the same kind of answer about rhetoric as well. What kind of thing is it knowledge of?

---

[6] Like Protagoras (*Prot.* 335a; cf. 316c-d), Gorgias draws attention to his success among the Greeks in general.

[7] Compare Protagoras's reported versatility (*Prot.* 335a).

GORGIAS: Speaking.

SOCRATES: What sort of speaking? Is it the sort which makes clear to e those who are sick what regimen they must follow if they are to regain their health?

GORGIAS: No.

SOCRATES: In which case, rhetoric is not concerned with *all* speaking.

GORGIAS: No, certainly not.

SOCRATES: Though speaking *is* what it makes people good at.

GORGIAS: Yes.

SOCRATES: And also presumably understanding the things they speak about?

GORGIAS: Of course.

SOCRATES: Now, take the science of medicine we've just been talking 450 about. Does it make people good at understanding and speaking about the sick?

GORGIAS: No question.

SOCRATES: In which case, medicine is also to do with speaking, apparently.

GORGIAS: Yes.

SOCRATES: Speaking about diseases, if nothing else.

GORGIAS: Precisely.

SOCRATES: And the science governing physical training also has to do with speaking – about the fitness or unfitness of our bodies.

GORGIAS: Exactly.

SOCRATES: And the other arts and sciences, too, Gorgias, are the same. Each of them has to do with just that branch of speaking which is con- b cerned with the subject belonging to the particular art or science it is.

GORGIAS: Apparently so.

SOCRATES: Then how come you don't call the other arts which are to do with speaking arts of rhetoric – if you call any art to do with speaking an art of rhetoric?

GORGIAS: Well, Socrates, for the other arts, virtually all their knowledge is to do with manual techniques and activities of that sort, whereas rhetoric has no manual output of that kind. Its whole operation and authority depends on speaking. That's why I hold that the art of rhetoric is about c speaking. And rightly, I maintain.

SOCRATES: So, do I understand now the kind of thing you want to say rhetoric is? Well, I shall soon have a clearer idea. Answer me this: we have arts and sciences, don't we?

GORGIAS: Yes.

SOCRATES: And of all the arts and sciences, I take it some consist mainly in production, and have little need of speaking. Indeed, some have no need at all, and the object of the art or science could be achieved in complete silence – painting, for example, and sculpture, and many others. I think those are the kind you mean, aren't they – the ones you say rhetoric d has nothing to do with?

GORGIAS: You have an excellent grasp of my meaning, Socrates.

SOCRATES: But then there are others of the arts and sciences where they get the whole thing done by means of speaking, and there is virtually no additional action needed at all – or very little. For example, the study of numbers, the study of ratios, geometry, playing draughts even, and a whole lot of others.[8] Some of them have roughly the same amount of speaking and activity, but most of them use speaking more, and their e whole operation and power to get things done comes entirely through speaking. I think you're saying that rhetoric is one of the arts of this kind.

GORGIAS: You're right.

SOCRATES: And yet I don't think you'd be at all inclined to call any of these rhetoric, though what you actually said in your formulation was that the art which gets things done by means of speaking is rhetoric. If someone wanted to be argumentative, his reaction might be: 'Are you in that case saying, Gorgias, that the study of numbers is rhetoric?' But I don't think you regard either the study of numbers or geometry as rhetoric.

451 GORGIAS: You're right, Socrates, I don't. Your assumption is correct.

SOCRATES: Come on, then, your turn. Complete your answer in the terms of my question. Since rhetoric turns out to be one of these arts which use speaking for the most part, but there are in fact others of the same kind, try and specify the particular sphere in which rhetoric, by speaking, gets things done. For example, suppose someone were to ask me about one of the sciences I mentioned: 'Socrates, what is the science b concerned with the study of numbers?' I would say to him, as you did just now, that it was one of the sciences which gets things done by means of

---

[8] The mention of playing draughts comes as a bit of a surprise. What qualifies it for inclusion here is presumably that it involves calculation of a sort. It is interesting that Socrates thinks of all these activities as proceeding principally through speech (not, as we might have supposed, through silent manipulation of symbols or the like).

speaking. And if he went on to ask me 'About what?', I would say 'About the even and the odd, irrespective of the actual magnitudes involved.'

Or again, if he asked: 'And the study of ratios? To which science do you give that name?' I would say that this science too was one of those which gets the whole thing done by means of speaking. And if he went on to ask: 'About what?' then (in the style of those who bring forward motions for debate before the people)[9] I would say, 'In other respects the study c of ratios is like the study of numbers – since it is about the same thing, the even and the odd – but with this difference, that the study of ratios is concerned with the quantitative relationship of the odd and the even both to themselves and to one another.'[10]

And if somebody then asked me about astronomy, and I said that it too gets everything done by means of speaking, then he might ask: 'And these astronomical speeches – what are they about, Socrates?' And I would say: 'They're about the motion of the stars and the sun and the moon, about their velocity relative to one another.'

GORGIAS: And you'd be quite correct, Socrates.

SOCRATES: Come on then, Gorgias, over to you. Rhetoric is in fact one d of the arts or sciences which uses speaking to get everything accomplished and settled, isn't it?

GORGIAS: It is.

SOCRATES: Speech about what? Tell me. What kind of thing are they concerned with, these speeches employed in rhetoric?

GORGIAS: The greatest of human affairs, Socrates, and the best.

SOCRATES: But that's still not clear, Gorgias. It's still open to argument. You must have been at drinking parties where you've heard people sing- e ing that song where they count blessings: 'First is good health, then looks, then wealth,' so the songwriter has it, 'that is honestly come by.'

GORGIAS: Yes, I have heard it. What of it?

SOCRATES: I'll tell you. Imagine the people who create these things 452 praised by the songwriter – the doctor, the fitness expert, the business-man – standing before you, here and now. The doctor might start off

---

[9] Socrates refers to the use in formulating amendments to motions before the assembly that speakers made of the blanket expression 'in other respects ... like ...', to avoid repetition of detail.

[10] 'The study of ratios' translates *logistikē*, often rendered as 'calculation'. As Socrates explains, it is closely related to *arithmētikē*, 'the study of numbers'. In the *Republic* he will use the expressions in harness (e.g. at *Rep.* 7.525a), although in Plato's account of the mathematical sciences there *logistikē* seems to be the preferred general term to designate the science of number as a whole. See further C. Huffman, *Archytas of Tarentum*, pp.68–76.

by saying: 'Gorgias is deceiving you, Socrates. It is not his art that is concerned with the greatest good for humanity, but mine.' And imagine me then asking him: 'And you? Who are you to be making this claim?' He would presumably say he was a doctor. 'What do you mean?' I'd say. 'The product of your art is the greatest good?' 'Of course, Socrates,' he would say, 'since its product is health. What greater good is there for

b people than health?'

And then after him, imagine the fitness expert saying: 'I'd be equally astonished, Socrates, if Gorgias can point to a greater good resulting from his own art than I can from mine.' And I'd say to him in his turn: 'And you, sir, who are you? What is your job?' 'I'm a fitness expert,' he would say. 'My job is to make people good-looking and physically strong.'

After the fitness expert, the businessman might say (with an air of complete contempt, I suspect, for the world in general): 'Ask yourself,

c Socrates, whether it isn't clear that there is no greater good than wealth – either in Gorgias' possession or in anyone else's.' 'And are you the person who creates it?' we might say to him. 'Yes,' he would say. 'And what are you?' 'A businessman.' 'What are you saying, then?' we will ask. 'Is wealth, in your judgment, man's greatest good?' 'Of course.' 'And yet Gorgias here takes issue with that,' we would say. 'He says the art in his possession is the cause of a greater good than yours.' So then the next thing he would

d say would obviously be 'What *is* this good? Let's hear Gorgias' answer.'

So come on, Gorgias. Take it you are being asked by me as well as by them, and give us your answer. *What* is it that you say is the greatest good people can have, and that you can create it?

GORGIAS: The thing, Socrates, which is in truth the greatest good and the cause both of freedom for people themselves and at the same time of each person's rule over others in his own city.[11]

SOCRATES: Yes, but *what* are you saying it is?

e GORGIAS: Persuasion, I would say. The ability to persuade by means of speeches, whether it be jurymen on a jury, councillors in the council-chamber, assembly members in the assembly – or any other meeting which is a meeting of citizens. In fact, by this power you will make a slave of the doctor, a slave of the fitness expert. And as for this businessman,

---

[11] This view of the greatest good – freedom for oneself, control over others – parallels the conception of what is most at stake for a city that Thucydides puts in the mouth of the Athenian orator Diodotus in the course of his debate with Cleon about the action Athens should take to deal with its recalcitrant ally Mytilene (3.45.6). In the *Meno* Meno confirms that Gorgias defined virtue as 'the capacity to rule over people' (*Men.* 73c–d):

it will become clear that he is not in business for his own benefit, but for someone else's – yours, since you are the one who has the ability to speak and persuade large groups of people.

SOCRATES: Now, Gorgias, I think you're getting pretty close to making clear what art you think rhetoric is. If I understand you at all, you're saying 453 that rhetoric is what creates persuasion. Its whole activity, its whole point, comes down to this. Can you suggest anything else, apart from persuasion, which rhetoric has the power to produce in the minds of its hearers?

GORGIAS: No, Socrates. I think that is a very satisfactory definition you have given. That is indeed its whole point.

SOCRATES: Then listen to me, Gorgias. Make no mistake about it, if there has ever been anyone who was keen, when discussing things with b others, to know precisely what the discussion was about, then I like to think I come in that category. As I am sure you do too.

GORGIAS: And if I am, Socrates?

SOCRATES: I'll tell you. This persuasion which is the result of rhetoric – I don't know for certain, believe me, what exactly it is and what subjects it is persuasion *about*, though I've a pretty shrewd idea what I think you're saying it is, and what it is concerned with. All the same, I'm going to ask you c what exactly you say the persuasion resulting from rhetoric is, and what it is concerned with. Why will I ask you, and not say myself, if I have a shrewd idea? For the sake of the argument – nothing personal. I'd like it to advance in such a way that we can see as clearly as possible the subject under discussion. Ask yourself whether you think this is a fair question for me to put to you? If I were asking you, for example, what kind of painter Zeuxis was, and you told me he was the one who paints living creatures, wouldn't it be a fair question for me to ask you what sort of living creatures, and where?[12]

GORGIAS: Perfectly fair.

SOCRATES: And is that because there are different painters painting d many different living creatures?

GORGIAS: Yes.

SOCRATES: Whereas if there were no other painter apart from Zeuxis, your answer would have been a good one?

GORGIAS: Yes, of course.

SOCRATES: Come on, then, answer the same question about rhetoric. Is it only rhetoric, do you think, which produces persuasion? Or are there other arts

[12] Dodds comments (*Plato: Gorgias*, p.204) that Zeuxis 'is probably the same as the Zeuxippus of *Prot.* 318b, who was "lionised" by the young people when he first appeared at Athens'.

which produce it as well? The kind of thing I mean is this: anyone who teaches anything – does he persuade, in what he teaches? Or does he not persuade?

GORGIAS: Quite the reverse, Socrates. He, more than anyone, does persuade.

e SOCRATES: Then let's go back to the same arts and sciences we were talking about a moment ago. Doesn't the study of numbers – and the person who is an expert in it – teach us everything to do with number?

GORGIAS: It certainly does.

SOCRATES: And does it also persuade?

GORGIAS: Yes.

SOCRATES: In which case, is the study of numbers also a creator of persuasion?

GORGIAS: It looks like it.

SOCRATES: So if someone asks us what kinds of persuasion, and concerned with what, the answer we shall give him, I suppose, will be that it is a teacher's persuasion about the entire series of even and odd. As for

454 the other arts we were talking about just now, we shall be able to demonstrate, shan't we, that they are all creators of persuasion – and what kind of persuasion, and concerned with what?

GORGIAS: Yes.

SOCRATES: In which case, it's not only rhetoric that is a creator of persuasion.

GORGIAS: You're right.

SOCRATES: Since, therefore, it is not the only art which performs this function, but there are others in addition, we would be justified in going on to ask the speaker the further question, as we did with the painter: 'All right, so rhetoric is the art of persuasion. What kind of persuasion? And in connection with what?' Or do you not think it would be justifiable to

b ask him that further question?

GORGIAS: No, I do think it would be justifiable.

SOCRATES: Then answer, Gorgias, since you agree on that.

GORGIAS: Very well, Socrates. I mean the persuasion that goes on in the lawcourts and in other large gatherings, as I said a little while ago – in connection with what is just and unjust.[13]

---

[13] Athenian juries regularly ran into the hundreds. For example, the orator Demosthenes refers to juries of 'two hundred or a thousand or whatever number the city empanels' (*Against Meidias* 223); the jury that condemned Socrates to death numbered 501. One imagines an experience in some ways more like the theatre, or a reality show before a live audience, than the modern American or British court.

SOCRATES: Yes, I rather suspected that this was the persuasion you meant – and in that connection, Gorgias. But don't be surprised if I ask you another question of the same sort in a moment or two – when something seems to be clear, and yet I ask you a further question anyway. As I say, I ask with a view to completing the argument in an orderly way – c nothing personal. This way we won't get into the habit of too quickly snatching at one another's meaning on the basis of guesswork, and you can develop your own views, in line with your thesis, in whatever way you choose.

GORGIAS: I think it's quite correct, what you are doing, Socrates.

SOCRATES: Very well. Then here's another question for us to examine. Is there something you call 'having learned'?

GORGIAS: Yes, there is.

SOCRATES: And something you call 'having been convinced'?

GORGIAS: Yes.

SOCRATES: And do you think having learned and having been d convinced – learning and conviction – are the same thing? Or are they different things?

GORGIAS: Different, Socrates, if you want my opinion.

SOCRATES: And you're right, as you will see if you look at it like this. Suppose someone asked you: 'Is there such a thing, Gorgias, as a false, and a true, conviction?' I imagine you'd say there was.

GORGIAS: Yes.

SOCRATES: What about knowledge? Is there a false and a true knowledge?

GORGIAS: No.

SOCRATES: In which case it's clear they are not the same thing.

GORGIAS: True.

SOCRATES: And yet both those who have learnt and those who have been convinced have been persuaded. e

GORGIAS: That is so.

SOCRATES: Do you want us, then, to postulate two forms of persuasion – one producing conviction without knowledge, the other producing knowledge?

GORGIAS: By all means.

SOCRATES: Which sort of persuasion does rhetoric create, in the law-courts and other large gatherings, on the subject of what is just and unjust? The sort which gives rise to being convinced without knowing, or the sort which gives rise to knowing?

17

GORGIAS: It's obvious, I take it, Socrates, that it's the sort which gives rise to being convinced.

SOCRATES: In which case, it seems, rhetoric is a creator of the per-
455 suasion which produces conviction, not the persuasion which teaches, on the subject of justice and injustice.[14]

GORGIAS: Yes.

SOCRATES: And the orator is not someone capable of teaching juries and other gatherings, on the subject of justice and injustice, but only of persuading them. Presumably he wouldn't be able to teach matters of such importance to a gathering that size in a short time.

GORGIAS: No, he wouldn't.

SOCRATES: Very well, then. Let's see what it is we are actually saying
b about rhetoric. For my part, I can't yet understand myself what it is I am saying. When the city holds a meeting about the selection of doctors or shipwrights or specialists of some other kind, it surely won't be the expert in rhetoric who gives his advice then, will it? It's obvious that in each choice it should be the most skilled person who does the choosing. And when it's a question of building walls or fitting out harbours or dockyards, again it won't be the expert in rhetoric, it will be the master builders. Or if there's a debate on the selection of generals, or some mobilisation against
c the enemy, or the occupation of strategic positions, again it will be those with expertise in generalship who will then give their advice, not those with expertise in rhetoric.[15] What is your view, Gorgias, in cases like this? After all, you claim both to be an orator yourself and to make other people skilled in oratory, so it is a good idea to come to you for answers to questions about your art.

You must regard me as having your interests at heart in this: there may in fact quite well be some member of the present company who wants to become your pupil – as I think I can see some, indeed quite a number – and they might possibly not have the nerve to question you. So when you
d are questioned by me, regard yourself as being questioned by them as well. 'What good will it do us, Gorgias, if we spend time with you? What

---

[14] Socrates' argument and the vocabulary in which it is couched echo Gorgias's own formulations in *Encomium of Helen* 13, where in detailing the achievements of persuasion Gorgias mentions as one example the power of a speech over a large gathering (*ochlos*) – it 'delights and persuades on account of the art (*technê*) with which it is written, not because it is spoken with truth'.

[15] As Dodds points out (*Plato: Gorgias*, p.209), in the *Protagoras* 'Socrates remarks (319b5) that on questions involving expertise the Athenians will listen only to qualified specialists, and Protagoras agrees (322d5)'.

will we be able to advise the city about? Will it be only about justice and injustice, or will it also be about the things Socrates was referring to just now?' Try and give them an answer.

GORGIAS: I will try, Socrates, to unfold clearly the power of rhetoric in its entirety, now that you have so admirably shown the way. You are aware, I take it, that your dockyards here, and the walls of Athens, and the build- c ing of the harbours, owe their origin to the advice of Themistocles – or in some cases Pericles – not to the advice of the experts.

SOCRATES: So it is said, Gorgias – of Themistocles. As for Pericles, I heard him myself when he was offering us his advice on the middle wall.[16]

GORGIAS: And when it's a question of selecting one of the specialists 456 you were mentioning just now, Socrates, you can see that the orators are the ones who give advice and whose proposals on these decisions win the day.

SOCRATES: Yes, and that's what surprises me, Gorgias. It's why I keep asking just what the power of rhetoric is. When I look at it in this way, a power so great seems to have something supernatural about it.

GORGIAS: Ah, if only you knew, Socrates – how rhetoric embraces virtu-ally all powers, and gathers them under its wing. I can give you convincing proof of this. I have often been with my brother and his doctor colleagues, b and visited someone who was ill but who refused either to drink medi-cine or put himself in the doctor's hands for surgery or cauterisation. And when the doctors couldn't persuade him, I have persuaded him, using only rhetoric and no other art or science. Indeed, I maintain that a rhetoric expert and a doctor can go to a city, anywhere you like, and if they are set against one another, in an assembly of the people or any other gathering, to argue which of them should be chosen as doctor, then the doctor will make no showing, and the one with the ability to speak would c be chosen, if that was what he wanted. And in competition with any other skilled practitioner you like, the rhetorician would be better than any of them at persuading people to choose him, since there is no subject on which the rhetorician would not speak more persuasively, before a large

---

[16] It was ultimately due to Themistocles' advice years before that the Athenians built two long walls enclosing the city and its two harbours of Peiraeus and Phaleron within a tri-angle, bounded on its third side by the sea, probably in the 450s BC. The 'middle wall' is usually thought to signify a third wall built later within this space parallel to the more northerly of the long walls (to Peiraeus), fortifying the military road between Athens and what had by the 440s become its major port.

crowd, than any skilled practitioner you care to name.[17] Such is the extent and nature of this science's power.

But when it comes to using rhetoric, Socrates, it should be used like d any other competitive skill. With other competitive skills, you shouldn't use them against everybody – just because you have learnt boxing, or no-holds-barred fighting, or fighting in armour, with the result that you are stronger than friends and enemies alike. That's not a good reason to start beating up your friends, or stabbing them and killing them. Or again, for heaven's sake, if somebody goes to the training ground regularly, is in good shape physically, and has learnt boxing, and then beats up his father and mother, or some other member of his household or his friends, e that's not a reason for hating physical fitness experts and those who teach fighting in armour, and banishing them from their cities. They passed on their skills on the understanding that those skills would be used in the cause of justice, against enemies and wrongdoers – not to start a fight, 457 but in self-defence. It is they – the recipients – who have perverted their strength and skill, using them for the wrong purposes. So it is not those who taught them who are evil, nor is this a reason for saying their art is to blame or evil, but rather, I think, those who do not use it for the right purposes.

Exactly the same argument applies to rhetoric. The orator has the *power* to speak against anyone, and about anything, in a way which makes him more persuasive among large crowds about – to put it in a nutshell – any-b thing he pleases. But the mere fact that he *could* do it is no sort of reason for him to deprive the doctors of their reputation, nor the other skilled practitioners. No, he should employ rhetoric too – like the competitive skills – in a just cause. If someone becomes a rhetoric expert, and then uses his power and his art to act unjustly, I don't think people should hate and banish from their cities the person who taught him. *He* passed on the c skill to be used justly; it is the recipient who abuses it. So it is right to hate and banish and put to death the person who uses the art incorrectly, but not the person who taught him.

SOCRATES: I imagine you, like me, Gorgias, have had a lot of experience of discussions, and there's something I expect you've noticed in the course of them, which is that people don't find it easy to define for one another the things they are trying to discuss, or to learn from one

---

[17] The scenario Gorgias imagines is less hypothetical than one might think: see note on 457c below.

another, so bringing their meetings to a conclusion. No, if they disagree d
about something, and one of them says the other is wrong or hard to
understand, they lose their tempers, and think the other is speaking out
of malice, trying to win an argument rather than investigating the subject put forward for discussion. Some of them end up parting in a way
they should be thoroughly ashamed of, hurling abuse at one another, and
exchanging the kind of remarks which make the bystanders annoyed as
well – on their own account, for ever thinking it was worth listening to
such people.

Why am I saying this? Because I think you are saying things now about e
rhetoric which don't quite follow from, or agree with, what you said to
begin with. But I hesitate to question you too rigorously, in case you
think I'm trying to win a victory over you. The only victory I want to
win is bringing clarity to the subject under discussion.[18] For my part, I
would gladly carry on with my questioning, if you are one of that group 458
of people to which I myself belong. What group is that? I am one of those
people who would be very glad to be proved wrong if I say something not
true, and very glad to prove someone else wrong, should he turn out to
be saying something not true – and every bit as glad to be proved wrong
as to prove wrong. In fact, I regard that as the greater good, to the extent
that ridding oneself of a very great evil is a greater good than ridding
someone else of one. And there is no greater evil for a human being, in my
opinion, than false opinion on the subjects we are actually talking about b
now. So if you claim to be the same kind of person as well, let us continue
our discussion. But if you think we should call it a day, let's do that now,
and bring our talk to a close.

GORGIAS: I certainly do claim, Socrates, that I too am the kind of person you are describing. But maybe we should also give some thought to
these people here. Earlier, before you arrived, I gave a long presentation
to those who were here, and it may be that we shall be dragging things
out unduly if we go on with our discussion. We ought to think about c

[18] Socrates is much given to stressing the distinctiveness of his attitude to discussion, with its
focus on getting clear about the merits of the argument, not on outperforming the person
he converses with (although that is not always how his interlocutors interpret him – not
without some justice). The issue is made the topic of an entire episode in the *Protagoras*
(333b–338e), where Protagoras is represented as explicitly articulating the alternative
competitive model (335a; see also 471e, 472c, 474a below). It wasn't just sophists and
professionals in oratory who vied with each other by delivering 'performance' set pieces
(*epideixeis*). Doctors too appear to have competed in this way (see the Hippocratic treatise
On the Nature of Man 1).

them as well. We don't want to keep any of them here if they have other things to do.[19]

CHAEREPHON: You can hear the reaction for yourselves, Gorgias and Socrates. All these men here are willing to listen to anything you have to say. And for my part, I hope I shall never be so busy that I find myself having to say no to talk of this kind, conducted in this way, because I have something more important to do.

d   CALLICLES: I couldn't agree more, Chaerephon. I too have been present at many discussions, and I'm not sure I have ever enjoyed one as much as this. As far as I'm concerned, you will be welcome to continue your discussion all day, if you want to.

SOCRATES: There's certainly no objection on my side, Callicles, if Gorgias is happy about it.

GORGIAS: Well, it would be humiliating after all that, Socrates, if I refused, when I was the one who proclaimed that I would answer any
e   question anyone chose to ask. If that is what these people want, continue the discussion and ask what you want to ask.

SOCRATES: Then listen, Gorgias, and I'll tell you what I find surprising in the things you are saying. It may be that what you say is correct, and that I am not understanding you correctly. You are saying, are you, that you can make a rhetorician of somebody, if he is willing to learn from you?

GORGIAS: Yes.

SOCRATES: You mean he'll be convincing in a large gathering on any subject at all, by means of persuasion rather than instruction?

GORGIAS: Absolutely.

459   SOCRATES: And you were saying a few moments ago that even on the subject of health the orator is more persuasive than the doctor.

GORGIAS: Yes, I was – certainly at a large gathering.

SOCRATES: And this 'at a large gathering' – isn't it just 'in front of those who don't know'? I don't imagine he will be more persuasive than the doctor with those who do know.

---

[19] A critical moment in the dialogue. Socrates' last speech encapsulates not only his insatiable appetite for intellectual discussion as uncompetitive pursuit of truth, but also his key conviction that to be in a state of false opinion on some issue of significance for living one's life is the greatest evil that can befall a human being. Gorgias, by contrast, is ready to call it a day, out of consideration for the company that has gathered (he is consistently portrayed as courteous and reasonable throughout the dialogue: see 462c–463a, 497b, 506a–b). When in response to the enthusiasm of Chaerephon and Callicles (the leading associates of the two discussants) he agrees to carry on, Socrates will produce an argument to show that the various claims Gorgias makes about rhetoric are mutually inconsistent.

GORGIAS: True.

SOCRATES: And if he's going to be more persuasive than the doctor, does this then make him more persuasive than someone who knows?

GORGIAS: It certainly does.

SOCRATES: Though he's not a doctor. Is that right?   b

GORGIAS: Yes.

SOCRATES: And the person who is not a doctor, I take it, is ignorant of the things which the doctor knows.

GORGIAS: Obviously.

SOCRATES: In which case, when the orator is more persuasive than the doctor, someone who doesn't know will be more persuasive, with those who don't know, than someone who does know. Is that what happens? Or something different?

GORGIAS: In that situation, this is what happens.

SOCRATES: And with all the other arts and sciences too, the position is the same for the orator – and for rhetoric. There's no need for him to know how things are in themselves, merely to have discovered some device for persuading people, so that he can appear to those who don't   c
know to know more than those who do know.

GORGIAS: Doesn't that make life a lot easier, Socrates? You don't have to learn the other arts and sciences, only this one, and you're on a par with the experts.

SOCRATES: Whether being like this puts the orator on a par, or not on a par, with the others is something we can look at presently, if it turns out to be at all relevant. As it is, there's another question to ask first. Does the rhetoric expert turn out to be in the same position with regard to what's just and unjust, what's ugly and beautiful, good and bad, as   d
he is with health and all the various objects of the different sciences? Is he in the position of not knowing the things themselves – what is good or what is bad, what is beautiful or what is ugly, or just or unjust – but of having contrived some device for persuading people about them? So that, despite not knowing, to those who don't know he still seems to know more than the person who does know? Or is knowing essential? Does the   e
person who is going to learn rhetoric have to know these things already, before coming to you? And if he doesn't know them, will you, the teacher of rhetoric, teach the person who comes to you none of these things – that not being your job – but will you make him seem to know these things, in the eyes of the many, even though he doesn't know them, and seem to be good even though he isn't good? Or will you be completely unable to

teach him rhetoric unless he knows the truth of these things before he
460 starts? How do matters stand here? Do for heaven's sake 'unfold' for us,
as you put it just now, what exactly the power of rhetoric is.

GORGIAS: Very well. In my view, Socrates, if he doesn't in fact know
them already, then these are things he will learn from me as well.[20]

SOCRATES: Hold it there. That's very important. So if you make someone an expert in rhetoric, then he must necessarily know the things which
are just and the things which are unjust – either beforehand, or by learning them from you later.

GORGIAS: Exactly.

b SOCRATES: Now, what about this? Is someone who has learned things to
do with carpentry a carpenter, or not?

GORGIAS: Yes, he is.

SOCRATES: And someone who has learnt things to do with music a
musician?

GORGIAS: Yes.

SOCRATES: And someone who has learnt things to do with medicine a
doctor? And the same with other activities, following the same principle –
in each case is the person who has learnt the things related to the activity
the kind of person this sort of knowledge always produces?

GORGIAS: Indeed he is.

SOCRATES: In that case, according to this argument, isn't the person
who has learnt the things that are just also just?

GORGIAS: Absolutely. No question.

SOCRATES: And presumably the just person does just things.

GORGIAS: Yes.

c SOCRATES: So doesn't it necessarily follow that the rhetorician is just –
and that the just person wants to do just things?

GORGIAS: It certainly looks that way.

SOCRATES: In which case, the rhetorician will never be willing to act
unjustly.

GORGIAS: Apparently not.

---

[20] Up to this point Gorgias's responses have been what we might have expected from the
author of *Encomium of Helen* and *Defence of Palamedes*. Elsewhere Plato represents Meno,
one of his followers, as denying that Gorgias ever claimed to teach virtue like the sophists
(*Men.* 95b–c; cf. 519c–520b below). But the battery of questions Socrates has just fired at
him put him on the spot (after all, he has insisted that his teaching is given on the basis
that it will be used justly: 457b–c), and the fatal concession he makes here is accordingly
extracted. Polus will shortly protest at the argumentative tactic employed (461b–c).

SOCRATES: Do you remember saying a little earlier that there was no call to prosecute fitness experts, or banish them, if the boxer uses his boxing d skill in an unjust cause? And in just the same way, if the orator uses the art of rhetoric in an unjust cause, that there was no call to prosecute his teacher or banish him from the city, but rather the person who is acting unjustly and using his rhetorical skill incorrectly? Was that what was said, or not?

GORGIAS: It was.

SOCRATES: Whereas now it's clear, isn't it, that this same person, the e rhetorician, couldn't possibly have acted unjustly?

GORGIAS: Yes, it is clear.

SOCRATES: And at the beginning of our discussion, Gorgias, was it claimed that rhetoric was to do with speaking concerned not with the even and odd, but with what is just and unjust?

GORGIAS: Yes.

SOCRATES: Yes, well, I inferred from those statements of yours then that rhetoric could never be something unjust, since it spends all its time composing speeches about justice. But when you said, a little later, that the orator could use rhetoric in an unjust way as well, that's what surprised 461 me, and I thought things were being said which were out of tune with one another. And that's why I said what I did, to the effect that if you, like me, thought there was some benefit in being proved wrong, then it was worth going on with the discussion, but if you didn't, then we should call it a day. And now, as we go on with our enquiry, you can see for yourself that it is again being agreed that the rhetorician is incapable of using rhetoric in an unjust way or being prepared to act unjustly. So how these things really are – ye dogs,[21] Gorgias, it would be no short discussion we'd need b to examine that properly.

POLUS: Honestly, Socrates! Do even you really believe what you are now saying about rhetoric? Or do you imagine – just because Gorgias was embarrassed not to go on and agree with you that the rhetoric expert knows what things are just, beautiful and good, and said that if he didn't know it to start with, he himself would teach him, and then from this agreement some inconsistency perhaps found its way into what he was saying – which is just what you love, when it's you who've led people c

---

[21] Literally 'by the dog'. The expression recurs at 466c and 482b (where a more grandiose version is used: 'by the dog of the Egyptians', i.e. Anubis, a dog-headed divinity). This comic oath – used by a slave in Aristophanes (*Wasps* 83) – was apparently a favourite with Socrates.

on into that kind of questioning – since who do you imagine is going to deny that he knows what things are just himself and that he can teach them to others? It is real boorishness to direct the conversation into those channels.

SOCRATES: Good for you, Polus. It's lucky we make friends and have sons. It means when we older ones lose our footing, you younger ones can be on hand to put us straight again – both in our actions and in our words.
d Just as now, if Gorgias and I are losing our footing in our discussion, you are on hand to put us straight – and quite right too. For my part, if you think anything that has been agreed has been wrongly agreed, I'm quite prepared to let you take back whatever you want to take back – with one small proviso, please.

POLUS: What is that?

SOCRATES: That preference of yours for lengthy speeches, Polus – you tried to indulge it back at the start – could you just keep that in check?[22]

POLUS: What? Will I not be allowed to say as much as I want to say?
e SOCRATES: That would indeed be hard on you, my fine friend – if you came to Athens, where there is the greatest freedom of speech of anywhere in Greece, and found, when you got there, that you alone did not get the benefit of it. But – sauce for the goose – if you speak at great length, and refuse to answer the question which is put to you, wouldn't that be hard on me in my turn, if I am not to be allowed to go away and
462 stop listening to you? No, if there's something you're not happy with in the discussion we've been having, and you want to put it to rights, then take back anything you want, as I've just said, and take turns at asking and answering questions (as Gorgias and I did): examine and be examined. I imagine you claim, don't you, that what Gorgias knows, you know as well?

POLUS: I do.

SOCRATES: In which case, do you also make a practice of telling people to ask you any question they like, in the belief that you know the answer?

POLUS: I certainly do.
b SOCRATES: Well, now's your chance to do whichever of those things you choose – ask the questions or answer them.

---

[22] Gorgias had on occasion spoken at length (notably at 456a–457c), but Socrates raised no objection at any point to his conduct as interlocutor. What he seems to be seeking to pre-empt here is more of the studied pre-prepared rhetoric Polus inflicted on the company in his first intervention in the conversation (at 448c).

POLUS: All right, I'll do that. Answer me this, Socrates. Since you think Gorgias is confused about rhetoric, what do you say it is?[23]

SOCRATES: Are you asking me what science I say it is?

POLUS: Yes, I am.

SOCRATES: I don't think it's a science at all, Polus, to tell you the truth.

POLUS: What *do* you think rhetoric is, then?

SOCRATES: Something you claim to make into a science in the treatise of yours I read the other day.   c

POLUS: What thing do you mean?

SOCRATES: I mean a kind of skill gained by practice.[24]

POLUS: So you think rhetoric is a skill?

SOCRATES: I do, unless you say otherwise.

POLUS: Skill at what?

SOCRATES: At producing pleasure and enjoyment of some sort.

POLUS: Don't you think rhetoric is a fine thing, then, if it is capable of giving people pleasure?

SOCRATES: Hang on, Polus! Have you discovered from me already what I say it is? You're going on to the next question when you ask me if I don't d think it is a fine thing?

POLUS: Haven't I discovered that you say it's a kind of skill?

SOCRATES: Very well. Since you're so keen on the idea of bringing pleasure to people, how about doing one small thing to please me?

POLUS: By all means.

SOCRATES: Ask me now about cookery – what science I think it is.

POLUS: All right, I'm asking you. What science is cookery?

SOCRATES: No science at all, Polus. 'What is it, then?' you must say.

POLUS: All right, I say it.

SOCRATES: A kind of skill. 'Skill at what?' you have to say.

POLUS: All right, I say it.

[23] Having Polus ask the questions allows Plato to represent Socrates – unusually in a 'Socratic' dialogue – as advancing and elaborating at length a theory of his own: the classification of sciences and skills he presents over the next four pages.

[24] The Greek expression is *empeiria*, from which English derives 'empirical', 'empiricism'. The fifth-century Presocratic philosopher Anaxagoras had claimed that humans are differentiated from the other animals by '*empeiria* and memory and wisdom and *technê*' (Fr.21b). In the early Hippocratic treatise *On Ancient Medicine*, the fact that medicine has relied on a gradual and methodical process of discovery like cookery constitutes the basis of its claim to *be* a science. Polus formulates a similar idea specifically in terms of *empeiria* (in its root sense of 'experience') in his speech at 448c. Socrates will have none of this (see 463a–c). For him *empeiria* is nothing more than a 'knack' (*tribê*) of doing things with a certain kind of intention (what he calls 'sycophancy') and effect (gratification).

e   SOCRATES: At producing pleasure and enjoyment of some sort, Polus.
POLUS: Does that mean cookery is the same thing as rhetoric?
SOCRATES: Certainly not. Though it is a subdivision of the same activity.
POLUS: What activity do you mean?
SOCRATES: Well, I hope nobody minds me calling a spade a spade – though I hesitate to do so with Gorgias here. I'm afraid he'll think I'm making fun of his activity. For my part, I have no idea whether this is
463 the rhetoric Gorgias practises – nothing in the discussion we've just had made it at all clear what exactly he thinks rhetoric is – but the thing *I* call rhetoric is a subdivision of something which is anything but 'fine'.
GORGIAS: Subdivision of what, Socrates? Tell us. Don't worry about me.
SOCRATES: Very well, Gorgias. I think it's an activity which is not scientific, but characteristic of a soul which is intuitive, bold, with a natural gift for handling people.[25] If you want a name for it, I'd say it boils down to
b   sycophancy, sucking up to people.[26] I think it's an activity with a number of subdivisions, of which cookery is another. And though it looks like a science, it is not a science, on my way of reckoning, but a skill, a knack. Rhetoric too I would call a subdivision of it, along with the skills of the fashion expert and the sophist – these four subdivisions for four different kinds of thing. If Polus wants to find out more, it's up to him to find out.
c   So far he hasn't found out what kind of subdivision of sycophancy I say rhetoric is. And not realising I haven't answered his question yet, he goes on and asks me the further question, whether I don't think it is a fine thing. But I'm not going to give him an answer to the question whether I think rhetoric is a fine thing or an ugly thing without first answering the question *what* it is. That's not the right way of going about it, Polus. But if you want to find out, ask me what kind of subdivision of sycophancy I say rhetoric is.

[25] The expression 'a soul which is intuitive, bold' may be an echo of a similar phrase applied to the skill of the orator in *Against Sophists* 17, by Gorgias's follower Isocrates, published around 390.
[26] The word translated 'sycophancy, sucking up to people' is *kolakeia*. 'Sycophant' is in origin itself a Greek expression, *sukophantēs*. As the Oxford Classical Dictionary says, nobody has yet come up with a good explanation of how the word got its modern sense of 'flatterer' – which is the connotation intended here. At Athens sycophants were people who earned a dubious and often corrupt living by initiating prosecutions (there being no public prosecutors). Understandably the word was often used as a term of abuse, and that carries over into the modern usage.

POLUS: All right, I'm asking you. Tell me what kind of subdivision it is.

SOCRATES: Would you be any the wiser if I told you? What rhetoric is, d on my way of reckoning, is an imitation of a subdivision of the science of politics.

POLUS: Well, fine or ugly? Which do you say it is?

SOCRATES: Ugly, in my view – I call what's bad ugly – since you force me to give you an answer as if you already knew what I meant.

GORGIAS: But heavens, Socrates, even I don't understand what you say.

SOCRATES: I'm not surprised, Gorgias. I haven't said anything intell- e igible so far. But our colt here is young and eager to be off.[27]

GORGIAS: Never mind him. Tell me what you mean when you say rhetoric is an imitation of a subdivision of the science of politics.

SOCRATES: I'll try and explain to you what rhetoric seems to me to be. If that's not in fact what it is, the colt here will prove me wrong. I take it there's something you call 'body' and 'soul', isn't there? 464

GORGIAS: Of course.

SOCRATES: Do you also think, for each of these, there is a particular condition of well-being?

GORGIAS: I do.

SOCRATES: What about a condition which appears to be well-being but isn't really? I'll give you an example. Lots of people seem to be in good shape physically, and you wouldn't find it easy to see they weren't unless you were a doctor or one of the physical fitness experts.

GORGIAS: True.

SOCRATES: What I'm saying is that that kind of thing occurs both with the body and with the soul. It makes the body and the soul seem to be in good condition, though they are none the more so for all that. b

GORGIAS: True.

SOCRATES: Very well. Now I'll show you more clearly, if I can, what I mean. For these two things I say there are two sciences: the one which looks after the soul I call politics; as for the one which looks after the body, I can't give you a single name for it, just like that. And though the care of the body is a single science, I say it has two subdivisions – physical fitness training and medicine. In politics, I say that legislating corresponds to fitness training, while the counterpart to medicine is justice.[28] The

---

[27] 'Colt' translates Greek *pôlos*: Socrates puns on Polus's name.
[28] By 'justice' Socrates seems to mean the administration of justice, or more specifically of what Aristotle would call corrective justice, rather than justice as a quality of soul. There is actually support in the manuscripts for thinking that Plato may have written 'the judicial

c members of each pair have in common with one another the fact that they
are concerned with the same thing. So medicine has something in common with fitness training, and justice with legislating – though there is
also some difference between them. Now, there being these four sciences,
two taking care of the body and two of the soul, and always with a view
to what is best, when sycophancy realises this – I won't say knowing for
certain, but intuitively – it divides itself into four, impersonates each of
d the subdivisions, and pretends to be the thing it impersonates. It has no
concern with what is best, but uses the pleasure of the moment to ensnare
and deceive folly, masquerading as something of the greatest value. So
cookery impersonates medicine, pretending that it knows the best foods
for the body, so that if a cook and a doctor had to be in competition before
an audience of children, or men with as little understanding as children,
e to see which of them – the doctor or the cook – was the expert on beneficial and harmful foods, the doctor would die of starvation.

Well, anyway, sycophancy is what I call it, and I say it's an ugly kind
465 of thing, Polus – this is my answer to your question – because it makes
an intuitive guess at what is pleasant, with no interest in what is best.
And I say it is not a science but a skill, because it can give no rational
explanation of the thing it is catering for, nor of the nature of the things
it is providing, and so it can't tell you the cause of each. And I don't give
the name 'science' to something which is unreasoning. For all this, if you
disagree, I am happy to render account.

b The mask of medicine, as I say, is worn by the sycophancy which is
cookery; that of fitness training, in just the same way, by fashion, since it
is pernicious, illusory, demeaning and slavish, deceiving with shapes and
colours, smooth skin and clothes. It makes people import an alien beauty
and neglect that beauty of their own which comes from training.[29] I don't
want to be speechifying, so I'll just say, in the language of geometry – and
c here you might be able to follow me – that as fashion is to training, so
cookery is to medicine. Or rather, as fashion is to training, so the skill of
the sophist is to the science of the legislator; and as cookery is to medicine, so rhetoric is to justice.[30] This is the natural division between them,

---

art' (*dikastikê*) here, not 'justice' (*dikaiosunê*), as they agree when it comes to the brief
reprise of the classification at 520c.

[29] Socrates takes it for granted that physical beauty is principally a matter of the body beautiful – the general Greek assumption, as evidenced most obviously by the representation of
the nude male body in sculpture.

[30] The comparisons Socrates introduces are *proportionalities*: hence the reference to geometry. The suggestion that Polus might find proportionality talk particularly helpful is an

but as I say they are all very closely related, so that sophists and orators get mixed up, working as they do in the same area and dealing with the same things. They don't know what to make of themselves, nor do other people know what to make of them. Indeed, if it weren't the case that the soul supervises the body, if the body supervised itself, and cookery d and medicine were not scrutinised and distinguished by the soul, but the body made its own discriminations on the basis of the pleasures available to it, then Anaxagoras' saying – very familiar to you, I'm sure, my dear Polus – would have a wide application.[31] All things would be mixed up together, with no attempt to distinguish what relates to medicine, health or cookery.

Well, now you've heard what I say rhetoric is. It relates to the soul as cookery does to the body. You may think I am a bit out of order, making e a long speech myself while not allowing you to speak at length. I can be forgiven for that. I did speak briefly, but you didn't understand me. You couldn't make head or tail of the answer I gave you, and needed an explanation. So if I can't make anything of your answers, then you too can 466 make what you say longer. If I can make something of it, then let me do so. That's only fair. For now, if you can make something of the answer I have given, please do so.

POLUS: So what are you saying? You regard rhetoric as sycophancy?

SOCRATES: A subdivision of sycophancy, was what I said. Problems with your memory, Polus? At your age? How will you manage when you get a bit older?

POLUS: Well, but do you think good orators are rated very lowly, as sycophants, in their cities?

SOCRATES: Are you asking a question? Or is that the beginning of a b speech?

POLUS: It's a question.

SOCRATES: I don't think they are 'rated' at all.

---

implicit reference to his training by Gorgias. In the *Encomium of Helen*, for example, Gorgias had written: 'The power of speech bears the same ratio to the ordering of the soul as does the ordering of drugs to the nature of bodies' (*Helen* 14; Socrates substitutes 'justice' for 'the power of speech' in this formula).

[31] In the opening sentence of his work on cosmology, Anaxagoras had described the original state of things, before any world or worlds were created, in a famous phrase: 'All things were together' (Fr.1). Socrates' apparent assumption that Polus will be familiar with the formula tends to confirm the hypothesis (see note on 448b) that Polus was someone who acknowledged an intellectual debt to Anaxagoras.

POLUS: What do you mean, not rated? Don't they have the greatest power in their cities?[32]

SOCRATES: No. At least, not if you say having power is a good thing for the person who has it.

POLUS: Well, of course I say that.

SOCRATES: In that case, I think of the people in the city, orators have the least power.

POLUS: What? Aren't they like tyrants? Don't they put to death anyone
c they will, confiscate property, and banish from their cities anyone they please?

SOCRATES: Ye dogs, Polus! Every time you open your mouth, I really have no idea whether you're saying something of your own, revealing your own opinion, or whether you're asking me a question.

POLUS: I'm asking you a question.

SOCRATES: Very well, my friend. In that case, you're asking me two questions at the same time.

POLUS: What do you mean, two?

SOCRATES: Didn't you just say something like this: 'Don't orators put to
d death those whom they will, like tyrants? Don't they confiscate property, and drive whoever they please out of their cities?'

POLUS: Yes, I did.

SOCRATES: In which case, I tell you there are two questions there, and I will give you an answer to both. I maintain, Polus, that both orators and tyrants have the least power in their cities, as I said a moment ago.
e They do virtually nothing of what they will – though they do do as they please.[33]

POLUS: And isn't that having great power?

SOCRATES: No, not according to Polus.

POLUS: Not according to me? But I *do* say it is having great power.

---

[32] Socrates has given some explanation of his classification of rhetoric as sycophancy, but his view is clearly open to challenge. Polus effectively objects: 'Aren't orators admired in a way sycophants aren't, because they exercise power sycophants don't?' Socrates accordingly next proceeds to try to demolish the idea that oratory endows people with great power.

[33] The distinction between 'what they will' and 'what they please' – crucial to the argument Socrates now develops (to 468e) – is no more obvious in Greek than in English. In both 'will' (Greek *boulesthai*) can sometimes be used to mean something like '*really* want' (or would want if one thought hard about it), and Socrates exploits this usage in forcing a sharp contrast with 'please' (Greek *dokein*). See further notes on 467d, 468e.

SOCRATES: Ye d—No, you don't. You say having great power is a good thing for the person who has it.

POLUS: I certainly do.

SOCRATES: Do you think it is a good thing, then, if a person of no understanding does what he pleases? Do you call that having great power?

POLUS: No, I don't.

SOCRATES: Are you then going to demonstrate that orators do have understanding, that rhetoric is a science, and not sycophancy – and so 467 prove me wrong? If you let me get away with it, and don't prove me wrong, then the orators who do as they please in their cities, and tyrants, will be no better off. Power is, you say, a good thing; but doing what you please without understanding, even you agree that is a bad thing, don't you?

POLUS: Yes, I do.

SOCRATES: How then can orators or tyrants have great power in their cities, unless Polus proves Socrates wrong – proves that they do do what they will?

POLUS: Listen to the man –   b

SOCRATES: I maintain that they do not do what they will. Prove me wrong.

POLUS: Didn't you just agree, a moment ago, that they do as they please?

SOCRATES: I did. And I still agree now.

POLUS: Doesn't that mean they do what they will?

SOCRATES: I maintain not.

POLUS: Even though they do as they please?

SOCRATES: Yes.

POLUS: That's outrageous, Socrates. Preposterous.

SOCRATES: No need for abuse, my peerless Polus – you see, I can address you in your own style.[34] No, if you have a question to ask me, then show c me I am wrong. If you don't, then you be the one to answer.

POLUS: All right, I don't mind answering. I'd like to know what you mean.

SOCRATES: In that case, do you think people always will what they do on any particular occasion, or do they will the thing which is the reason *why* they do the thing they do? People who drink medicine prescribed by their doctors, for example. Do you think they will the thing they are doing,

---

[34] 'peerless Polus' attempts to capture the Gorgianic jingle of *ô lôiste Pôle*.

drinking medicine and feeling discomfort? Or do they will the thing – namely health – which is the reason why they are drinking it?

POLUS: Obviously the thing they will is health.

d SOCRATES: And people going to sea, or making money in other ways – what they will is not the thing they are doing at any particular moment (after all, who has a will to go to sea, with all its danger and inconvenience?), but the thing which I imagine is the reason why they are going to sea, namely to get rich. Riches are the reason why they go to sea.[35]

POLUS: Very much so.

SOCRATES: And isn't it the same with everything else? If someone does something for a reason, doesn't he will the thing which is the reason why he does it, rather than the thing which he does?

POLUS: Yes.

e SOCRATES: Now, is there anything of the things that there are, which is not either good or bad or somewhere in between – neither good nor bad?

POLUS: No, there can't possibly be.

SOCRATES: And do you say that wisdom is a good thing, and health and riches and things of that sort, and that their opposites are bad things?

POLUS: I do.

SOCRATES: And the things which are neither good nor bad, do you say they are the kinds of things which sometimes share in the good, some-
468 times in the bad, and sometimes in neither – for example, sitting, walking, running or going to sea, or again stones, wood and things of that sort? Aren't those what you mean? Or are there some other things to which you give the label 'neither good nor bad'?

POLUS: No, I mean those things.

SOCRATES: Now, do people do these in-between things – when they do do them – for the sake of the good things? Or do they do the good things for the sake of the in-between things?

POLUS: The in-between things for the sake of the good things, I imagine.

---

[35] Subsequently Socrates will restate the point (468b–c): it's not that we can't properly be said to will such things as drinking medicine or going to sea, but rather that we will them in a derivative sense – only if they really bring us benefit, only if the reason why we perform them really turns out good. The Greeks did not go to sea for pleasure. A celebrated passage of Hesiod expatiates on the dangers and miseries of seafaring (*Works and Days* 618–93).

SOCRATES: So it is in pursuit of the good that we walk, when we do   b
walk, because we think it is better – or again, stand still when we do
stand still, for the same reason, for the sake of the good, isn't it?

POLUS: Yes.

SOCRATES: And do we put to death, if we do put anyone to death, and
banish, and confiscate property, because we think it is better for us to do
this than not to do it?

POLUS: We certainly do.

SOCRATES: So it is for the sake of the good that the people who do all
these things do them?

POLUS: Yes.

SOCRATES: And didn't we agree that we don't will the things we do for
the sake of some other thing, but only the thing which is the reason why   c
we are doing them?[36]

POLUS: Indeed we did.

SOCRATES: It is not our will, in that case, to butcher people, or banish
them from our cities, or confiscate their property, just like that. No, if
these things are of benefit, then it is our will to do them; if they are harmful, then it is not our will. And that's because, according to you, we will
the things which are good, while the things which are neither good nor
bad we don't will – nor the things which are bad, do we? Do you think
what I say is true, Polus, or not? Why don't you answer?

POLUS: Yes, it's true.

SOCRATES: Well, if we agree on that, then if one person – be he tyrant or   d
orator – puts another to death, or banishes him, or confiscates his property, supposing that to be better for him, but in fact it turns out to be
worse, then I take it this person is doing as he pleases, isn't he?

POLUS: Yes.

SOCRATES: And is he also doing what he wills, if these things in fact turn
out to be bad for him. Why don't you answer?

POLUS: No, as far as I can see he doesn't do what he wills.

SOCRATES: Can it be, then, that such a person has great power in that
city, if having great power is, on your own admission, something good?   e

POLUS: No, it can't.

---

[36] A reference back to 467c–e, where Polus agrees (i) that what people will is the rationale for
their actions (e.g. health), and (ii) that health is something good.

SOCRATES: In which case, what I said was true, when I said it was possible for a man to do as he pleases in a city, and yet not have great power and not do what he wills.[37]

POLUS: Oh yes, Socrates! And of course you'd be the first to say no if you had the chance to do as you please in the city, rather than not! You wouldn't feel envious when you saw someone putting to death whoever he pleased, or confiscating his property, or imprisoning him!

SOCRATES: Do you mean justly or unjustly?

469 POLUS: Whichever he does, isn't it an enviable thing either way?

SOCRATES: Sh! Don't say things like that, Polus.

POLUS: Why not?

SOCRATES: Because we shouldn't envy those who are not to be envied, nor those who are wretched. We should pity them.

POLUS: What? Is that how you think things are for the people I am talking about?

SOCRATES: Of course.

POLUS: So the person who puts to death whoever he pleases – and puts him to death justly – do you think he is wretched and deserving of pity?

SOCRATES: No, I don't. But I don't regard him as enviable either.

POLUS: Didn't you just say he was wretched?

b SOCRATES: If you mean the person who puts people to death unjustly, my friend, then yes I did – and deserving of pity into the bargain. The one who puts people to death justly I say is unenviable.

---

[37] The nature and validity of the distinction Socrates has drawn between doing what you will and doing what you please has been much disputed by commentators. Something like the following seems to be what he articulates: I *will* X if I want it either because *it* is good, or because it leads to Y and Y is in truth good; whereas the X I want is merely my *pleasure* if, although it may lead to Y, Y isn't actually good for me. Socrates' thought does capture the point that we want *real* goods, not ones that fail to live up to expectations that they will be good – at any rate in one important sense of 'want'. Three additional points: (1) The formulation suggested here leaves it unclear whether I have to know that something is good if I am to be said to will it or anything that leads to it. Although there is no explicit reference to knowledge in the course of the argument at 467b–468e, Socrates perhaps implies the condition when he contrasts doing what you will with doing what you please *without understanding* (467a). (2) Socrates makes it obvious that there is a question over whether banishing or killing people or confiscating their property satisfies the conditions set on doing what you will, and so (Socrates concludes) on having great power. But substantive argument that the conditions are failed is yet to come. (3) Although he draws no attention to the point, the original suggestion (467c–d) that health and wealth are the sorts of things which motivate behaviour and therefore count as 'willed' is effectively to be regarded similarly as provisional: if they turn out *not* to be truly good, they won't be the objects of willing.

POLUS: Well, at any rate the one who is put to death unjustly is both to be pitied and wretched.

SOCRATES: Less so than the person who puts him to death, Polus. And less so than the person who is put to death justly.

POLUS: How come, Socrates?

SOCRATES: For the simple reason that acting unjustly is in fact the greatest of evils.

POLUS: Is it really the greatest? Isn't being treated unjustly a greater evil?

SOCRATES: Far from it.[38]

POLUS: So for choice, you'd be treated unjustly rather than act unjustly?

SOCRATES: I wouldn't want either, personally. But if I were compelled c to act unjustly or be treated unjustly, then I would choose to be treated unjustly rather than act unjustly.

POLUS: So you wouldn't say yes to being a tyrant?[39]

SOCRATES: Not if what you mean by being a tyrant is what I mean by it.

POLUS: Well, I mean what I meant just now: the power to do whatever you please in the city – putting to death and banishing and in general doing as you please.

SOCRATES: Bless you, Polus! Now, let me tell you what *I* think, and you can find fault with that. Suppose I were in a market-place full of people, d with a dagger up my sleeve. I could say to you: 'Polus, I have just acquired tremendous and tyrannical power. If it pleases me that one of these people you can see is to die, here and now, then die he will – whichever one I please. And if it pleases me that one of them should have his head broken, then broken it will be, just like that. His cloak torn to shreds? Then torn to shreds it will be. So great is the power I have in this city.' If you didn't e believe me, then I could show you the dagger; and maybe when you saw

---

[38] Socrates' responses here to Polus mark his commitment to a conception of what good and bad in life consist in that constitutes a radical departure from conventional Greek views. The whole of the rest of his conversation with Polus attempts to explain and justify this revaluation of values, and particularly the thesis that doing what is just is better for the agent than behaving unjustly, whatever ostensible advantages injustice achieves.

[39] Polus now reverts to explicit discussion of tyranny, first broached by him at 466c, and will shortly introduce the paradigm case of Archelaus, ruler of Macedonia (470d). Oratory drops out of the picture until the last page or two of the conversation with him (from 479a), except for Socrates' remarks about methodology at 471d–472c. The switch of focus enables him to tackle issues at the moral heart of the dialogue: justice and happiness (cf. 472c–d).

it you would say: 'On that basis, Socrates, anyone could have great power. Any house you please could be burnt down in this way, along with the dockyards and triremes of the Athenians, and all their sailing vessels, both publicly and privately owned.' In which case, it isn't having great power, this doing what one pleases. Or do you think it is?

POLUS: Well, in that situation, no.

470 SOCRATES: Can you say what your objection is to power of this sort?

POLUS: Yes, I can.

SOCRATES: What is it? Tell me.

POLUS: He's bound to be punished, the person who acts like this.

SOCRATES: And being punished is an evil, isn't it?

POLUS: It certainly is.

SOCRATES: Polus, you're a marvel! You've finally come round to the view that if a person does as he pleases, and it turns out to his advantage, then it is good, and this, it seems, is having great power. If it doesn't turn out well, it is bad, and this is having little power. And there's another point

b for us to consider. Do we definitely agree that doing the things we've just been talking about – putting people to death, banishing them, confiscating their property – is sometimes for the better and sometimes not?

POLUS: We certainly do.

SOCRATES: Well, that's at least one thing, by the looks of it, which is agreed on your side and mine.

POLUS: Yes.

SOCRATES: So when do you say that doing those things is for the better? Tell me where you draw the line.

POLUS: You answer that one, Socrates.

c SOCRATES: Very well. What I say, Polus, if you'd rather hear it from me, is that when someone does those things justly, then it is for the better; if he does them unjustly, then for the worse.

POLUS: Prove you wrong, Socrates? Now there's a challenge! Why, a child could prove that what you say is not true.

SOCRATES: In which case, I shall be most grateful to the child – and equally to you, if you prove me wrong, and rid me of some piece of nonsense. You're doing a friend a favour, so stick at it – prove me wrong.

POLUS: Well, no need to use examples from history, Socrates. There are

d things which happened only yesterday which are quite enough to prove you wrong, and demonstrate that lots of people who act unjustly are happy.

SOCRATES: What kind of things?

38

POLUS: Take this fellow Archelaus, son of Perdiccas, who rules over Macedonia. You know him?

SOCRATES: Well, if I don't, I've certainly heard of him.

POLUS: Do you think he is happy or wretched?

SOCRATES: I don't know, Polus. I've never met the man.

POLUS: What, you mean you'd know if you met him, but otherwise you e can't tell straight away that he is happy?

SOCRATES: Heavens, no.

POLUS: And obviously, Socrates, you're going to say you're not even sure if the Great King is happy.[40]

SOCRATES: And I'll be right. I don't know how well off he is in terms of education and justice.

POLUS: What? Is that where the sum total of happiness lies?

SOCRATES: Yes, if what I say is true. I claim that the man – or woman – who is noble and good is happy, and that the one who is unjust and wicked is wretched.[41]

POLUS: So he's wretched, is he, this Archelaus fellow, on your 471 reckoning?

SOCRATES: If he's unjust, my friend, then yes.

POLUS: Well, of course he's unjust! He shouldn't by rights have had anything to do with the throne he now occupies, since his mother was a slave of Perdiccas' brother Alcetas, and so far as justice goes he was Alcetas' slave. If he'd wanted to act justly, he could have gone on being a slave to Alcetas, and he'd be happy, on your reckoning. As it is, he has carried out the greatest injustices, and so become spectacularly wretched. First of all he sent for this Alcetas in person, his master b and uncle, saying he was going to give him back the kingdom which Perdiccas had taken away from him. He gave him hospitality, and then got him drunk, together with his son Alexander, his own cousin and about the same age as him. Then he threw them into a cart, took them out under cover of darkness, cut their throats and disposed of them both. After these acts of injustice, he didn't realise he had become incredibly wretched, so he didn't repent, but not long after turned his attention to his brother, Perdiccas' legitimate son, a boy of about seven, c to whom, so far as justice goes, the kingdom was due to come. He didn't

---

[40] The Great King of Persia was the most powerful man in the world, in the eyes of the Greeks.

[41] It was a Socratic thesis that virtue is gender neutral: not one thing for a man, another for a woman. See *Men.* 72d–c; Xenophon, *Symposium* 2.9; Aristotle, *Politics* 1.13, 1260a20–2.

want to become happy by doing what was just – bringing the boy up and restoring the kingdom to him. Instead he threw him into a well and drowned him, and told his mother Cleopatra that he had been chasing a goose, had fallen in and died. Which is why now, having carried out the greatest injustices of anybody in Macedonia, he is the most wretched of all the Macedonians, not the happiest. And no doubt there

d are Athenians, starting with you, who would settle for being any other Macedonian at all rather than Archelaus.

SOCRATES: Right back at the beginning of our discussion, Polus, I complimented you on the fine education in rhetoric I think you have received – but I said you had neglected question and answer. And now, is this really the argument with which a child could prove me wrong? And when I say that the person who acts unjustly is not happy, have I now been proved wrong by you, using this argument – is that what you think? How can you possibly believe that, my friend? Why, I disagree with every word you say.

e POLUS: That's because you won't allow yourself to agree, though what you really think is as I say.

SOCRATES: Bless you, no! It's because you're using the orator's way of trying to prove me wrong, just like those who think they are proving people wrong in the lawcourts. There one side thinks it's proving the other wrong if they produce lots of reputable witnesses to the things they are saying, and their opponent produces only one – or none. But proving people wrong like this is of no value when it comes to getting at the truth.

472 It can happen that somebody is the victim of wholesale perjury – and from a lot of people who have some reputation.

Today, for example, the things you are saying now – practically everybody, Athenians and foreigners alike, will agree with you and testify that what I say is not true, if you choose to produce them as witnesses against me. Among those who will give evidence for you, if you want, are Nicias the son of Niceratus, and his brothers with him; it is their tripods which stand in a row in the precinct of Dionysus. Or Aristocrates, if you want, the son

b of Scellias; he in his turn has that handsome offering in the precinct of Pythian Apollo.[42] Or again, if you want, the whole household of Pericles,

---

[42] Nicias was a major politician, who opposed the proposal for a military expedition against the Sicilian city of Syracuse in 415 BC, but was the commander whose questionable decision-making precipitated the final crushing defeat of the Athenian forces in 413. Aristocrates was to be a member of the regime of Four Hundred, the oligarchic party which controlled Athens briefly in 411. The tripods would have been prizes won by a

or any other family you may wish to select from those here in Athens. I
am just one person, but I do not agree. You do not, after all, *compel* me to
agree with you; instead you bring lots of false witnesses against me, and
try to dislodge me from my patrimony, from the truth. Whereas I reckon,
if I can't produce one person, you yourself, as a witness confirming what
I say, then I have achieved nothing worthwhile so far as the object of our
discussion is concerned. Any more than you have, in my view, unless I, one c
single person, act as witness for you, and you forget about all these others. So there is that way of proving people wrong, as you think and many
others think. But there is also another way, the way I on my side think.
Let's set them side by side, and ask ourselves if we're going to find any
difference between them. After all, the things we disagree about really are
anything but trivial – broadly speaking, they are those where knowledge is
most admirable, and ignorance most disgraceful. What it boils down to is
recognising, or failing to recognise, who is happy and who is not.

For a start, to take the subject of our present discussion, you believe d
that a man acting unjustly and being unjust can have fortune's blessing,
if you believe Archelaus is unjust and yet happy. Are we right in taking
this to be your view?

POLUS: You certainly are.

SOCRATES: But I say it's impossible, so there's one thing we disagree
about. Very well – acting unjustly he will be happy. Even if he meets his
just deserts and is punished?

POLUS: No. In that case he will be most wretched.

SOCRATES: But if he doesn't meet his just deserts, the person who acts e
unjustly, then on your view he will be happy.

POLUS: That is what I maintain.

SOCRATES: Whereas in my opinion, Polus, the person who acts unjustly –
the unjust person – is altogether wretched, but more wretched if he does
not pay for his crimes or meet with punishment when he acts unjustly,

play successful in one of the city's annual drama festivals, presented to the citizen who
as *chorêgos* had funded its production, and then dedicated by him to Dionysus (patron
deity of most of the festivals), or in Aristocrates' case to Apollo. Socrates evidently selects
examples of eminent Athenian families notable for wanting the popular acclaim they had
won by lavishly competitive expenditure to be on permanent public display. His thought
is presumably that these people above all could be expected to go along with conventional
opinion on a topic such as the happiness of a tyrant – although as he goes on to suggest,
practically any Athenian family would harbour similar sentiments: all are captive to conventional values. According to the *Laws*, 'being a tyrant and doing whatever you desire'
was generally held to be one of the good things in life (*Laws* 2.661a–b).

and less wretched if he does pay for his crimes and does meet with justice at the hands of gods and men.

473   POLUS: These are extraordinary views you are putting forward, Socrates.

SOCRATES: Yes, and I'm going to try and make you, my friend, put forward the same views as me. You see, I regard you as a friend. For now, what we disagree on is this – see if you agree. I suppose what I've been saying earlier on was that acting unjustly was worse than being treated unjustly.[43]

POLUS: Exactly.

SOCRATES: Whereas you said being treated unjustly was worse.

POLUS: Yes.

SOCRATES: I maintained that those who act unjustly are wretched, and I was proved wrong by you.

POLUS: You certainly were.

b   SOCRATES: As you think, Polus.

POLUS: And rightly.

SOCRATES: Maybe. You, by contrast, regard those who act unjustly, if they don't pay for their crimes, as happy.[44]

POLUS: Indeed I do.

SOCRATES: Whereas I claim they are most wretched, and those who pay for their crimes are less wretched. Do you want to prove that wrong as well?

POLUS: Help! That's even harder to prove wrong than the first one, Socrates!

SOCRATES: No, not harder, Polus. Impossible. What is true is never proved wrong.

POLUS: What do you mean? Suppose a person is caught acting unjustly –
c   with designs on tyranny, say. When he is caught he is put on the rack, castrated, he has his eyes burnt out and suffers all kinds of other torments himself, and has to watch his wife and children suffering them as well. Finally he is impaled, or used as a human torch. Is this person going to be happier than if he had got away with it and made himself tyrant, and lived his life as ruler in the city, doing whatever he wished, envied and
d   congratulated by the citizens and foreigners too? Are those the things you are saying it is impossible to prove false?

---

[43] The reference is to the passage at 469a–b.
[44] Socrates recapitulates Polus's language at 470c.

SOCRATES: Now you're trying to make my flesh creep, noble Polus, not proving me wrong. A moment ago you were calling witnesses. Anyway, refresh my memory on one small point. Unjust designs on tyranny, did you say?

POLUS: Yes, I did.

SOCRATES: Then neither of them will ever be happier, neither the one who has unjustly achieved the tyranny nor the one who pays for his crimes – you can't have a 'happier' out of two wretched people. All the same, the one who gets away with it and becomes tyrant is the more   e
wretched. What, Polus? Are you laughing? Is this yet another way of proving someone wrong – laughing at him when he says something, instead of proving him wrong?

POLUS: Don't you think you've already been proved wrong up to the hilt, Socrates, when you say the kinds of things no one in the world would say? I mean, ask any of these people here.

SOCRATES: I'm not one of your politicians, Polus. Last year I was chosen by lot to serve on the council, and when it was my tribe's turn to provide the executive committee, and it was up to me to put something to the vote, I made a bit of a fool of myself by not knowing how to put it to the   474
vote.[45] So don't now tell me to put it to the vote with these people here. No, if that's the best you can do in the way of proving me wrong, then do as I suggested a moment ago. Let me have a turn, and then you can see what I think a proof should be like. I only know how to produce one witness for the things I'm saying – and that's the person I'm actually having the discussion with. I've no time for the many. But if it's one person, then I do know how to put it to the vote. As for the many, I can't even begin to have a discussion with them. So see if you'll be willing in your turn to   b
give me a chance to prove you wrong, by answering the questions which

[45] At Athens the council prepared the business for the assembly of all citizens (the body which took major decisions), although it also had responsibility for managing the city's finances, not least expenditure on buildings and armaments, through boards whose work it had a duty to oversee. It acted on the advice of an executive committee consisting – through a system of rotation – of one of the ten tribal contingents (of fifty citizens each) that constituted its membership. Each day of the year a different member of the contingent in charge for that month chaired any meeting of the assembly or council being held, with nobody permitted to do the job more than once. There is no other evidence relating to the incident Socrates recounts. It is sometimes supposed that the reference is to the motion to put on trial as a group the generals commanding the fleet at the battle of Arginusae (406 BC), mentioned by Socrates elsewhere as opposed by him alone among members of the executive committee (*Apol.* 32b). But there is nothing to indicate that the two occasions were the same.

are put to you. You see, it's my opinion that you and I and the rest of mankind believe that acting unjustly is worse than being treated unjustly, and that not paying the penalty is worse than paying the penalty.

POLUS: Whereas it's my opinion that neither I nor anyone else in the world believes that. I mean, would you choose to be treated unjustly rather than act unjustly?

SOCRATES: Yes. And so would you. And so would everybody else.

POLUS: You couldn't be more wrong. I wouldn't. Neither would you. And neither would anyone else.

c SOCRATES: Does that mean you won't answer?

POLUS: No, I certainly will answer. I really want to know what in the world you are going to say.

SOCRATES: Well, if you want to know, then tell me, as if I were starting my questions again from the beginning – which do you think is worse, Polus, acting unjustly or being treated unjustly?[46]

POLUS: Being treated unjustly, in my view.

SOCRATES: How about which is more disgraceful, acting unjustly or being treated unjustly? Don't stop answering.

POLUS: Acting unjustly.

SOCRATES: In which case it is also worse, if it is more disgraceful.

POLUS: No, it isn't.

d SOCRATES: I see. You don't, apparently, think that fine and good are the same thing. Nor bad and disgraceful.

POLUS: No.

SOCRATES: Here's a question for you. All fine things – such as bodies or colours or shapes or sounds or practices – do you always call them fine, when you do, without reference to some standard? For instance, let's start with a fine body. Don't you call it fine either with respect to its use – whatever it is each one is useful for – or with respect to some pleasure, if it causes those who look at it to delight in looking at it? Can you suggest any consideration apart from these with regard to what is fine in a body?

POLUS: No, I can't.

e SOCRATES: Is it the same with all the others on my list? Do you call shapes and colours fine either because of some pleasure they give, or some benefit, or both?

---

[46] Socrates now launches an argument for this conclusion, reluctantly agreed by Polus at 475d–e. In Callicles' view, Polus concedes too much to conventional views (cf. 475d) when he allows here that acting unjustly is more disgraceful than being unjustly treated – which is what enables Socrates to tie him in knots.

POLUS: Yes.

SOCRATES: And isn't it just the same with sounds, and everything to do with music?

POLUS: Yes.

SOCRATES: And then again, anything to do with laws and practices – anything fine, that is – there's nothing else to this apart from being either beneficial or pleasurable or both.

POLUS: No, I don't think there is.   475

SOCRATES: And what is fine in branches of learning – is it the same with that?

POLUS: Absolutely. This is a fine definition you're giving now, Socrates, using pleasure and good to mark out what is fine.

SOCRATES: And when I use the opposite, pain and evil, to mark out what is disgraceful?

POLUS: That must follow.

SOCRATES: In which case, when one of two fine things is more fine, is it more fine because it surpasses in one or both of these two things – either pleasure or benefit or both?

POLUS: Indeed it is.

SOCRATES: And when one of two disgraceful things is more disgraceful, b it will be more disgraceful because it surpasses in painfulness and badness. Isn't that inevitable?

POLUS: Yes.

SOCRATES: Very well. Now, what was said a moment ago on the subject of acting unjustly and being treated unjustly? Weren't you saying that being treated unjustly was worse, but that acting unjustly was more disgraceful?

POLUS: I was.

SOCRATES: In which case, if acting unjustly is more disgraceful than being treated unjustly, wouldn't it be more disgraceful either because it is more painful and surpasses in painfulness, or in badness, or both? Isn't this also inevitable?

POLUS: Of course.

SOCRATES: So let us first ask ourselves: 'Does acting unjustly surpass c being treated unjustly in painfulness? Do those who act unjustly suffer more than those who are treated unjustly?'

POLUS: That can't possibly be the case, Socrates.

SOCRATES: In which case, it doesn't surpass it in painfulness.

POLUS: Certainly not.

SOCRATES: And if not in painfulness, there can no longer be any question of its surpassing it in both.

POLUS: Apparently not.

SOCRATES: The only thing left, then, is that it surpasses it in the other.

POLUS: Yes.

SOCRATES: In badness.

POLUS: It looks that way.

SOCRATES: And it is because it surpasses it in badness that acting unjustly would be worse than being treated unjustly.

POLUS: Well, obviously.

d SOCRATES: Now, isn't it agreed by most people – and by you at an earlier point in our discussion – that acting unjustly is more disgraceful than being treated unjustly?

POLUS: Yes.

SOCRATES: And now it has been shown to be worse.

POLUS: Apparently.

SOCRATES: Well, would you choose the worse and more disgraceful in preference to the less? [*silence*] Don't be afraid of answering, Polus. You won't come to any harm. Put yourself in the hands of the argument, there's a brave fellow – think of it as a doctor – and answer. Either say yes to my question, or say no.

e POLUS: No, I wouldn't choose the more disgraceful, Socrates.

SOCRATES: Would anyone else in the world?

POLUS: I don't think so. Not on this argument, at any rate.[47]

SOCRATES: In that case, I was speaking the truth when I said neither you nor I nor anyone else in the world would choose to act unjustly in preference to being treated unjustly. And that is because it is in fact a worse thing.

POLUS: So it seems.

SOCRATES: You see, Polus. If you compare this method of proving somebody wrong with the other, it is nothing like it. In yours, everyone else agrees with you except me, whereas in mine, all I need is you on your

---

[47] There is general if not universal agreement among commentators that Socrates' argument is flawed. One way of articulating the complaint is to object that throughout it treats pleasurable and painful, beneficial and bad (which here means 'disadvantageous' or 'harmful', not 'wicked') as absolute terms, not allowing for consideration that something may be pleasurable for A but painful for B, or beneficial for B but bad for A. All Polus needed to do, on this view, was to reply to Socrates' suggestion: 'And now it has been shown to be worse' (475d) with the qualification: 'Yes, worse in its consequences for others, but not for the agent' – and then it's not clear that the agent *hasn't* reason to choose it.

own, just one person, agreeing with me and giving evidence for me. I can 476
put it to just your vote, and forget about everyone else. Well, so much for
that. But following on from it, let's examine the second thing we disagreed
about: when a person who acts unjustly pays for his crimes, is it the greatest of evils, as you thought, or is not paying for his crimes a greater evil, as
I on my side thought? Let's look at it like this. Do you call paying for one's
crimes and being justly punished for acting unjustly the same thing?[48]

POLUS: Yes, I do.

SOCRATES: And can you deny that all things which are just, to the extent b
that they are just, are fine? Think carefully before you speak.

POLUS: No, I think they are all fine, Socrates.

SOCRATES: Now, think about this. If somebody does something, mustn't
there also be another thing which has something done to it by the doer?

POLUS: Yes, I think so.

SOCRATES: Does it have done to it precisely what the doer does, and in
precisely the way the doer does what he does? Look, this is what I mean:
if someone gives a beating, must there necessarily be something which is
being beaten?

POLUS: Yes, there must.

SOCRATES: And if the person giving the beating does the beating vio-
lently or rapidly, must the thing which is being beaten be beaten in pre- c
cisely the same way?

POLUS: Yes.

SOCRATES: In which case, is what is done to the thing being beaten done
in precisely the same way as the beating is done by whatever is giving the
beating?

POLUS: Very much so.

SOCRATES: And if someone does some burning, must there necessarily
be something which is being burnt?

POLUS: Of course.

SOCRATES: And if he does the burning fiercely or painfully, then must
the thing which is being burnt be burnt in just the way that whatever is
doing the burning burns?

---

[48] Socrates' proof that *not* being punished for your crimes is worse than paying for them,
in fact the worst thing that can happen to a person, extends for the whole of the rest of
the conversation with Polus. It employs the same principle as in the previous argument
(that what's fine is so because it's either beneficial or pleasurable). This time, however, it
becomes explicit that the benefit is benefit to someone in particular, namely the person
paying for his crimes.

POLUS: Absolutely.

SOCRATES: And if someone does some cutting, does the same apply? I mean, something is being cut.

POLUS: Yes.

SOCRATES: And if the cut is large, or deep, or painful, does the thing
d being cut get a cut of just the sort made by whatever does the cutting?

POLUS: It looks like it.

SOCRATES: In general, then, see if you agree with what I said originally: in every case, in whatever way the doer does something, what has something done to it has it done in precisely the same way.

POLUS: Yes, I do agree.

SOCRATES: Then if these things are agreed, is paying for your crimes having something done to you, or doing something?

POLUS: Having something done to you, Socrates. Must be.

SOCRATES: By someone who is doing it, presumably?

POLUS: Of course. By the person doing the punishing.

SOCRATES: And does the person who punishes correctly punish justly?
e POLUS: Yes.

SOCRATES: Doing things which are just, or not?

POLUS: Things which are just.

SOCRATES: So the person being punished, in paying for his crimes, is he having just things done to him?

POLUS: Apparently

SOCRATES: And things which are just have been been agreed, I take it, to be fine?[49]

POLUS: Indeed they have.

SOCRATES: In which case, one of them is doing things which are fine, and the other, the one being punished, is having them done to him.

POLUS: Yes.

477 SOCRATES: And if fine, then good, since they are either pleasurable or beneficial?

POLUS: That must be so.

SOCRATES: In which case, does the person paying for his crimes have good things done to him?

POLUS: It looks like it.

SOCRATES: Is he, in that case, benefited by them?

POLUS: Yes.

[49] See 476b.

SOCRATES: And is the benefit what I take it to be? Does he become better in his soul if he is justly punished?[50]

POLUS: Probably.

SOCRATES: In which case, is the person who pays for his crimes released from evil affecting his soul?

POLUS: Yes.

SOCRATES: And is he released from the greatest evil? Look at it this b way. In the state of someone's finances, can you see any evil other than poverty?

POLUS: No. Just poverty.

SOCRATES: What about the state of the body? Would you say that evil there was weakness, disease, ugliness – things like that?

POLUS: Yes, I would.

SOCRATES: And in the soul as well? Do you think there can be some badness there?

POLUS: Of course.

SOCRATES: And don't you call it injustice, ignorance, cowardice – that sort of thing?

POLUS: Absolutely.

SOCRATES: So for one's finances, body and soul – that's three things – c have you named three kinds of badness: poverty, disease, injustice?

POLUS: Yes.

SOCRATES: Which of these forms of badness, then, is the most disgraceful? Isn't it injustice and, in general, the bad condition of the soul?

POLUS: It certainly is.

SOCRATES: And if it is the most disgraceful, is it also the worst?

POLUS: How do you mean, Socrates?

SOCRATES: Like this. What is most disgraceful is always most disgraceful because it produces either the greatest pain, or harm, or both – that follows from what has been agreed earlier on.

POLUS: Absolutely.

SOCRATES: And hasn't it just now been agreed by us that the most disgraceful thing is injustice and bad condition of soul generally?

[50] Socrates' introduction of the crucial idea that it is the soul (i.e. the mind or personality) that punishment benefits enables him to achieve two objects: first, to identify the badness or disadvantage (*kakon*) that afflicts an unjust person as moral evil (which as Polus agrees is what *ponêria*, 'badness', 'bad condition', as a state of the soul consists in); and then to return in effect to his earlier classification of sciences, and present punishment as having a remedial effect on the soul much as medicine does on sick bodies – to the extent that it makes people self-controlled and their behaviour more just.

d POLUS: Yes, it has.

SOCRATES: Is it then the most disgraceful either because it is the most distressing, and surpasses in distress, or in harm, or in both?

POLUS: Yes, it must be.

SOCRATES: And is being unjust, undisciplined, cowardly and foolish a more painful thing than being poor or being ill?

POLUS: I don't think so, Socrates. Not on these considerations, at any rate.

SOCRATES: In which case, the thing which makes the bad condition of the soul the most disgraceful of all must be that it surpasses the rest by

e reason of some monstrously great harm, some incredible evil, since on your own argument it does not surpass them in painfulness.

POLUS: Apparently.

SOCRATES: But then, I imagine, what surpasses the rest by reason of the greatest harm would be the greatest evil to be found anywhere.

POLUS: Yes.w

SOCRATES: In which case, are injustice, intemperance, and bad condition of the soul generally, the greatest evil to be found anywhere?

POLUS: Apparently.

SOCRATES: Well then, which art or science gets rid of poverty? Isn't it skill at business?

POLUS: Yes, it is.

SOCRATES: And which gets rid of disease? Isn't it medicine?

478 POLUS: It must be.

SOCRATES: And which gets rid of badness and injustice? [*long silence*] If you're stuck for an answer, look at it like this. Where, and to whom, do we take people who have something wrong with their bodies?

POLUS: We take them to doctors, Socrates.

SOCRATES: And where do we take those who act unjustly and without restraint?

POLUS: To appear before judges, do you mean?

SOCRATES: So that they can pay for their crimes?

POLUS: Yes.

SOCRATES: Well then, don't those who punish correctly employ justice of some kind in their punishment?

POLUS: Yes, obviously.

SOCRATES: So skill at business gets rid of poverty, medicine gets rid of

b disease, and the administration of justice gets rid of intemperance and injustice.

POLUS: Apparently.

SOCRATES: And which of these is the finest?

POLUS: Which of which is the finest?

SOCRATES: Skill at business, medicine, the administration of justice.

POLUS: There's no comparison, Socrates. The administration of justice.

SOCRATES: Well then, if it is the most admirable, doesn't it again produce either the greatest pleasure or the greatest benefit or both?

POLUS: Yes.

SOCRATES: And is being treated by a doctor pleasant? Do people enjoy being treated?

POLUS: No, I don't think so.

SOCRATES: But it is beneficial, isn't it?

POLUS: Yes.

SOCRATES: Yes, because he's getting rid of a great evil, and so it pays   c
him to endure the pain and be healthy.

POLUS: Of course.

SOCRATES: Well then, as far as his body is concerned, which way would a person be happiest – undergoing treatment, or not being ill in the first place?

POLUS: Not being ill, obviously.

SOCRATES: Yes, because that's not what you take happiness to be, it seems, a release from evil, but never acquiring the evil in the first place.

POLUS: That is so.

SOCRATES: Next question: of two people who have an evil either in their   d
body or their soul, which is the more wretched – the one who receives treatment and gets rid of the evil, or the one who does not receive treatment, and still has the evil?

POLUS: The one who does not receive treatment, as it seems to me.

SOCRATES: Well, did paying for one's crimes turn out to be a release from the greatest evil – badness?

POLUS: Yes, it did.

SOCRATES: Yes, because just punishment teaches people self-control, and makes them more just. It is medicine for badness.

POLUS: Yes.

SOCRATES: In which case, the happiest person is the one who does not have evil in his soul, since evil in the soul was shown to be the greatest of evils.   e

POLUS: Obviously.

SOCRATES: Second, presumably, is the person who is getting rid of an evil.

POLUS: It looks that way.

SOCRATES: And this is the one who is being taken to task and reproved, and who pays for his crimes.

POLUS: Yes.

SOCRATES: In which case the worst life is that of the person who has an evil and doesn't get rid of it.

POLUS: Apparently.

SOCRATES: And is this in fact the person who does the greatest wrongs, acting with the greatest injustice, in such a way as to be neither taken 479 to task nor punished, nor to pay for his crimes, which is what you say Archelaus has managed to achieve – along with all the other tyrants, orators and ruling groups?

POLUS: It looks that way.

SOCRATES: With all due respect, what these people have managed to do is pretty much the same, I take it, as someone in the grip of severe illnesses managing not to pay the penalty, to his doctors, for the faults in his body, and not undergoing treatment, fearing the cautery and surgery the way a b child does, because it hurts. Or don't you agree that that is how it is?

POLUS: No, I do agree.

SOCRATES: Because he doesn't know, seemingly, what kind of a thing health is, or excellence of body. And from what has now been agreed by us, people who avoid just punishment are also probably doing the same kind of thing, Polus. They can see the painful side to it, but are blind to the beneficial side. They don't know how much more wretched it is to live with a soul which is not healthy, but rotten, unjust, unholy, than c to live with an unhealthy body. That's why they will go to any lengths to avoid paying for their crimes – and avoid getting rid of the greatest evil – providing themselves with money, friends and the most persuasive oratory they can muster. But if the things we have agreed on are true, Polus, do you see the things that follow from the argument? Would you like us to reckon them up?

POLUS: All right – since you're going to anyway.

SOCRATES: Well then, does it follow that injustice and acting unjustly are the greatest evil?

d POLUS: Apparently it does.

SOCRATES: And what is more, was paying for one's crimes shown to be a release from this evil?

POLUS: Possibly.

SOCRATES: Whereas not paying was the continuation of the evil?

POLUS: Yes.

SOCRATES: In that case, acting unjustly comes second in the scale of evils. It is acting unjustly and not being punished which is, in the nature of things, the first and greatest of all evils.

POLUS: It looks that way.

SOCRATES: And wasn't that the thing, my friend, we disagreed about? You were congratulating Archelaus on his good fortune in acting unjustly on the grand scale without paying for his crimes, whereas what I thought, e by contrast, was that, whether it was Archelaus or anyone else on earth who acted unjustly and didn't pay for it, this person was deservedly the most wretched of mankind; that the person who acts unjustly is always more wretched than the person who is treated unjustly; and that the person does not pay for his crimes is more wretched than the person who does pay. Aren't those the things I said?

POLUS: Yes.

SOCRATES: And has it been demonstrated that what I said was true?

POLUS: Apparently it has.

SOCRATES: Good. Now, if those things are true, Polus, then what is the 480 point of rhetoric?[51] On what has now been agreed, a person should be his own guardian, to avoid acting unjustly at all costs, since acting unjustly will bring trouble enough. Isn't that right?

POLUS: Indeed it is.

SOCRATES: And if he acts unjustly – either himself or one of the people he cares for – he should go in person, of his own accord, to some place where he can pay for his crimes as quickly as possible, going before the judge as he would to a doctor, in his determination not to allow the disease of injustice to become chronic, leaving his soul festering and incurable. b What else can we say, Polus, if the things we agreed earlier still stand? Doesn't this have to be the only way of making what we are saying now harmonise with what we said then?

POLUS: Well, what *are* we to say, Socrates?

SOCRATES: For defending injustice, then – his own, or that of his parents or friends or children, or his country when it acts unjustly – rhetoric

---

[51] At long last Socrates returns to consideration of rhetoric, and spells out some paradoxical conclusions in the light of the theory developed over the last five pages.

482 is in our view no use at all, Polus, except perhaps for someone who takes
   c it to be of use for the opposite purpose – deciding that he ought to accuse
   first and foremost himself, but also any among his family or anybody else
   among his friends who on any particular occasion acts unjustly – not shel-
   tering them, but bringing the unjust action into the light of day, so that he
   may pay for his crime and become healthy. He should compel himself and
   the others not to play the coward, but grit his teeth and present himself
   well and bravely, as if to a doctor for surgery or cautery, in pursuit of the
   good and fine, taking no account of the pain. If the unjust things he has
   done deserve the lash, he should offer himself for a beating; for imprison-
   d ment, if they deserve prison; he should pay a fine, if they deserve that; go
   into exile, if they deserve exile; or be put to death, if they deserve death.
   He should himself be the first accuser both of himself and of the rest of
   his family, and that is what he should use rhetoric for – to make sure their
   unjust actions come to light, and they rid themselves of the greatest evil,
   which is injustice. Are we to say this, Polus, or not say it?
   e POLUS: Well, it seems extraordinary to me, Socrates, but I dare say you
   find it agrees with what went before.
   SOCRATES: Must we then either undo what went before as well, or necessarily accept what we are saying now?
   POLUS: Yes, that much at least is true.
   SOCRATES: Then again, turning it round the other way, if there is ever the
   need to do someone an injury[52] – either an enemy or anyone at all – then
   provided we are not ourselves being treated unjustly by our enemy – we
   have to watch that – no, so long as it's someone else our enemy is treating
   unjustly, then we should do everything we can, in deed and word, to stop
481 him paying for his crimes or coming before the judge. And if the case
   does come to court, we should engineer his acquittal, and make sure our
   enemy does not pay for his crimes. If he has stolen a large sum of money,
   we should make sure he does not pay it back, but keeps it and spends it
   on himself and his friends, unjustly and godlessly. If his unjust actions
   deserve death, we should see that he does not suffer death – preferably not

---

[52] Elsewhere Socrates argues that there isn't (*Crito* 49b–d, *Rep.* 1.333b–336a). Here he shows
   that the common Greek attitude 'help friends, harm enemies' will entail strange consequences, given the conclusions he and Polus have reached about benefit and harm. Dodds
   describes these consequences as 'comic fantasy' (*Plato: Gorgias*, p.259), but at the same
   time they are meant with all seriousness insofar as they dramatise Socrates' commitment
   to the view of good and evil they express. He will recur to them in the discussion with
   Callicles (508b; cf. 507d).

ever, so that he can be immortal in his wickedness, but failing that, see that
he lives as long as possible the way he is. For that sort of purpose, Polus, I b
think rhetoric is some use, since for the person who is not planning to act
unjustly I don't think its use is very great – if indeed it is any use at all,
which it hasn't been shown to be anywhere in our earlier discussion.

[*stunned silence*]

CALLICLES: Tell me, Chaerephon, is Socrates serious? Or is he
joking?

CHAEREPHON: If you want my opinion, Callicles, deadly serious.
Nothing like asking the man himself, though.

CALLICLES: Ye gods, I'd like to! Tell me, Socrates, are we to take you
seriously in this? Or are you joking? If you're serious, and if the things c
you say are in fact true, wouldn't our whole human life have been simply turned upside down? Aren't we all, on the face of it, doing the exact
opposite of what we should be doing?

SOCRATES: If human beings didn't have some experience in common,
Callicles – some sharing one experience, some another – if one of us
had some private experience not shared by others, then he wouldn't find
it easy to explain his own feelings to another. I say this because I have d
noticed that you and I do in fact now share a common experience. The
two of us are each in love twice over – I with Alcibiades, son of Cleinias,
and with philosophy, and you twice over – with the Athenian demos and
with Demos the son of Pyrilampes. And I notice that, clever as you are,
it's the same every time. Whatever your darlings say, however they say
things are, you have no power to oppose them, but keep changing your
ground this way and that.[53] e

In the assembly, if you say something and the Athenian demos disagrees, you change your ground and say what it wishes; and with the son
of Pyrilampes, that beautiful young man, the same kind of thing happens
to you. You are incapable of resisting the proposals and arguments of
your darlings, with the result that, if anyone were ever to express surprise
at the absurdity of what they are getting you to say on any particular
occasion, you would probably say – if you wanted to tell the truth – that

[53] Socrates goes on the attack right away. The charge that an orator like Callicles is thoroughly dependent on the whims of his audience picks up Socrates' earlier characterisation
of rhetoric as sycophancy (463a–c), and will become a major theme in the last part of the
long conversation that is starting here (512d–522e). The Demos referred to was the son
of Plato's stepfather, and became a wealthy man, serving as trierarch (which carried the
responsibility of equipping and provisioning an Athenian warship).

482 unless someone makes your darling give up this way of talking, then you won't ever stop saying these things either.

Make up your mind, then, that you're going to have to listen to the same kind of thing from me, and don't be surprised by my saying these things. What you have to do is get philosophy, which is my darling, to give up saying them. What philosophy keeps saying, my dear friend, is what you are now hearing from me; and as I see it, she is much less capricious than my other darling. We all know the son of Cleinias – now of one opinion, now of another – whereas philosophy is always of the same opinion.

b She says the things you now find so surprising, though you were here yourself when they were being said. So, as I was saying just now, you can either prove her wrong by showing that acting unjustly, and getting away with it when you do act unjustly, is not the most extreme of all evils – or if you let it go without proving it wrong, then by the dog of the Egyptians, Callicles, you will not have Callicles agreeing with you. He will be out of tune with you in his whole life. And yet for my part, with all due respect, I think it is better that my instrument should be discordant and out of tune – along with any chorus I may be responsible for putting on the

c stage – and that the greater part of mankind should disagree with me and contradict me, than that I, this one person, should be out of harmony with myself and contradict myself.

CALLICLES: If you ask me, Socrates, you're arguing like an adolescent – really playing to the gallery. And here you are playing to the gallery again, now the same thing has happened to Polus that Polus blamed Gorgias for letting happen to him when he was talking to you. He said, if I remember rightly, that Gorgias was asked by you, in the situation where the per-

d son wanting to learn rhetoric came to him not knowing what was just, whether Gorgias would teach him. And he said that out of embarrassment Gorgias said he would teach him, having an eye to conventional morality, which would take exception to someone who said he wouldn't. Agreeing to this, in Polus's view, compelled Gorgias to contradict himself, which is just what you love. At that point Polus was laughing at you – quite rightly, in my view. But now he himself has allowed exactly the same thing to happen to him in his turn. And there's one point on which I personally am less than impressed by Polus – namely his concession to you that acting unjustly was more disgraceful than being treated unjustly.

e It was agreeing to that which got him too, in his turn, tied up in knots and gagged by you during the argument, all because he was too embarrassed to say what he thought.

Gorgias

What you're really doing, Socrates, for all your talk about the pursuit of truth, is dragging the discussion down to commonplace appeals
to public opinion – to things which are fine by convention, but not in
nature. These are for the most part opposed to one another, nature and
convention. So if someone, out of embarrassment, shrinks from saying
what he thinks, he is bound to contradict himself. You've spotted this 483
little trick too, and you're quite unscrupulous about using it in argument.
If people talk about the way things are by convention, you question them
about the way things are in nature. If they talk about how things are in
nature, then you ask them about how things are by convention.

Just now, for example, in this question of acting unjustly and being
treated unjustly, when Polus talked about what was more disgraceful by
convention, you pursued the argument in terms of nature. In nature,
anything is more disgraceful which is also worse – being treated unjustly,
for example – though by convention acting unjustly is more disgraceful.
And that's because a real man doesn't have this happen to him, this b
being treated unjustly. It only happens to some slave for whom death
is preferable to life – who when he is treated unjustly and downtrod-
den is incapable of defending himself or anyone else he cares for. If you
ask me, the people who put laws – conventions – in place are the weak,
the many.[54] It is with an eye to themselves and their own advantage that
they put the laws in place, praise the things they praise, and blame the
things they blame. They intimidate the more forceful among mankind, c
the ones capable of getting the better of others, and to stop them getting
the better of *them*, they say that getting the better of others is disgraceful
and unjust, and that this is what injustice is – trying to get the better of
everyone else. For themselves, I imagine they are well pleased if they can
have an equal share, given their inferiority.

That is why, by convention, this is said to be unjust and disgraceful –
trying to get the better of the many – and they call it acting unjustly. In

[54] So far Greek *nomos* has been 'convention', and opposed to *phusis*, 'nature'. But it is also
(as here) the standard word for 'law'. Callicles will eventually speak approvingly of 'the
law of nature' (483c), meant to sound paradoxical in view of the earlier contrast, but in
fact a coherent enough conception (although not at all what is nowadays meant by the
expression). Callicles' theorising about *nomos* and *phusis* echoes ideas we can document
particularly in the fifth century sophist Antiphon (Fr.44A), although many other thinkers
of the period deployed the contrast to argumentative effect, and in a variety of ways (see
W.K.C. Guthrie, *A History of Greek Philosophy*, Vol. 3, Pt I, Ch.IV). The view that law and
justice are no more than a compact struck between humans too weak to inflict harm on
others with impunity is worked out by Glaucon in a famous passage at the beginning of
Book 2 of the *Republic* (358c–359b).

my view, however, nature itself shows clearly what is just – for the better
d man to have more than the worse, and the more powerful more than the
less powerful. It is evident in many areas that this is how things are, both
in the animal world and among humans, in whole cities and races – that
justice has been adjudged to be precisely this – the stronger ruling over,
and getting the better of, the weaker. By what right, after all, did Xerxes
lead his expedition against Greece – or his father against the Scythians?
e You could give any number of similar examples.[55] These people, I take it,
act as they do in accordance with nature – the nature of the just. Yes, by
heaven, and in accordance with law – the law of nature, though possibly
not with this law which we put in place. We take the best and most forceful among us – catching them young, like lions – mould them with spells
484 and bewitchments, and enslave them. We tell them they should have what
is equal, and that this is what is admirable and just. But as I see it, if a
man is born with a strong enough nature, he shakes all this off, breaks
through it, makes his escape from it. He tramples on our prescriptions,
our charms, our spells, our laws which all run counter to nature, and rising up he stands revealed as our master, this slave, and there what is just
in nature shines forth.[56]
b   I think Pindar, too, is pointing to what I mean in the poem where he
talks of 'Law, king of all the mortals and immortals'. Law, he says:

> With powerful hand makes the most violent just.
> For this I call as witness Heracles,
> Who in his labours never paid …

Something of the sort, I don't remember the poem. Anyway, he says
that without paying for them, and without Geryon giving them to him,
c Heracles drove off Geryon's cattle, in the belief that what is just by nature
is for the cattle and other goods of those who are lesser and weaker to be
the property of the one who is better and stronger.[57]

---

[55] A reference to expeditions by successive kings of Persia to conquer the Scyths, a nomadic
people living north and east of the Black Sea (about 510 BC), and the Greeks (in 480:
Xerxes' unsuccessful attempt to achieve what his father Darius failed to accomplish in
490). Does Callicles admire the assertion of power as much as its effectiveness?

[56] Readers have often been reminded here of Nietzsche's 'superman'. There is a good brief
discussion of the topic in the Appendix to Dodds, *Plato: Gorgias.*

[57] For the tenth of his twelve labours Heracles was required to fetch the cattle of the
monstrous giant Geryon without demand or payment. Pindar's poem does not survive,
although the subsequent lines (about Heracles' theft of the cattle) are preserved elsewhere
(Fr.169 Snell).

Anyway, that's the truth of it, as you will realise once you say good-bye to philosophy and move on to things which are more important. I tell you, Socrates, philosophy is a charming thing for anyone who gets a modest dose of it at the right age. But if he carries on with it further than he should, it is the ruin of any human being. However able he may be, if he carries on with philosophy to an advanced age, he will inevitably be without experience of all the things you need to have experience of if you d are going to be a man – fine, upstanding and well respected. Philosophers are without experience of the laws of the city, of the language required in dealings with people, whether private or public, of human pleasures and desires – in fact, altogether ignorant of the ways of the world. The result is that when they enter upon any private or public undertaking, they make themselves a laughing-stock – just as I imagine politicians do e when they in their turn enter upon your lot's discussions and ways of talking.[58] Euripides is right: this is where each person shines, and this is what he strives for:

> Keeping the main part of the day for things
> In which he's at his best.[59]

Where he's weak, that's territory he avoids, pouring scorn on it, while 485 the other he praises, out of self-regard, thinking that in this way he is praising himself.

Most appropriate, I suppose, is to have a share of both. It's fine to partake of philosophy to the extent that education requires, and for a boy there's no disgrace in pursuing philosophy. But for a person who's grown up to be still going on with philosophy – the thing's ridiculous, Socrates. What I feel about people doing philosophy is very like what I feel about b people lisping or playing. When I see a child, who is still of an age to talk that way, lisping or playing, I like it. I find it charming, an assertion of freedom, and suited to the age of the child, whereas hearing a little child speaking with great clarity is a thing I find distasteful. It offends my ears, and seems to have something slavish about it. But when you hear a man lisping, or see him playing, it strikes you as ludicrous and unmanly. He c deserves a beating, you feel.

[58] Socrates has already confessed to his own political ineptitude (473e). In the later *Theaetetus* (173c–175b) Plato makes him digress from the main epistemological preoccupations of the dialogue, to offer an extended exploration of the unworldly philosopher's helplessness and of the ridicule he attracts on that account.

[59] Words taken from a speech by Zethus in Euripides' play *Antiope* (Fr.183 Nauck²), further quoted and paraphrased by Callicles below (485c–486c).

Well, speaking for myself, that's exactly how I feel about people doing philosophy. When I see philosophy in a young lad, I am charmed; I find it appropriate, and I think 'This is somebody who expresses his freedom, this person.' The one who doesn't do philosophy I think of as unfree and unlikely ever to expect any admirable or noble achievement from himself.

d But when I see an older person still going on with philosophy, and not giving it up, then in my view, Socrates, what this man needs is a good beating. As I said just now, what happens to a person like this, however able he may be, is that he becomes unmanly, avoiding the city centre and the meeting places in which, says the poet, men win distinction.[60] He disappears from view, and spends the rest of his life whispering in a corner

e with three or four adolescents, without ever giving voice to anything free, or great, or effective.

For my part, Socrates, I feel pretty friendly towards you. I suppose I feel now what Euripides' Zethus, whom I mentioned earlier, felt about Amphion.[61] I find myself wanting to say to you very much what Zethus said to his brother: 'Socrates, you pay no attention to the things you ought to attend to. Fate has given you a natural nobility of soul, yet you present

486 yourself to the world in the guise of an adolescent. You couldn't make a proper speech in the halls of justice; you're never going to come up with the plausible or the persuasive, or put forward a bold proposal in support of someone else.' And yet, my dear Socrates – and don't be angry with me, it's for your own good I'm saying this – don't you think it's a disgrace to be in the state I think you're in, along with rest of those who spend their whole time pressing on with philosophy? As things stand now, if someone seized hold of you or one of your kind, and carted you off to prison, claiming you were acting unjustly when you weren't acting unjustly, you know

b you'd have no way of helping yourself. You'd go dizzy, and stand there gawping, with no idea what to say. You'd be had up in court, find yourself facing some altogether contemptible and vicious accuser, and if he chose to demand the death penalty for you, you'd be put to death.[62]

---

[60] Callicles quotes from Homer on speaking in an assembly: *Iliad* 9.446.

[61] The lost *Antiope* contained a scene in which Zethus and his brother Amphion debate the merits of their different ways of life: Zethus as spokesman for the active life of political engagement (Callicles quotes further from him now: Fr.185), Amphion representing the 'quiet' life devoted to pursuit of leisured activities such as music (his own pastime) or philosophy. Socrates agrees with Callicles that the key issue between them is indeed the choice between philosophy and politics (at least as ordinarily conceived): see 487c–488a, and especially 500b–d, 506b–c.

[62] Plato no doubt expects us to hear a reference to Socrates' trial and death, as also subsequently at 521b–522c.

How can this be wisdom, Socrates – 'an art which takes an able man and makes him worse', with no power to help himself, or save himself or anyone else from the greatest dangers? All he can do is watch his whole property being plundered by his enemies, and live in the city as an absolute nobody. c With someone like this, to put it a bit crudely, you can give him a knuckle sandwich and get away with it. I mean it, listen to me. Stop this questioning people, and 'practise the music of affairs' – practise where 'for wisdom you will get repute'; 'to others leave these subtleties' – call them follies, call them nonsenses – which will 'bring you a life in empty halls'.[63] Model yourself, not on men who ask these nitpicking questions, but on those who possess life and reputation and many other good things besides.   d

SOCRATES: Suppose it were in fact made of gold, Callicles, this soul I have, don't you think I'd be delighted to find one of those stones – and the very best – they use for testing gold? I could apply my soul to it, to see if the stone agreed that my soul had been well cared for; that way I could finally be sure that I was in satisfactory shape and that I had no need of any further test.

CALLICLES: What are you getting at, Socrates?   e

SOCRATES: I'll tell you. I think that in finding you I have found a godsend of just that kind.

CALLICLES: How so?

SOCRATES: I'm quite sure that if *you* agree with me about the opinions my soul is forming, then these are finally the real truth.[64] It strikes me that the person who is going to be an adequate touchstone for the soul, to see 487 whether or not it lives rightly, must in fact possess three things – understanding, goodwill, and a willingness to speak his mind – all of which you do possess. I meet many people who cannot possibly act as my touchstone because they are not wise the way you are. Others are wise, but refuse to tell me the truth because they don't care about me the way you do. As for our two visitors here, Gorgias and Polus, they are both wise, and both my friends; but they're a bit unwilling to speak their minds, and a b

[63] Callicles' final rhetorical flourish weaves together yet more excerpts from Zethus's speech (Fr.186, 188).

[64] Commentators ask whether Socrates is being ironic when he claims to be sure that agreement between him and Callicles will constitute the truth (cf. 487e). Since the claim is premised on Callicles' 'understanding' or 'knowledge' (*epistêmê*) or 'wisdom' (*sophia*: 487c), we can hardly take it at face value. Socrates no more thinks that Callicles has understanding than that Gorgias and Polus are 'wise' (*sophoi*: 487a; cf. 527a–b). Callicles for his part makes emphatic assertions about the truth, incompatible with Socratic tenets, at strategic points in the conversation; e.g. 492c, 493d.

bit anxious – more than they should be – about what people will think. That must be it. They've both taken concern for what people will think to the point where, out of embarrassment, each of them resolutely contradicts himself, before a large number of people, and about things of the greatest importance at that. Whereas you have all these qualities which other people do not have. You have had a good enough education, in the opinion of many Athenians, and you are well-disposed towards me. What
c evidence do I have for that? I'll tell you.

I know there are four of you, Callicles, who are associates in wisdom – you, Teisandros from Aphidnae, Andron the son of Androtion, and Nausicydes of Cholargos.[65] I overheard you once discussing how far the practice of wisdom should be taken, and I know that the opinion which prevailed among you was something like this: you shouldn't throw yourselves into the philosophising that sets store by extreme precision, rather
d you were urging one another to be careful not to acquire more wisdom than was called for, and so come to grief without realising it. When I hear you giving me the same advice you give your own closest friends, that's evidence enough for me that you really are well-disposed towards me. As for your ability to speak your mind without embarrassment, I have your own statement, borne out by the speech you have just made. So for
e our present purposes the position is clearly this: if you agree with me on something in our discussion, then that point will thereby have been sufficiently tested by me and by you. There will no longer be any need to apply it to some further touchstone. After all, you wouldn't have agreed to it from lack of wisdom, nor from over-attention to what people think; and you wouldn't agree with me with a view to deceiving me, because you're my friend, as you yourself say. So the agreement between me and you really will, finally, bring us to our goal, which is truth.

Of all possible enterprises this enquiry is the finest, Callicles – though you criticised me for it. It's about the kind of person a man should be, be
488 he older or younger, what he should pursue, and up to what point. For my part, if there is some way in which I am not doing the right thing in my own life, then believe me, I am not doing wrong on purpose, but as a

---

[65] Dodds surveys the little that is known about Callicles' 'associates in wisdom', and concludes (*Plato: Gorgias*, p.282): 'The general picture which the evidence suggests is that of a group of ambitious young men, drawn from the *jeunesse dorée* of Athens, who have acquired just enough of the "new learning" to rid them of inconvenient moral scruples.' In the *Protagoras* Andron is one of the young Athenians assembled in Callias's house to listen to the sophists (*Prot.* 315c).

result of my own stupidity. So it's up to you. You've started taking me to task, so don't give up, but make it absolutely clear to me what this thing is I should be pursuing, and in what way I might be able to acquire it. And if you catch me agreeing with you now, but at some later time not doing the things I have agreed to, then you can regard me as a complete numskull, and never take me to task again, since I'll not be worth bothering with. b

Start again at the beginning, please. How do you say it is with justice, you and Pindar? What's just in nature, that is. That he who is more powerful should carry off by force the things that belong to those who are less powerful, that he who is better should rule over those who are worse, and that the superior should have more than the inferior? Am I remembering it right? You're not saying justice is anything other than that, are you?

CALLICLES: No, that's what I said. And what I still say.

SOCRATES: And do you call the same man better and more powerful? I wasn't able earlier to find out from you what exactly your meaning is. c Is it the stronger you are calling more powerful, and is it the stronger that the weaker should obey? That's the kind of thing I think you were suggesting earlier, when you said that great cities attack small cities in accordance with what is just in nature, because they are more powerful and stronger, as though 'more powerful', 'stronger' and 'better' were the same thing.[66] Or is it possible to be better, but less powerful and weaker, or more powerful but more wicked? Does the same definition apply to 'the better' and 'the more powerful'? What you must define clearly for d me is this: are 'more powerful', 'better' and 'stronger' the same thing? Or are they different things?

CALLICLES: I can tell you that, quite clearly. They are the same thing.

SOCRATES: And in nature, are the many more powerful than the single individual? They even pass laws to control the individual, as you were saying just now.

CALLICLES: Of course they're more powerful.

SOCRATES: In which case, the rules prescribed by the many are the rules of the more powerful.

CALLICLES: Absolutely.

SOCRATES: Are they then the rules of those who are better? After all, I e take it the more powerful are the better, by your own admission.

[66] Even more than Callicles' original version of the thesis, Socrates' reformulation recalls Thucydides' representation of the Athenians' arguments in the dialogue he represents them as conducting with envoys from the island of Melos (5.85–113), and their subsequent act of genocide. But the Athenians made no suggestion that the natural dominance of the strong constituted any sort of justice.

CALLICLES: Yes.

SOCRATES: And in the nature of things, are the rules of these people, since they are more powerful, fine?

CALLICLES: That is what I maintain.

SOCRATES: Well then, do the many regard it as a general rule – and again it was you who were saying this just now – that it is just to have what is equal, and more disgraceful to act unjustly than to be treated unjustly?

489 Is that how it is, or not? And mind you in your turn don't get caught answering out of embarrassment. Do they regard it as a rule, the many, or don't they, that having what is equal rather than what is greater is just, and that acting unjustly is more disgraceful than being treated unjustly? [*silence*] Please don't refuse me this answer out of pique, Callicles. If you agree with me, then I'll be getting full corroboration from you, since it will be a man of discernment who has agreed.

CALLICLES: Yes, if it's the many you're talking about, they do regard that as a general rule.

SOCRATES: In which case, it's not only by convention that acting unjustly
b is more disgraceful than being treated unjustly, or that having what is equal is just. It is so in nature as well. So it looks as if what you said earlier was not true, and your accusations against me were wide of the mark. You said that convention and nature are opposed – and that this is something I am well aware of when I make malicious use of it in argument, appealing to convention, if someone speaks about how things are in nature, and to nature, if he speaks about how they are by convention.

CALLICLES: Honestly! Will the man never stop drivelling? Tell me, Socrates, aren't you ashamed at your age to be catching at words, and
c thinking it's a real stroke of luck if somebody slips up in a statement? I mean, do you think I'm saying that for people to be more powerful is anything other than for them to be better? Haven't I been telling you for some time that I maintain the better and the more powerful are the same thing? Or do you think I'm saying that if a rabble of slaves gathers, or some ill-assorted collection of humanity good for nothing except perhaps the exercise of physical strength, and if these people make some claim, that this is what is lawful?

SOCRATES: Very well, Callicles, fount of all wisdom. Is that your position?

CALLICLES: Absolutely.

d SOCRATES: Good for you! I have myself been suspecting for a while now that that was the kind of thing you meant by 'more powerful', and my questions are prompted by my eagerness to get a clear idea what you mean. You of all people don't believe, presumably, that two are better than one, nor that your own slaves are better than you, just because they are stronger than you are. No, start again from the beginning and tell me, what exactly do you mean by those who are better, since you don't mean those who are stronger? And be gentle with me, maestro, in your teaching; otherwise I shall leave your lessons.

CALLICLES: You're teasing, Socrates. e

SOCRATES: Far from it, Callicles. I swear by Zethus, whom you have made use of in all those teasing remarks you have just been directing at me. So come on, tell me, who do you say the better people are?

CALLICLES: I mean superiors.

SOCRATES: You see? Now you are the one catching at words, without making anything clear. Won't you tell me, when you talk about those who are better and more powerful, do you mean those with more understanding,[67] or some other group?

CALLICLES: Yes, by Zeus, I do mean them. Emphatically so.

SOCRATES: In which case, according to your argument, one person 490 who does have understanding is often more powerful than a multitude who don't. This is the one who should rule, the others should be ruled, and the ruler should have more than the ruled. This is what I think you mean – I'm not trying to catch you out verbally – if the one is more powerful than the multitude.

CALLICLES: Yes, that is what I mean. This is what is just in nature, I think, that one who is better and has more understanding should rule over, and have more than, his inferiors.

SOCRATES: Hold it there. What exactly is it you are saying this time? b Suppose a number of us are gathered in one place, as we are now, and we have a lot of food and drink to share between us, though we're all very different – some strong, some weak. And suppose one of us has more understanding of these things, because he's a doctor. And suppose, as is likely, he is stronger than some and weaker than others. Won't he, by understanding more than we do, be better and more powerful in this area?

CALLICLES: Indeed he will.

[67] The word for 'having understanding' here is *phronimos* (verb *phronein*). Socrates' subsequent contrast between 'one' and the 'multitude' echoes Heraclitus, Fr.49 ('One man is for me a multitude, if he is the best'), and comes close to articulating a view of what entitles someone to be a ruler that might be inferred from passages in Socratic dialogues such as *Crito* 48a or *Laches* 184c (cf. *Statesman* 297b–c, 301a–e).

c SOCRATES: Should he then have more of these foods than us, because he is better? Or should he, by virtue of being the ruler, distribute it to everybody, and not be greedy in consuming it and using it for his own body, unless he wants to suffer for it? Shouldn't he in fact have more than some and less than others, and if he turns out to be weakest of all, shouldn't the smallest share of all go to the best person, Callicles? Isn't that, with all due respect, how it should be?

CALLICLES: There you go, talking about food and drink and doctors and
d any old rubbish. That's not what I'm talking about.

SOCRATES: Do you say the person with more understanding is better? Yes or no?

CALLICLES: Yes, I do say that.

SOCRATES: But not that the better person should have more?

CALLICLES: Not of food and drink, anyway.

SOCRATES: I see. Of cloaks, maybe? Should the person who is best at weaving have the largest cloak, and go around wearing the most and the finest cloaks?

CALLICLES: Cloaks? What *are* you talking about?

SOCRATES: And shoes. Clearly the person who understands most about
e them and is best at them should have more. Maybe the leather cutter should walk around wearing the biggest shoes, and the greatest number of them.[68]

CALLICLES: What do you mean, shoes? You keep talking nonsense.

SOCRATES: If that's not the kind of thing you mean, how about this? A man who's into farming, perhaps, with the wisdom of the soil, a fine, upstanding person – should he perhaps have a greater share of the seed, and use as much seed as possible on his own land?

CALLICLES: You really do keep on saying the same things, Socrates.

SOCRATES: Yes, and not just that, Callicles, but *about* the same things as well.

491 CALLICLES: Ye gods, it's leather cutters and cleaners and cooks and doctors, the whole time. You never stop. As if they were the people our discussion was about.

SOCRATES: Well, who are we talking about, then? Will you tell us? When the more powerful person, the person of superior understanding, rightly has more, what is it he has more of? Will you neither tolerate my suggestions nor tell us yourself?

---

[68] Leather cutters functioned primarily as shoemakers and cobblers.

CALLICLES: I *have* told you – some time ago. In the first place, the more powerful, who they are – I don't mean leather cutters and cooks, but those who are people of understanding where the affairs of the city are con- b cerned, and the way in which they might be well run. And not just people of understanding, but brave as well, and capable of carrying through the things they plan – people who won't give up from weakness of spirit.

SOCRATES: Do you see, excellent Callicles, how different the things you accuse me of are from the things I accuse you of? According to you, I am for ever saying the same things. You blame me for it. I, by contrast, accuse you of just the opposite – of never saying the same things about the same things. First you defined the better and more powerful people c as the stronger, then again as those with superior understanding, and now here you are with something else again, and it's some collection of braver people who are said by you to be the more powerful and better. For heaven's sake, tell me once and for all who exactly you say the better and more powerful are – and what at.

CALLICLES: I've already told you. People of understanding where the affairs of the city are concerned, brave people. They are the ones who should by rights be ruling their cities, and what is just is for these peo- d ple to have a greater share than the rest – the rulers than the ruled.

SOCRATES: And in relation to themselves, my friend?[69]

CALLICLES: *What*?

SOCRATES: Are they rulers or ruled?

CALLICLES: What do you mean?

SOCRATES: I mean each one being himself his own ruler. Or is there no need for him to rule himself, just everyone else?

CALLICLES: What do you mean, his own ruler?

SOCRATES: Nothing complicated. I mean what most people mean, being moderate, his own master, ruling the pleasures and desires within himself. e

CALLICLES: You simpleton. By 'the moderate' you mean 'the foolish'.

SOCRATES: Far from it. Nobody could fail to realise that's not what I mean.

CALLICLES: It's exactly what you mean, Socrates. How can a human being be happy if he is a slave to anyone at all? No, what is admirable

[69] By this question Socrates begins to switch discussion from politics to psychology, and to an examination of Callicles' conception of desire and (connectedly) the limits of his rejection of conventional morality.

and just according to nature is what I am now telling you, speaking my mind quite freely: the person who is going to live in the right way should allow his own desires to be as great as possible, without restraining them.

492 And when they are as great as can be, he should be capable of using his courage and understanding in their service, and giving them full measure of whatever it is, on any particular occasion, his desire is for. This is impossible for most people, in my view, which is why they are ashamed of themselves, and condemn people like this as a cloak for their own powerlessness. They even go so far as to claim that lack of restraint is something disgraceful, as I was saying earlier, enslaving those people who are by nature better; and being themselves incapable of providing for the fulfil-

b ment of their pleasures, they praise moderation and justice because of their own lack of manliness.

But those who've had the chance, right from the beginning, either to be sons of kings or to have the natural ability to win some position of authority for themselves – as tyrant or part of a ruling élite – for these people, what could in truth be more disgraceful or worse than moderation and justice? It's open to them to enjoy the good things in life – what is to stop them? – and yet they choose to bring in, as master over themselves, the general population's law, reasoning and values. How can they

c have been made anything other than wretched by this prize possession of yours – justice and moderation – when they hand out no more to their own friends than to their enemies, and that despite being rulers in their own city? Whereas if you want the truth, Socrates – something you claim always to be on the track of – here is how things are. Luxury, lack of restraint, freedom – given the resources, that is what virtue and happiness are; the other stuff – the window-dressing, the manmade agreements which run counter to nature – are rubbish, and of no value.

d SOCRATES: Spoken like a man, Callicles. You certainly don't mince words when you get your teeth into an argument. You're now saying in so many words what the rest of the world thinks, but isn't prepared to say. I beg you, therefore, not to ease up in any way, so that it really can be made crystal clear how we should live our lives. Tell me this: you are saying, are you, that a person should not restrain his desires, if he is to be as he ought

e to be, but allow them full rein, giving them fulfilment from whatever source he can – and that this is virtue?

CALLICLES: Yes, that is what I maintain.

SOCRATES: In which case it isn't right, is it, to say that those who want nothing are the happiest?

CALLICLES: No. On that basis stones and dead bodies would be the happiest.

SOCRATES: But then again, the life of the people you are talking about is d pretty odd too. I wouldn't be surprised if Euripides was right about these things when he said:

> Who knows if life be death, and death be life?[70]

In our own case, maybe we really are dead. Indeed, I myself have cer- 493 tainly heard one of the wise say we are already dead – that we leave the womb for a tomb – and that this part of the soul where the desires are is in fact highly susceptible to persuasion, and easily turned topsy-turvy. In fact, some ingenious story-teller,[71] probably some Sicilian or Italian, has made a play on the name, and because you have to be canny when it comes to persuasion, has called it a can, or jar. He called the unintell-igent uninitiated, and with regard to the unintelligent, said of the part of the soul where the desires are – or rather its unrestrained, unwatertight b condition – that it was a leaky jar, the point of the comparison being the impossibility of filling it. He completely disagrees with you, Callicles. He is trying to show that among those in Hades – meaning by that the place of Shades – these people are the most wretched, these uniniti-ated, carrying water to the leaky jar by using a similarly leaky thing, a sieve. By the sieve, according to the person who told me about the story, he means the soul, comparing the soul of the unintelligent to a sieve c because it leaks, and because its unreliability and forgetfulness make it incapable of holding anything.[72] Well, this is maybe rather strange stuff, but it does illustrate my point. I'd like to use it to persuade you, if in any way I can, to change your mind, and choose the ordered life,

---

[70] Socrates counters Callicles' use of Euripides with a quotation of his own, from a play now lost (Fr.638 Nauck²; cf. Heraclitus Fr.62, 88).

[71] 'Socrates does not claim to know, and we cannot know, the identity of the *kompsos aner*' ('ingenious man'): so Dodds, *Plato: Gorgias*, p.297.

[72] For the Greeks of southern Italy and Sicily in the classical period, there is a lot of evidence, much of it tantalisingly fragmentary and hard to interpret, for mystery cults and initiation rituals relating to the afterlife. Plato represents Socrates as summarising an allegorised version of a myth of 'water carriers' (perhaps the daughters of Danaus, condemned to an endless and endlessly frustrating task, in punishment for the murder of their husbands on their wedding night), further interpreted by the informant in epistemological terms. The allegory works largely by extracting significance from what we would regard as punning etymologies and verbal jingles. The translation given here tries to capture these, with some inevitable sacrifice of literal accuracy. For example, 'leave the womb for a tomb' renders 'the body (*sóma*) is a tomb (*séma*)'. (Dodds' proposed addition of *suneis* to the text at 493b2 seems unnecessary, and is not translated.)

a life where what you have at any particular moment is adequate and sufficient, in preference to the insatiable, unrestrained life. Am I per-
d suading you at all? Are you changing your mind? Do you think those whose life is ordered are happier than those who are unrestrained? Or can I tell you any number of stories like this without you changing your mind in the least?

CALLICLES: That's much closer to the truth, Socrates.

SOCRATES: All right. Let me give you another picture – from the same school as the one I've just given you. Ask yourself this question about each of these two lives, the moderate and the unrestrained. Imagine two men, each with a number of jars. One of them has sound, full jars – full of
e wine, of honey, of milk – and many other jars full of many things, though for each of these things his supplies are scanty and not easily come by, and acquiring them is just one hard struggle after another. So this man, having got his jugs filled, can cut off the flow of supplies to them and stop worrying about them. He can relax where they are concerned. For the second man, as for the first, the sources of supply are capable of providing for him, though with difficulty, but his containers are leaky and rotten. He is compelled to spend his whole time filling them, night and day, or
494 else suffer the most extreme hardships. If that is what each of their lives is like, are you saying the life of the unrestrained man is more fortunate than the life of the ordered man? Do I at all persuade you by this description to agree that the ordered life is better than the unrestrained? Or do I not persuade you?

CALLICLES: You do not persuade me, Socrates. The one who has done all his filling no longer has any pleasure left. No, this is, as I was saying
b earlier, the life of a stone, with no more enjoyment or discomfort, once he is filled. Whereas living an enjoyable life simply consists in having as much flowing in as possible.

SOCRATES: And inevitably, if there is a lot flowing in, then there must also be a lot going out; the holes for the outflow must indeed be large.

CALLICLES: Yes, very.

SOCRATES: So. Some kind of stone-curlew's life,[73] then, that you in your turn are talking about. Not the life of a corpse or a stone. Tell me, do you mean something like being hungry, and eating when you are hungry?

CALLICLES: I do.

---

[73] This translates Greek *charadrios*, 'a bird of messy habits and uncertain identity' (Dodds, *Plato: Gorgias*, p.306).

SOCRATES: And being thirsty, and drinking when you are thirsty?   c

CALLICLES: Yes, that is what I am talking about. And having all the rest of the desires and being able to enjoy satisfying them, and so leading a happy life.

SOCRATES: Bravo, sir! Now, continue as you have begun, don't hold back out of embarrassment. And I mustn't be embarrassed either, by the looks of it. So tell me this for a start: if you feel an itch and want to scratch, and are able to scratch to your heart's content, and spend your life scratching, is that living a happy life?

CALLICLES: That's absurd, Socrates. You're just scoring points.   d

SOCRATES: Yes, Callicles, that's how I unnerved Gorgias and Polus, and made them embarrassed. But you're a brave chap, you won't be unnerved or get embarrassed. Just keep answering.

CALLICLES: Very well. In that case I maintain that even the person scratching would be living pleasantly.

SOCRATES: And if pleasantly, then also happily?

CALLICLES: Absolutely.

SOCRATES: And do you mean if he just scratches his head, or – well,   e how much further do I have to go with my questions? I mean, what will your answer be, Callicles, if someone asks you, step by step, about all the things which are linked to these? To take the crowning instance of this sort of thing, what about the life of a bumboy. Isn't it horrible, disgraceful, wretched? Or will you bring yourself to say that these people are happy if they can get an unlimited amount of what they need?

CALLICLES: Aren't you ashamed to drag the discussion down to such depths, Socrates?

SOCRATES: Well, my high-born friend, am I really the one dragging it down? Or is it the person who makes this blanket claim that people who are enjoying themselves are happy, no matter how they are enjoying themselves, without making any distinction among pleasures,   495 which are good and which bad? So tell me, do you still say the pleasant and the good are the same thing? Or is there, among pleasant things, something which is not good?

CALLICLES: Well, to avoid a contradiction in my position if I say it's different, I do say the pleasant is the same as the good.[74]

---

[74] Callicles' response indicates that the issue is not one on which he has an antecedent position. See further note at 499b.

71

SOCRATES: That destroys what we said at the beginning, Callicles. You can't share the job of examining the truth about things with me properly if you're going to say things that aren't what you really think.

b CALLICLES: Yes, I can, Socrates. *You* do.

SOCRATES: Well, if I do, I'm certainly in the wrong. And so are you. Seriously, think about it. The good can't just be pleasure in all its forms, because if it is, the obvious result is all those shameful things hinted at just now. And many more besides.

CALLICLES: According to you, Socrates.

SOCRATES: And you? Do you really affirm this position, Callicles?

CALLICLES: I do.

c SOCRATES: Are we then to set about this discussion on the assumption that you are serious?

CALLICLES: Absolutely serious.

SOCRATES: Very well, if that's your decision, can you draw a distinction for me, please. I take it there is something you call knowledge?

CALLICLES: Yes.

SOCRATES: And weren't you saying a few moments ago that there was a form of courage accompanied by knowledge?[75]

CALLICLES: I was.

SOCRATES: So weren't you talking of them as two things, taking courage to be something different from knowledge?

CALLICLES: I certainly was.

SOCRATES: What about pleasure and knowledge? The same thing, or different?

d CALLICLES: Different, obviously, O fount of all wisdom.

SOCRATES: And do you also say courage is different from pleasure?

CALLICLES: Of course.

SOCRATES: Good. Let's keep it on record,[76] then, that Callicles from the deme of Acharnae said that pleasant and good were the same thing, but that knowledge and courage were something different, both from each other and from the good.

---

[75] Socrates refers to Callicles' final articulation of his main thesis (at 491a–d), there expressed in terms of understanding (*phronimos, phronein*) rather than knowledge (*epistēmē*).

[76] Socrates employs the language appropriate to a legal deposition, including specification of Callicles' native deme (local district), to indicate first the proposition (about pleasure and the good) he will be examining in the two arguments that follow (495c–497d, 497d–499b), and then a key premise (about knowledge and courage) to be deployed in the second.

CALLICLES: And Socrates from the deme of Alopece, does he disagree with us? Or does he agree?

SOCRATES: He disagrees. And so, in my view, will Callicles, once he e looks at himself in the right way. Tell me this. People who are doing well, don't you think what has happened to them is the opposite of what has happened to people who are doing badly?

CALLICLES: Yes, I do.

SOCRATES: In which case, if these things are opposites, is it inevitably the same with them as it is with health and sickness? A person is not healthy and sick at the same time, I take it, nor does he get rid of health and sickness at the same time.

CALLICLES: What are you getting at?

SOCRATES: Well, for example, take any part of the body you like and think about it, just by itself. A person can have something wrong with his 496 eyes, I imagine, for which the name is ophthalmia?

CALLICLES: Of course.

SOCRATES: And presumably he's not also at the same time in a healthy condition where his eyes are concerned?

CALLICLES: No, not at all.

SOCRATES: What about when he gets rid of his ophthalmia? Does he at that point get rid of health where his eyes are concerned, and finish up having got rid of both at the same time?

CALLICLES: No.

SOCRATES: No. If you ask me, that's paradoxical and against reason, isn't it?

CALLICLES: Quite. b

SOCRATES: I think he gains and loses each of the two conditions in turn, doesn't he?

CALLICLES: Yes.

SOCRATES: And the same with strength and weakness?

CALLICLES: Yes.

SOCRATES: And speed and slowness?

CALLICLES: Very much so.

SOCRATES: And good things and happiness, and their opposites – bad things and wretchedness – does he gain them in turn and get rid of each of them in turn?

CALLICLES: Absolutely – that must be right.

SOCRATES: In which case, if we find things which a person both gets rid c of and possesses at the same time, these things clearly wouldn't be the good and the bad. Do we agree on that? Think carefully before you answer.

CALLICLES: I do agree. Couldn't agree more.

SOCRATES: Very well. Now turn to the things which were agreed earlier. You mentioned hunger – did you say it was pleasant or painful? I mean the actual hunger itself.

CALLICLES: Painful, in my view. But being hungry and eating is pleasant.

d SOCRATES: I agree. I can see that. But just the hunger by itself is painful, isn't it?

CALLICLES: Yes, it is.

SOCRATES: And thirst too?

CALLICLES: Very much so.

SOCRATES: Do I need to go on asking you questions, or do you agree that all want and desire is painful?

CALLICLES: I agree. No need to go on asking questions.

SOCRATES: Very well. And being thirsty and drinking – you're saying that is pleasant?

CALLICLES: I am.

SOCRATES: And in this statement of yours, I take it, 'being thirsty' is 'being in discomfort'?

CALLICLES: Yes.

e SOCRATES: And drinking is both a satisfaction of the need and a pleasure?

CALLICLES: Yes.

SOCRATES: So you're talking about enjoyment from drinking?

CALLICLES: Absolutely.

SOCRATES: When you're thirsty, you mean.

CALLICLES: Yes.

SOCRATES: And in discomfort?

CALLICLES: Yes.

SOCRATES: In which case, do you see what the consequence is? When you talk about being thirsty and drinking, you're talking about being in discomfort and getting enjoyment. Or is this not something which takes place in the same location, either of soul or body – call it which you like, I don't think it makes any odds? Is that how it is, or not?

497 CALLICLES: It is.

SOCRATES: But surely you say it's impossible for someone who is doing well to be doing badly at the same time.

CALLICLES: Yes, I do say that.

SOCRATES: And yet you've agreed that it is possible for someone who is in pain to get enjoyment.

CALLICLES: Apparently.

SOCRATES: In which case, getting enjoyment is not doing well, nor is being in pain doing badly, and the pleasant turns out to be something different from the good.

CALLICLES: I don't know about all this clever stuff of yours, Socrates.

SOCRATES: Yes, you do, Callicles. You're just playing the dunce. Come on, take the next step into what lies ahead.

CALLICLES: Why do you persist with this drivel?

SOCRATES: I want you to be aware how smart you are being when you take me to task. Doesn't each of us stop being thirsty and getting pleasure b from drinking at the same time?

CALLICLES: I don't know what you're getting at.

GORGIAS: No, but answer, Callicles. It's for us as well, so that the discussion may be brought to a conclusion.

CALLICLES: But this is how Socrates always is, Gorgias. He asks you little footling questions, and then proves your answers wrong.

GORGIAS: What does that matter to you? You're certainly not the one who thinks they're important, Callicles. Let Socrates prove you wrong in whatever way he chooses.

CALLICLES: [*to Socrates*] All right, then, you'd better carry on with your c finicky little questions, since Gorgias thinks it's a good idea.

SOCRATES: You're fortunate, Callicles, to have been initiated into the higher mysteries before the lower.[77] I didn't think it was permitted. Continue with your answers, then, at the point where you left off. The question was, doesn't each of us stop being thirsty and getting pleasure at the same time?

CALLICLES: Yes.

SOCRATES: And stop being hungry, and feeling the other desires and pleasures, at the same time?

CALLICLES: That is so.

SOCRATES: Don't we then stop feeling pains and pleasures at the same time?

[77] As often Socratic irony is at work: the big picture ('the higher mysteries') Callicles has painted in his speech at 482c–486d isn't really more important than the clarity and precision Socratic dialectic demands ('the lower mysteries'). For an account of the very various mystery cults known in Greco-Roman antiquity, see the Oxford Classical Dictionary. Athenians might be initiated into the higher mysteries at Eleusis and its cult of Demeter and Persephone in the autumn (involving among other things disclosure of sacred objects, secret explication of myth, and a form of collective purification), after the lower mysteries at Agrae in the spring.

d CALLICLES: Yes.

SOCRATES: But we don't stop having good things and bad things at the same time, as you yourself agreed. Or do you now not agree?

CALLICLES: No. I do agree. What of it?

SOCRATES: Just that the good things turn out, my friend, to be not the same as the pleasant things, nor the bad things the same as the painful things. In the one case, both things stop at the same time, in the other they don't, implying that the things are different. So how could the pleasant things be the same as the good things, or the painful as the bad?

Here's another way of looking at it, if you prefer, since I don't think
e there is much agreement with your position this way either.[78] Consider this question: do you call good people good because of the presence in them of good things, just as you call people beautiful because they have beauty present in them?

CALLICLES: I do.

SOCRATES: And what about calling foolish, cowardly people good men? No. Not just now, at any rate. You said it was the brave and the understanding. Or aren't these the people you call good?

CALLICLES: They certainly are.

SOCRATES: Now, how about a foolish child enjoying himself? Have you ever seen that?

CALLICLES: Yes, I have.

SOCRATES: And a man, foolish and enjoying himself? Did you ever see that?

CALLICLES: I think I have. What of it?

498 SOCRATES: Nothing. Just keep on answering.

CALLICLES: Yes, I've seen that.

SOCRATES: How about a sensible man in pain and enjoying himself?

CALLICLES: Yes.

SOCRATES: Which group gets more enjoyment and feels more pain, those with understanding or the foolish?

CALLICLES: Personally, I'd say there wasn't much in it.

---

[78] It appears that Socrates does not wish to insist on the argument against Callicles he has just deployed. Perhaps this is because Plato is conscious that discussion has moved rather far away from any of the issues that preoccupied Callicles when setting out his views initially or in subsequent clarification of them. The next argument will by contrast focus on the difficulty of reconciling hedonism with Callicles' claims about knowledge and courage – key elements in the final articulation of his main thesis.

SOCRATES: Well, even that's good enough. Now, have you ever seen a cowardly man in time of war?

CALLICLES: Of course I have.

SOCRATES: When the enemy withdrew, which did you think were more pleased, the cowardly or the brave?

CALLICLES: I thought both were pleased, but maybe the cowards more b so. If not, then both about equally.

SOCRATES: It's neither here nor there. So the cowards too are pleased?

CALLICLES: Very much so.

SOCRATES: As are the foolish, apparently.

CALLICLES: Yes.

SOCRATES: And when the enemy approach, is it only the cowards who are troubled, or the brave men as well?

CALLICLES: Both.

SOCRATES: Both equally?

CALLICLES: Maybe the cowards more.

SOCRATES: So do the foolish and the wise and the cowardly and the brave feel pain and pleasure about equally, according to you, though the cowards a bit more than the brave?   c

CALLICLES: Yes.

SOCRATES: And the wise and brave are good, while the cowardly and foolish are bad?

CALLICLES: Yes.

SOCRATES: In which case, do the good and the bad feel pleasure and pain about equally?

CALLICLES: Yes.

SOCRATES: So are the good and the bad about equally good and bad? Or are the bad even more good?

CALLICLES: For God's sake, Socrates! I have no idea what you are on d about!

SOCRATES: No idea that what you are saying is that the good are good as a result of the presence of good things, and the bad are bad by the presence of bad things? That the good things are pleasures, and the bad things pains?[79]

CALLICLES: No, I do have an idea of that.

---

[79] The crux of the argument: if the good is the same as the pleasurable, and the bad the same as the painful, then if the good is what makes a person good and the bad a person bad, fools and cowards are going to turn out just as good as anyone else – because they feel as much pleasure.

SOCRATES: And are the good things, the pleasures, present to those who are enjoying themselves, if they really are enjoying themselves?

CALLICLES: Of course.

SOCRATES: And if good things are present to them, are those who are enjoying themselves good?

CALLICLES: Yes.

SOCRATES: What about those suffering? Aren't the bad things – pains – present to them?

CALLICLES: Yes, they are.

e SOCRATES: Are you saying it is the presence of bad things which makes the bad people bad? Or are you no longer saying that?

CALLICLES: No, that is what I'm saying.

SOCRATES: So are those who are enjoying themselves good, and those who are suffering bad?

CALLICLES: Exactly.

SOCRATES: More so if enjoying themselves or suffering more, less so if less, and about the same if about the same?

CALLICLES: Yes.

SOCRATES: And do you say that the wise and the foolish and the brave and the cowardly enjoy themselves and suffer about the same – or the cowardly a bit more?

CALLICLES: I do.

SOCRATES: Then join with me in reckoning up what our conclusion is from the things that have been agreed. It is a fine thing, they say, 'twice, yes and thrice' to state and consider what is fine. We say that the wise and brave person is good, don't we?

499

CALLICLES: Yes.

SOCRATES: And that the foolish, cowardly person is bad?

CALLICLES: Certainly.

SOCRATES: And again, that the person enjoying himself is good?

CALLICLES: Yes.

SOCRATES: And that the person who suffers is bad?

CALLICLES: Inevitably.

SOCRATES: And that the good and the bad suffer and enjoy themselves equally, or maybe the bad person a bit more?

CALLICLES: Yes.

SOCRATES: In which case, does he become bad and good, the bad person, equally with the good person – or maybe more good? Isn't that what

b follows, together with those things we mentioned earlier, if someone says that pleasant things and good things are the same? Isn't that inescapable, Callicles?

CALLICLES: I've been sitting here listening to you for some time now, Socrates, and coming to the conclusion that if anyone makes the slightest concession to you, even jokingly, you're like a young boy in the delight with which you clutch hold of it. As if you could imagine that I, or anyone else in the world, would fail to regard some pleasures as better and others as worse.[80]

SOCRATES: Ouch, Callicles! That really is unscrupulous! Treating me c like a child. First you say things are one way, then later you say the same things are different, trying to mislead me. And yet back at the start I didn't think I was going to be deliberately misled by you. I thought you were my friend. Now it turns out I was deceived, and I have no choice, it seems, but to make the best of a bad job, in the words of the old saying, and accept what I am being given by you. Which is, apparently, what you are now saying, that there are pleasures, and that some are good and some bad. Isn't that it?

CALLICLES: Yes.

SOCRATES: And are the beneficial ones good, and the harmful ones d bad?

CALLICLES: Absolutely.

SOCRATES: And are the ones which do some good beneficial, and the ones that do some harm bad?

CALLICLES: Yes, they are.

SOCRATES: Do you mean things like the bodily pleasures we were talking about just now, the pleasures of eating and drinking? Of those, are the ones which produce health or strength in the body, or some other physical excellence – are these ones good, and the ones which produce the opposite bad?

CALLICLES: Absolutely. e

SOCRATES: And the same with pains? Are some good and others bad?

CALLICLES: Of course.

SOCRATES: And should we choose the good ones – pleasures or pains – and act on them?

CALLICLES: Absolutely.

SOCRATES: But not the bad ones?

[80] We recall that Callicles had already found the position on pleasure and desire he was getting into uncomfortable (494c–e), and opted for hedonism as what was required to stop it collapsing altogether (495a).

CALLICLES: Obviously not.

SOCRATES: No, because if you remember, good things were surely what we decided, Polus and I, should be the aim of everything we do. Do you agree with that as well – that the good is the goal of all actions and that everything else should be done for the sake of it, not it for the sake of 500 other things? Do you too cast your vote with us, making a third?

CALLICLES: Yes, I do.

SOCRATES: In which case, it is for the sake of good things that we should do pleasant things and everything else, not good things for the sake of pleasant things.

CALLICLES: Definitely.

SOCRATES: And is every man capable of distinguishing, among pleasant things, the kinds which are good and the kinds which are bad? Or do we need an expert for each kind?

CALLICLES: We need an expert.[81]

SOCRATES: Let us then also recall the things I found myself saying to Polus and Gorgias. I was saying, if you remember, that there are some activities which go no further than pleasure, providing this one thing b only, with no knowledge of what is better or what is worse, and other activities which do recognise what is good and what is bad. Among those concerned with pleasures I classed cookery as a skill, not as a science; and among those concerned with the good I classed medicine as a science.

Now, in the name of friendship, Callicles, please don't make up your mind this is a moment for joking. Don't give the first answer that comes into your head, contrary to what you believe, and don't, in your turn, take c the things I say to you like that – as if I were joking. You can see that nothing could be of more importance to anyone of the slightest intelligence than the subject we are discussing, which is this: how should we live our lives? There's the life you are urging upon me, doing the things a real man does – speaking before the people, practising rhetoric, engaging in politics the way you people now engage in it. Is that the way to live? Or should it be this life spent in philosophy? And why exactly does the one

---

[81] With Callicles' abandonment of hedonism, the dialogue can now return to consideration of rhetoric as Socrates had begun to approach it in the conversation with Polus, but with a sense – enhanced by Callicles' intervention at 482c–486c – that what is at stake is how we should choose to live our lives, and with clarity now about the difference between the good and the pleasurable (taken for granted without examination in the classification of sciences and skills at 464b–465a).

differ from the other? Maybe it's best to make distinctions, as I tried to do d
a little while back, and when we have made our distinctions, and agreed
with one another whether there really are these two distinct lives, then to
look into how they differ from one another, and which of them we ought
to live. But maybe you're not yet clear what I mean.

CALLICLES: No, I'm certainly not.

SOCRATES: I'll tell you more clearly. Since we have agreed, you and I,
that there is a good and a pleasant, and that the pleasant is a different
thing from the good, and that there is a practice and activity concerned
with the acquisition of each of them, the pursuit of the pleasant and the
pursuit of the good – well, tell me whether or not you agree with that, for
a start. *Do* you agree?   e

CALLICLES: Yes, that is my view.

SOCRATES: Come, then. Grant me the things I was saying to these
people, too, if you thought what I was saying was true then. I was saying, I fancy, that I don't think cookery is a science, but a skill, whereas
medicine is a science, because, I said, one of them has examined both
the nature of the things it looks after and the reason for the things it 501
does, and it can give an account of each of these things – that's medicine. But the other, in its concern for pleasure, towards which all its care
is directed – well, it just makes a beeline for it, quite unscientifically,
without undertaking any sort of examination of the nature of pleasure,
or its cause. It works in a completely unreasoning way, making virtually
no distinctions at all – it has the skill of using everyday experience to
keep just the memory of what usually happens, which is how it provides b
its pleasures.

For a start, then, see if you think this is an adequate description. Do
you think there are other practices of this kind that operate on the soul
as well, some of them scientific, having some thought for what is best for
the soul, and others again which think that is a waste of time, and instead,
as with the body, have considered only the soul's pleasure, and how it
may be brought into being? As for which of the pleasures is better or
worse, they give no thought to that, nor is it their concern to do anything
except produce enjoyment, be it better or worse. For my part, Callicles, c
I think there are such activities, and I maintain that this kind of thing is
sycophancy – whether it's the body or the soul or anything else whose
pleasure can be looked after without any thought being given to better or
worse. What about you? Do you set down the same opinion about these
things as we do? Or do you disagree?

CALLICLES: No, I don't. I'll go along with you, if it'll get your argument completed, and do Gorgias here a favour.[82]

d SOCRATES: And is it so for a single soul, but not so for two or more souls?

CALLICLES: No, it is so for two or more.

SOCRATES: And is it possible to give pleasure to an assembled gathering of souls all at the same time, with no thought for what is best?

CALLICLES: I think so, yes.

SOCRATES: Then can you say which are the practices which do this? Or rather, if you prefer, I'll ask you, and you say yes if you think it is one of these and no if you think it isn't. Let's start by thinking about playing the

e reed pipe. Don't you think it's one of that kind, Callicles – that its only aim is our pleasure, that it gives no thought to anything else?

CALLICLES: Yes, I do think it is.

SOCRATES: And all activities like it – playing the kithara in competitions, for example?[83]

CALLICLES: Yes.

SOCRATES: How about the training of choruses and the writing of dithyrambic poetry?[84] Isn't it clear to you that they're pretty much the same? Do you think Cinesias the son of Meles is remotely interested in saying the kind of thing which would make his hearers better people? Isn't he

502 just trying to give his rabble of an audience what they want?

CALLICLES: Yes, clearly, Socrates. Cinesias, at any rate.

SOCRATES: And what about his father Meles?[85] Did you really think he was singing his songs with a view to what was best? Or did he sing with no view even to what was most pleasant? His songs were certainly painful to his audience. Ask yourself whether you don't think that the whole business of singing to the kithara and writing dithyrambic poetry has been invented for the sake of pleasure.

CALLICLES: Yes, I do think that.

---

[82] From this point on Callicles gives answers in this spirit, but with increasing reluctance, until at 506c dialogue between them breaks down completely.

[83] For the reed pipe see the note on *Prot.*318c; for the *kithara* the note on *Prot.* 312b.

[84] A form of choral song, from the end of the sixth century BC onwards performed in competitions held at many of the major Athenian festivals honouring the god Dionysus. Cinesias was active in the last two decades of the fifth century, and a famous exponent of innovations in freer forms of poetry and music, such as provoked the comic playwright Aristophanes to ridicule and induced in Plato apocalyptic gloom.

[85] Cinesias's father Meles was described by Pherecrates in the *Savages* (see *Protagoras* 327d) as the worst performer on the *kithara* there had ever been.

SOCRATES: And what about that revered, awe-inspiring activity we know b
so well, the writing of tragedy? Is its undertaking and concern, in your
view, merely to give the audience what they want, or – if there is something they would find pleasant and enjoyable, but wicked – is it engaged
in a struggle to do its utmost not to say this, and if there is something
which is in fact unpleasant but beneficial, to say and sing this, whether
they like it or not? For which of these purposes do you think the writing
of tragedy is designed?

CALLICLES: Well, not much doubt about that, Socrates. Its impulse is c
mainly towards pleasure and giving the audience what they want.

SOCRATES: And did we say just now, Callicles, that that sort of thing was
sycophancy?

CALLICLES: Indeed we did.

SOCRATES: Come then, suppose you stripped away melody, rhythm and
metre from any verse composition, isn't what is left simply speech?

CALLICLES: Yes, it must be.

SOCRATES: Speech addressed to a great gathering, to the people?

CALLICLES: Yes.

SOCRATES: In which case, poetry is some kind of popular oratory.

CALLICLES: It looks like it. d

SOCRATES: And popular oratory counts as rhetoric. You do think poets
in the theatre practise rhetoric, don't you?

CALLICLES: Yes, I do think that.

SOCRATES: In which case, we've now discovered a rhetoric aimed at the
kind of popular audience which consists of children and women and men
all together, slave and free alike. And we don't really like it very much,
since we say it is sycophantic.

CALLICLES: Exactly.

SOCRATES: Very well. How about the rhetoric pitched at the popular
assembly of the Athenians and the popular assemblies of free men in e
the other cities? What exactly do we think *it* is? Do you think orators
always speak with a view to what is best, so that the effect of what they
say should be to make the citizens as good as possible? Is that their aim?
Or do you think their impulse too is towards giving the citizens what
they want, and that in pursuit of their own private good they neglect
the common good, addressing their popular assemblies as if they were
children, trying only to give them what they want, with no thought to
the question whether they will be better or worse as a result of what
they are saying? 503

CALLICLES: That's not such a simple question any more. There are those who say what they say out of concern for the citizens, and there are also the kind of people you are talking about.

SOCRATES: That's good enough. If there really are two sides to this, I take it one of these activities would be sycophancy, the worst kind of appeal to the public; the other would be admirable, bringing it about that the souls of the citizens are as good as possible, and battling to say what is best, regardless of whether this makes it more pleasing or unpleasing to those listening to them. But this is a rhetoric which you have never

b yet seen. Or if you *can* think of anybody like this among the orators, why won't you tell me who he is?

CALLICLES: Heavens! Certainly none of our present-day orators.

SOCRATES: How about orators of the past? Can you tell me one who is thought to be responsible for the Athenians having become better people after he first took up speaking in public, when they had been worse previously? For my part, I have no idea who it would be.

c CALLICLES: What about Themistocles? Don't you think he has the reputation of having been a good man? And Cimon, and Miltiades, and our own Pericles, who died not so long ago?[86] You must have heard him yourself.

SOCRATES: Well, if true excellence is what you said it was earlier, Callicles – namely satisfying desires, both one's own and other people's – then yes, they were good men. If it's not that, if it's what we were compelled to agree on later in the argument – that we should satisfy those

d desires whose fulfilment makes a person better, and not satisfy those which make him worse, and this, we thought, was a science – are you able to say that any of them was a man of that kind?

CALLICLES: I don't know what to say.

SOCRATES: But look at it in the right way and you will find an answer. Let's just examine the question calmly, and see if any of those we mentioned was a person of this kind. Very well, the good man, the one who speaks with a view to what is best, will he say the things he says not just

e anyhow, but with some end in view? It's the same with any skilled practitioner. Each one looks to his own particular job, and applies the measures he applies, selecting them not just anyhow, but with the intention that the object he is making shall have a certain form. Take painters, if you like,

---

[86] Socrates will launch a sustained onslaught on the high reputation enjoyed by these statesmen at 515b–519d.

or builders, or shipwrights, or any of the other skilled practitioners –
whichever of them you like. Each one positions each thing he positions in
some structure, and compels one thing to be appropriate and harmonise
with another, until he has composed the whole into a thing of order and   504
system. And it's not just the other skilled practitioners, it's the people we
were talking about just now, the ones who have to do with the body, fitness experts and doctors – they order and attune the body, I take it. Do we
agree on that, or not?

CALLICLES: We may as well say this is how it is.

SOCRATES: And would a house with design and order be some use,
whereas a house lacking design would be no good?

CALLICLES: Yes.

SOCRATES: And a ship the same?

CALLICLES: Yes.   b

SOCRATES: And our own bodies as well, do we say?

CALLICLES: Certainly.

SOCRATES: What about the soul? Will it be any good if it is without
design, or only if it does have design and order?

CALLICLES: From what has gone before, I have no choice but to agree
with that as well.

SOCRATES: In the body, what is the name for the thing which is the
result of design and order?

CALLICLES: Health and strength, I suppose you mean.

SOCRATES: I do. And what, in its turn, is the name for the thing in the c
soul which is the result of design and order? Try and find a name for this,
and tell me, as you did for the body.

CALLICLES: Why not tell us yourself, Socrates?

SOCRATES: If that's what you prefer, I will. And you must say if you
think I'm right. But if you don't think I'm right, then prove me wrong.
Don't let me get away with it. My view is that 'healthy' is the name for
a body with design in it, which is where the health in it comes from,
together with all other excellence of the body. Is that so, or not?

CALLICLES: It is so.

SOCRATES: And for design and ordered arrangement in the soul the d
names are 'lawful' and 'law', which is how people become law-abiding
and orderly. The things we're talking about are justice and self-control.
Yes or no?

CALLICLES: They may as well be.

SOCRATES: Those are the things our orator will have in view, then – our scientific, good orator – as he applies to souls the words he speaks, the actions he performs, the gifts he gives, or takes away anything he may take

c away.[87] He will be forever thinking about how he can breed justice in the souls of the citizens, and get rid of injustice, how he can breed restraint and get rid of indiscipline, how he can breed virtue in general and get vice to depart. Do you agree, or not?

CALLICLES: I agree.

SOCRATES: Because what's the use, Callicles, of giving lots of food – however delicious – or drink, or anything else to a body which is sick and in wretched shape? It won't do him any the more good – in fact, on a true reckoning, it will do him less. Is that right?

505 CALLICLES: It may as well be.

SOCRATES: Yes, because it's no benefit, I imagine, for a person to go on living if his body is in wretched shape. That way he will inevitably lead a wretched life as well. Isn't that so?

CALLICLES: Yes.

SOCRATES: And when it comes to satisfying desires such as eating as much as you want when you are hungry, or drinking when you are thirsty, do doctors mostly allow a healthy person to do that, but virtually never allow someone who is sick to be filled with the things he desires? Is that something you too go along with?

CALLICLES: It is.

b SOCRATES: And as for the soul, isn't it, with all due respect, just the same? For as long as it is in a bad condition, foolish, undisciplined, unjust and unholy, it should be kept away from its desires and not allowed to do anything other than the things which will make it better. Yes or no?

CALLICLES: Yes.

SOCRATES: Yes, because that way it's better for the soul itself, I imagine?

CALLICLES: It certainly is.

SOCRATES: And keeping it away from the things it desires is disciplining it?

CALLICLES: Yes.

---

[87] In democratic Athens an orator might persuade the body he was addressing to award invalided war veterans pensions or issue contracts for large public works (cf. 513c–514a), or again to confiscate the property of a traitor such as Alcibiades.

SOCRATES: In which case, being disciplined is a better thing for the soul than the state of indiscipline you were in favour of just now.

CALLICLES: I don't know what you mean, Socrates. Ask your questions c of someone else.

SOCRATES: Honestly! Here's a man who can't bear to be helped, or experience for himself the thing the argument is about – that is to say, being disciplined.

CALLICLES: I'm not interested in any of these things you are talking about. I've only been giving you these answers to please Gorgias.

SOCRATES: Very well! So what are we going to do? Are we breaking off the argument in the middle?

CALLICLES: That's up to you.

SOCRATES: Well, even with stories they say it is not permitted to break off in the middle. They say you should put a head on them, to stop them d going around headless. So do answer the remaining questions, and let our argument have a head.

CALLICLES: What a bully you are, Socrates. If you take my advice, you'll call it a day with this argument – or find yourself having a discussion with someone else.

SOCRATES: Who else is willing, then? We don't want to leave the argument unfinished.

CALLICLES: Couldn't you follow the argument to its conclusion by yourself? You could either speak in your own person, or answer your own questions.

SOCRATES: It'll be like that passage in Epicharmus:[88] 'What once two e men were saying', it's up to me alone to manage. Anyway, it looks as if I have no choice. Let's do it like this. My own view is that we should all be striving for the prize when it comes to knowing what is the truth of the things we are talking about, and what false. It is a general good for everybody, after all, that it should become clear. So what I will do is go through 506 with the argument in the way that seems best to me. If any of you thinks I am agreeing with myself on what isn't true, you must take me up on it and prove me wrong. After all, it's not as if I'm that sure either about the things I'm saying. It's a joint search, with the rest of you, so if the person who challenges me turns out to have a point, I shall be the first to agree with him. Anyway, I'm suggesting this on the assumption that you feel

[88] This line of Epicharmus (Fr.253 Kaibel) is quoted in full by Athenaeus, *Deipnosophistae* 308c, 362d.

the argument should be brought to a conclusion. If that's not what you want, let's call it a day now, and take our leave.

GORGIAS: Well, I for one don't think we should take our leave yet,
b Socrates. I think you should finish going through the argument. And it looks to me as if that's what the others think as well. For my part I would certainly like to hear you going through what remains by yourself.

SOCRATES: Well, Gorgias, I too would be very glad to continue my discussion with Callicles here, until I had given him the speech of Amphion in payment for the speech of Zethus. But since you refuse, Callicles, to join me in completing the argument, at any rate listen to what I have to
c say, and take me up on it if you think I am getting things wrong. And if you prove me completely wrong, I won't get angry with you, as you did with me, but have you put on record as my greatest benefactor.

CALLICLES: Do your own talking, mister. Finish the argument yourself.

SOCRATES: Listen, then, as I pick up the argument from the beginning.[89] Are the pleasant and the good the same thing?

— No, not the same, as Callicles and I agreed.
— Should the pleasant be done for the sake of the good, or the good for the sake of the pleasant?
— The pleasant for the sake of the good.
d — And is pleasant that which makes us pleased if it is there, and good that which makes us good if it is there?
— Absolutely.
— However, we are good — we and anything else which is good — because there is some excellence there?
— That seems to me inescapable, Callicles.
— But the excellence of each thing — of a tool, a body, yes and the soul too, and every living thing — is best produced not simply by chance, but in each case by the appropriate application of design, precision and skill. Is that right?
— Well, I for one maintain it is.
e — In which case, is it by design that the excellence of each thing is designed and ordered?

[89] In what follows, Socrates both asks and answers the questions. It gradually becomes clear that he is pretending to represent Callicles in the role of questioner, playing answerer himself. Down to 507a the reasoning simply recapitulates in summary form key points in the more discursive argumentation of 503d–505b (the point at which Callicles refused to give any more answers).

– If you ask me, yes.   d
– Is there then some order arising in each thing, each thing's own order,
  which produces each good thing among the things that are?
– I think so.
– And is a soul with its own order better than the soul without order?
– It must be.
– And the soul which has order is an orderly soul?
– Of course.
– And the orderly soul is self-controlled?
– It most certainly must be.   507
– In which case, the self-controlled soul is good.

Personally, my dear Callicles, I can't reach any other conclusion. But if
you can come up with anything, tell us.

CALLICLES: Say on, mister.

SOCRATES: Very well. I say that if the self-controlled soul is good, the
soul affected in the opposite way to the self-controlled soul is bad. And
this was the foolish, undisciplined soul.

– Absolutely.
– Furthermore, the self-controlled person would do what was appropriate both in his dealings with the gods and in his dealings with
  men. After all, he wouldn't be self-controlled if he did what was not
  appropriate.
– Necessarily so.
– Now surely, doing what was appropriate in his dealings with men   b
  would mean doing what is just, in his dealings with the gods doing
  what is holy. And the person who does what is just and holy must necessarily be just and holy.
– That is so.
– And brave in addition. He must be. After all, it is not the act of a self-
  controlled man either to pursue or to run away, where that is not appropriate, but rather to run away from and pursue whatever – things, people,
  pleasures, pains – he should run away from and pursue, and stand his
  ground and endure where he has to. So the inescapable conclusion,
  Callicles, is that the self-controlled person, as we have described him –   c
  just and brave and holy – must be a completely good man, and that the
  good man must do the things he does well and admirably, and that the
  person who does well must be blessed and happy, whereas the wicked
  person, the one who does badly, is wretched. And he would be the one

who is the opposite of the self-controlled person – the undisciplined person you were praising.[90]

Well, that's my position, and this is what I say is true.[91] And if it is true, then I say that anyone wanting to be happy must, by the looks of it, d pursue and practise self-control, and run away from indiscipline, each one of us as fast as our legs can carry us. We should arrange, preferably, to have no need of punishment, but if anyone does need it, whether himself or someone in his household, whether private individual or city, then we should apply the penalty and punish him, if he is to be happy. This, I believe, is the target we should be aiming at as we lead our lives. We should bend all our own and the city's efforts to achieve this one thing – that justice and self-control shall be present in the person who is going to be happy. That is how we should act, not allowing our desires to e be undisciplined or trying to satisfy them – an evil without end, living the life of a pirate. Such a person could be friend neither to any other human nor to god. He would be incapable of feeling any sense of community, and there can be no friendship for someone who has no sense of community.

508   What the wise say, Callicles, is that heaven and earth and gods and men are bound together by community, friendship, orderliness, self-control and justice, and this is why, my friend, they call the whole thing a world-order, not a disorder or indiscipline. In your wisdom, you pay no attention to these things, as far as I can see. You haven't realised that geometrical equality has great power among gods and among men, and so you think you have to practise grabbing as much as you can. You should do more geometry.[92]

---

[90] The claims Socrates has made since Callicles' last utterance constitute a complex moral psychology, which is no more than an unargued sketch as it stands. Key ingredients are the idea that behaviour in accordance with all the main traditional virtues will flow from self-control (*sôphrosunê*), because the self-controlled person will correctly judge what it is appropriate to want in any situation, and will act accordingly; and that such a person, as a completely good man, will in doing well and admirably attain happiness – something Socrates will further illustrate in the myth of judgment at the end of the dialogue.

[91] At this point Socrates drops the fiction of dialogue sustained since 506c.

[92] Socrates' appeal to a cosmic justice binding the universe together echoes a theme found in many Presocratic thinkers in various guises. But a more specific inspiration must inform the mysterious appeal to geometry, and to geometrical equality as what should replace 'getting as much as you can' (*pleonexia*, the principle Callicles had advocated: 483c). The likeliest candidate is the Pythagorean Archytas, whom Plato was probably to meet on his first visit to Sicily and southern Italy in the early 380s BC. Among the surviving fragments that have a good claim to authenticity, Fr.3 gives some indication of Archytas's application

Well, then: we must either prove this argument wrong, and show that it is not by the acquisition of justice and self-control that the happy are b happy, and by the acquisition of evil that the wretched are wretched, or if the argument is true, we must ask, what are the consequences? And the consequences, Callicles, are all those things I said earlier which made you ask if I was serious.[93] I said a person should accuse himself, his son, his friend, if he does wrong in any way, and that is what he should use rhetoric for. So it turns out that the things you thought Polus agreed with out of embarrassment were true after all: that the more disgraceful acting unjustly is, relative to being treated unjustly, the worse it is. And it turns c out that the person who is going to be the right sort of rhetorician really must be just and know what is just, which is what Polus in his turn said that Gorgias agreed to out of embarrassment.

These things being so, let us ask ourselves what exactly your complaint is against me. Is it fair comment or not, when you say the result is that I am incapable of helping either myself or any of my friends or even family, or of rescuing them from the greatest dangers, that I am at the mercy of the first passer-by – just as those who have lost citizen status are at anybody's mercy – whether he wants to give me a knuckle sandwich, to d use your forthright phrase,[94] or confiscate my money, or expel me from the city, or even, finally, put me to death? Being in this situation is the ultimate disgrace, in your view. As for what my view is, well, it's been said a few times now, but there's nothing to stop it being said again.

What I say, Callicles, is that being given a knuckle sandwich unjustly is not particularly disgraceful, any more than having either my body or my e purse cut. Striking me, or cutting me or my things up unjustly is both more disgraceful and worse – yes, and stealing, enslaving, housebreaking, in fact treating me and my things in any way unjustly is both worse and more disgraceful for the person acting unjustly than for me who am being treated unjustly. These things we saw to be clearly so, as I maintain, back

of geometry to ethics and politics: 'Once the study of ratios is discovered, it puts an end to faction and increases concord. For once this is available, there is no grabbing as much as you can, but equality. By this means we achieve reconciliation in our transactions. The consequence is that through this the poor receive from the powerful, and the wealthy give to those in need, both in the confidence that they will have equality by this means [i.e. a share equal to their status or deserts, not an absolute equality]. It serves as a standard and deterrent to those who practice injustice.'

93 See 480b–d.
94 See 486a–c.

there at an earlier point in our discussions.[95] They are held in place and
500 secured, if it's not offensive to say so, by arguments made of iron and
adamant – or so at least it would appear. And if you, or some other young
hero, do not untie them, then anyone who says anything different from
what I am saying now cannot be right.

For my part, my position is always the same: I don't myself know the
truth of these matters, but I do know that of all the people I have come
across, present company included, none is ever able to say anything different from this without making himself a laughing-stock. So for my part,
b I take the view that this is how things are. But if this *is* how they are, if
injustice *is* the greatest of evils for the person acting unjustly, and greater
still than this greatest, if such a thing were possible, is for the person acting unjustly not to pay the just penalty, what then is the 'help' of which
it really is true to say that if a person can't provide it for himself he will
become a laughing-stock? Isn't it that help which will avert the greatest
harm from us? It necessarily follows that this is the help it is most disgraceful not to be able to give, whether to oneself or to one's friends or
c family. Second would be help against the second greatest evil, third help
against the third, and so on. The credit of being able to help against each,
and the disgrace of being unable, depends in each case on the magnitude
of the evil. Is that wide of the mark, Callicles, or is that how it is?
CALLICLES: No, it's not wide of the mark.[96]
SOCRATES: Of the two, then – acting unjustly and being treated
unjustly – we are saying that acting unjustly is a greater evil, and being
treated unjustly is a lesser. What form of self-help, then, could a person
d equip himself with so as to have both these forms of protection – against
acting unjustly and against being treated unjustly? Is it power or will he
needs? Let me put it like this: will he avoid being treated unjustly if he
wants not to be treated unjustly, or if he equips himself with some power
of not being treated unjustly?
CALLICLES: Clearly the second – if he equips himself with some
power.
SOCRATES: And what about acting unjustly? Is it just a question of not
wanting to act unjustly? Will that be enough – he won't act unjustly – or
e is there a need in this case too to equip himself with some power and art
or science, because if he doesn't learn them and put them into practice,

95 See 474c–475c.
96 Callicles has apparently recovered some of his poise.

he will act unjustly? That's the question I need you to answer, Callicles. Do you think the agreement Polus and I were driven to earlier in the discussion was correct, when we agreed that no-one acts unjustly on purpose, but that all those who act unjustly do so unwillingly?[97]

CALLICLES: It may as well be, Socrates, if you like. Just so you can finish your argument. 510

SOCRATES: It looks, then, as if here too we do need to equip ourselves with some power and some art – to stop us acting unjustly.

CALLICLES: We certainly do.

SOCRATES: In which case, what *is* the art or science that equips people with the power of not being treated unjustly at all – or as little as possible? See if you think as I do. This is what I think it is: I think a person needs to be either ruler himself – or even tyrant – in his city, or else a friend of the existing regime.

CALLICLES: Now, Socrates, see how ready I am to give praise when you get something right. I think what you've just said puts it quite b admirably.

SOCRATES: Very well. Then see if you think I'm right about something else as well. I think one person is most a friend to another when it's a case, as wise men of old say, of 'like to like'.[98] Don't you think so too?

CALLICLES: I do.

SOCRATES: So where a tyrant is a savage and uncivilised ruler, if there were someone in the city much better than him, would the tyrant presumably fear him, and be incapable of ever becoming friends wholeheart- c edly with him?

CALLICLES: That is so.

SOCRATES: And even if there were someone much inferior, this person couldn't be his friend either. The tyrant would despise him. He'd never be able to take him seriously as a friend.

CALLICLES: That's true as well.

SOCRATES: The only friend left worth speaking of, then, for a person like this, is someone of the same character as himself, someone who condemns

[97] A version of the famous Socratic paradox: 'No one sins willingly' – although as Irwin points out (*Plato: Gorgias*, p.229), it has not in fact been articulated previously in the dialogue in so many words. Socrates and Polus have agreed (i) that nobody does something he wills if that turns out to be bad for him (468d), and (ii) that acting unjustly is harmful to the agent (480a).

[98] A proverb as old as Homer (*Od.* 17.218), but invoked as a physical principle by many fifth century Presocratic thinkers.

and approves the same things – but is prepared to be ruled and submit to
d the ruler. This person will have great power in this city, this person no-one
will treat unjustly without regretting it. Isn't that how it is?

CALLICLES: Yes.

SOCRATES: In which case, suppose one of the young men in this city
were to wonder: 'In what way could I have great power and make sure
nobody treats me unjustly?' There is a way for him, it seems, which is to
accustom himself, from an early age, to have the same likes and dislikes
as the despot, and take appropriate steps to resemble him as closely as
possible. Isn't that how it is?

CALLICLES: Yes.

SOCRATES: So for this person, the goal of not being treated unjustly and
c having great power in the city – as you and your lot would argue it – will
surely have been accomplished.

CALLICLES: Indeed it will.

SOCRATES: And not acting unjustly as well? Far from it, if he's going to
be like the ruler, who is unjust, and exercise great power alongside him.
No, I think it'll be just the opposite. He will so equip himself as to be able
to do as much injustice as possible, and not pay the penalty for it when
he does act unjustly.

CALLICLES: It looks that way.

511 SOCRATES: So the greatest evil will be his, maimed in soul and in a
bad way as he is through his imitation of the despot and the power it
gives him.

CALLICLES: I don't know how you keep twisting the argument,
Socrates – turning it upside down. Don't you realise that this person who
does imitate the tyrant will, if he feels like it, put the person who doesn't
imitate him to death, and confiscate his possessions?

b SOCRATES: Yes, I do realise that, my worthy Callicles. I'm not deaf. I've
heard it enough times today from you and Polus – and from pretty well
everybody else in the city. Now it's time for you to listen to me. Yes, he
will put him to death, if he feels like it, but it will be someone bad putting
a fine, upstanding individual to death.

CALLICLES: Isn't that what's so upsetting about it?

SOCRATES: Not if you look at it sensibly, as the argument shows. Do you
think a person's one aim in life should be to stay alive as long as possible,
practising those skills which always preserve us from danger – like the
c rhetoric which you instruct me to practise because it keeps us safe in the
lawcourts?

CALLICLES: Yes. Very sound advice. too, for goodness' sake.

SOCRATES: Is it really, sir? And what about knowing how to swim? Are you equally impressed by that as a branch of knowledge?

CALLICLES: Oh, for heaven's sake! Of course not.

SOCRATES: Yet it too saves people from death, when they find themselves in the kind of situation where this knowledge is required. Or if you think that's trivial, I'll give you a more serious example – the skill of the   d helmsman, which saves not only souls but also bodies and possessions from the most extreme dangers, just as rhetoric does. Helmsmanship is modest and decorous. It doesn't strike imposing attitudes, and claim to be accomplishing something out of the ordinary. No, it accomplishes exactly what advocacy accomplishes, and then for bringing you here safely from Aegina it charges two obols, I believe; and from Egypt or Pontus, for this   e great service, keeping safe everything I just mentioned – the man himself, his children, his possessions, his womenfolk – and putting them ashore in harbour, it charges two drachmas;[99] and the man himself who has this skill, and brought this about, disembarks and stretches his legs by the sea and his ship in a very unassuming way. He is quite capable of working out for himself, I imagine, how uncertain it is which of those who sailed with him he has helped, and which he has harmed, by not allowing them to be lost at sea. He knows they were no better when he set them ashore, either   512 in body or in mind, than when he took them on board. And so his reasoning is as follows: if someone whose body is in the grip of serious and incurable diseases was not drowned, then it is this person's misfortune not to have died, and he has received no help from him.

By the same token, if somebody has a host of incurable diseases in that which is of greater value than his body, namely his soul, it cannot be that this person should go on living, or that he will be doing him any favours if he saves him from the sea, or from prison, or from anywhere else. No, he knows that for a bad human being it is not better to go on living, since   b the life he leads will inevitably be a bad one.

That's why it is not the custom for the helmsman to strike attitudes, despite the fact that he keeps us safe, any more than it is for the maker of siege engines, for goodness' sake – though he can sometimes be a saviour quite as much as any general, let alone helmsman or anybody else, since

---

99 The island of Aegina lies not far south of Piraeus, so the fare of two obols (in the late fifth century roughly a third of what a labourer might earn in a day) was comparatively low. Pontus, by contrast, the coastal region off the south shore of the Black Sea, was a more expensive trip (on the same calculation two days' wages at maximum).

he sometimes saves whole cities. And you think he's not on a par with the advocate? And yet, if he chose to talk the way you people do, Callicles,
c making what he does sound important, he could bury you with his words. He'd tell you – urge on you – the necessity of becoming makers of siege engines, since nothing else amounts to anything. He could make an ample case. But that doesn't stop you despising him and his art. When you call him a maker of engines, it's by way of disparagement. You wouldn't be prepared to give your daughter to his son in marriage, nor would *you* take *his* daughter for your son. And yet, given your reasons for praising your own accomplishments, what justification do you have for looking
d down on the maker of engines and the other people I mentioned just now? I know you would say you are a better man, and of better family. Yet if better is not what I say it is, if human excellence just comes down to this – preserving oneself and one's possessions, whatever kind of person one may in fact be – then it becomes absurd, your finding fault with the maker of engines and the doctor and all the other arts and sciences which have been developed with a view to keeping us safe.

Would you deign to consider whether the noble and the good may not be something other than keeping safe and being kept safe? Maybe this is something – living for a particular length of time – which the real
e man[100] should forget about. Maybe he should not be too devoted to life, but should trust to god in these matters, and believe the old wives' tale that nobody can escape his destiny; on that basis he can decide how he can best live whatever time is given him to live. Is it by turning himself
513 into an exact copy of the political system in force where he is living? In which case, you should now be making yourself as much like the Athenian demos as you can, if you are going to endear yourself to it and have great power in the city. See if that is in your best interests and mine. Heavens, we don't want what they say happens to those who draw down the moon – the women of Thessaly – to happen to us.[101] We don't want our choice of this degree of power in the city to cost us the things which are dearest to us. And if you think that anyone in the world is going to pass on to you
b some art or science of the kind which will make it so that you have great

---

[100] 'Real man' echoes Callicles' emphatic use of the word 'man' in his opening speech (488b, 484d; cf. 500c).

[101] Witches were believed to pay for their special powers by suffering calamities such as blindness or the death of a family member. 'Pulling down the moon' (or as we might say, causing an eclipse) was a magical feat particularly associated with witches in Thessaly, home to the cult of the goddess Hecate.

power in this city – whether for better or for worse – without turning yourself into a copy of its political system, then in my view, Callicles, you are making a big mistake. It's not just a question of mimicking these people. You have to be like them in your very nature, if you are to make any real progress towards friendship with the Athenian demos – or with the son of Pyrilampes, come to that.[102] That's why it's the person who will make you most like these people – he's the person who will make you into a politician and rhetorician in the way you want to be a politician. All groups of people take pleasure in speeches which conform to their own c ethos, and are offended by an ethos which isn't theirs. Or do you disagree, dear friend? Do we have any answer to this, Callicles?

CALLICLES: I'm sure you're right, Socrates – in some sense which is beyond me. But I still feel what most people feel: I simply don't believe you.

SOCRATES: That's because you have the love of the demos in your soul, Callicles. That's what I'm up against. But if we examine these same questions often enough, and in a better way, you will be persuaded. Anyway, remember how we said the activities that are directed to looking after d each of these things – body and soul – were two in number. We said that one of them approaches its object with a view to pleasure, the other with a view to what is best, not indulging it but battling with it. Weren't those the definitions we laid down earlier?

CALLICLES: Indeed they were.

SOCRATES: And one of them – the one which has a view to pleasure – is ignoble, and simply amounts to sycophancy, doesn't it?

CALLICLES: It may as well be, if you like. Just to please you. e

SOCRATES: Whereas the other is nobler, and thinks about making the thing we are taking care of – it may be the body, it may be the soul – as good as possible.

CALLICLES: Exactly.

SOCRATES: Should this, then, be our approach to the city and its citizens, to take care of them, and make the citizens themselves as good as possible? Without that, as we've just discovered,[103] there's no point in bestowing any other benefit – if the character of those who are going to be 514 given large sums of money, or authority over others, or any other power at all, is not fine and upstanding. Are we to lay this down as a principle?

CALLICLES: By all means, if that is your pleasure.

---

[102] Socrates echoes his first words to Callicles (481d).
[103] See 504d–505b.

SOCRATES: Well, Callicles, suppose it were our intention to take part in public life, in the affairs of the city, and suppose we were encouraging one another in some building project – some major construction of city walls, dockyards or temples – ought we to examine ourselves, and ask ourselves
b a few questions? In the first place, is it an art we know, the art of building, or an art we don't know? And who did we learn it from? Is that what we should do, or not?

CALLICLES: Yes, that's exactly what we should do.

SOCRATES: And secondly, have we ever built a building as private individuals, either for one of our friends or a building of our own? And this building, is it handsome or ugly? If we find, when we ask these questions,
c that we have had good, well-known teachers, and that there are many fine buildings we have built with our teachers, and many all our own, after we had finished with our teachers – if that were our situation, then it would be sensible for us to embark on public works. If we had no teacher of ours we could point to, and no buildings, or a lot of worthless ones, that would surely be a daft basis on which to set about public works and encourage one another in that direction. Is this is a correct statement of the position,
d should we say, or not?

CALLICLES: It certainly is.

SOCRATES: And is everything like this? To take a specific example, suppose we had set about acting in public life, and were encouraging one another in the belief that we were competent doctors, we would presumably have had some questions to ask of one another – I of you and you of me: 'Tell me, as god is your witness, when it comes to bodily health, how is it with Socrates himself? Has anyone in the past – whether slave or free – been cured of an ailment because of Socrates?' And I would ask the same sort of questions, I imagine, about you. And if we couldn't
e find anyone who was now in better shape because of us – neither among foreigners nor among Athenians, neither man nor woman – then heavens, Callicles, wouldn't it be truly laughable for people to reach such a height of folly as to try and learn pottery on the wine jar, as the saying goes,[104] by trying to go into public practice ourselves and inviting others like us to do the same, without first, as private individuals, having done a lot of indifferent work and a lot of successful work, and so developed our skill fully? Don't you think it would be foolish to act in this way?

---

[104] 'Learning pottery on the wine jar' seems to have been the equivalent of the English expression 'running before you've learned to walk'.

CALLICLES: Yes, I do.

SOCRATES: But we're not trying to be doctors. You, most excellent of 515 men, are yourself just starting to take part in political life, and encouraging me to, and criticising me when I don't. Are we not going to ask each other some questions? Tell me, has Callicles in the past made any of the citizens better? Is there anyone who used to be wicked – unjust, undisciplined, unthinking – who has become a fine upstanding person because of Callicles? Any foreigner, any citizen? Any slave, any free man? Tell me, if somebody asks you these questions, Callicles, what will you say? What b human being will you claim to have made better by your association with him? Are you reluctant to answer, if indeed there is some achievement of yours when you were still a private citizen, before embarking on public life?

CALLICLES: How very competitive you are, Socrates.

SOCRATES: It's not competitiveness which makes me ask. I genuinely want to know just how you think political activity among us should be conducted. Shall we really find that you have gone into politics with anything in mind other than how we the citizens may be as good as possible? c Haven't we now agreed several times that this is what the man who knows how to practise politics ought to be doing? Have we agreed that, or not? Answer me. [*silence*] Yes, we have agreed – I will answer for you.[105] In which case, if this is the provision the good man ought to be making for his own city, cast your mind back now to those men you just mentioned, and tell me if you still think they were good citizens. I mean Pericles, Cimon, Miltiades and Themistocles. d

CALLICLES: Yes, I do think they were.

SOCRATES: And if they were good, then clearly each of them made the citizens better rather than worse. Did they do that, or not?

CALLICLES: Yes, they did.

SOCRATES: So when Pericles began to speak before the people, were the Athenians worse than when he made his last speeches?

CALLICLES: Maybe.

SOCRATES: Oh, come on! There's no 'maybe' about it. They must necessarily have been, on what has been agreed – if he really was a good citizen, that is.

CALLICLES: Well, what of it? e

---

[105] See 504d–e, 513c–514a.

SOCRATES: Nothing. But tell me something else as well: are the Athenians said to have become better because of Pericles? Or just the opposite? Are they said to have been corrupted by him? You see, what I hear is that Pericles turned the Athenians into idlers, cowards, chatterboxes and scroungers, by being the first to make them dependent on payment for civic services.

CALLICLES: You've been listening to the boys with cauliflower ears, Socrates.[106]

SOCRATES: Well, here's something which isn't just hearsay. I am well aware – as indeed are you also – that in the beginning Pericles was well thought of. The Athenians didn't bring any humiliating charges against him, or convict him, when they were worse. But once he had turned them 516 into fine, upstanding people, at the end of Pericles' life, they found him guilty of theft, and came very close to putting him to death, clearly in the belief that he was wicked.[107]

CALLICLES: So what? Does that prove Pericles was a bad person?

SOCRATES: Well, if the same thing happened with someone who had the care of donkeys, or horses, or oxen, you'd think he wasn't much good – if they didn't kick him or butt him or bite him when he took them on, but he left them fierce enough to do all those things. Or don't you think any b keeper of any animal is not much good, if he takes on his animals in a tamer state, and leaves them fiercer than when he took them on? Do you think that, or not?

CALLICLES: Yes, I really do – just to do you a favour.

SOCRATES: In which case, do me another favour, and answer this. Is a human being, too, one of the animals, or not?

CALLICLES: Of course.

SOCRATES: And Pericles had the care of human beings?

CALLICLES: Yes.

[106] Young Athenians of oligarchic sympathies who aped things Spartan took up boxing among other habits and pastimes (see *Protagoras* 342b–c); Callicles clearly distances himself from them. They might well have grumbled about the daily allowance for which citizens attending the assembly or serving on a jury or in the army were eligible, although able-bodied men could make better money working – with the result that the juries were often elderly in their composition, something Aristophanes satirises in the *Wasps*.

[107] In 430 BC Pericles appears to have been charged with embezzlement, convicted and fined. But he was restored to office the following year (for the evidence, see Thucydides 2.65, Plutarch, *Pericles* 32).

SOCRATES: Well, then. Shouldn't they, as we were agreeing just now, have been made more just by him rather than less just – that is, if he had the care of them and if he was good at politics?   c

CALLICLES: Indeed they should.

SOCRATES: And the just are gentle, according to Homer.[108] How about you? What is your view? Aren't they gentle?

CALLICLES: Yes.

SOCRATES: But he actually left them fiercer than when he took them over – and that against himself, which is the last thing he would have wanted.

CALLICLES: Do you want me to agree with you?

SOCRATES: Yes, if you think what I say is true.

CALLICLES: Very well. Let's say it is so.

SOCRATES: And if he left them fiercer, then also more unjust and worse?

CALLICLES: It may as well be so.   d

SOCRATES: So. Not much good at politics, Pericles, on this argument.

CALLICLES: Not according to you.

SOCRATES: Not according to you either, for heaven's sake. Not from what you have agreed. Or again, tell me about Cimon. Didn't these people he was looking after ostracise him, so that for ten years they wouldn't have to listen to his voice?[109] And Themistocles – didn't they do exactly the same to him, and punish him with exile as well? And Miltiades the hero of Marathon – didn't they vote to throw him into the pit, and but for the president of the council, wouldn't he have been thrown in?   e And yet if these people had been good men, as you maintain they were, these things would never have happened to them. Now it cannot be the case with good charioteers that to start with they don't get thrown out of their chariots, but then when they look after the horses, and become better charioteers themselves, then they get thrown out. That's not how

---

[108] See Homer, *Od.* 6.120, 9.175, 13.201.

[109] The institution of ostracism allowed the Athenian demos an annual opportunity to vote into exile for ten years any politician they disapproved of (six thousand votes were required). Cimon was ostracised in 461, but recalled in 457 (see Plutarch, *Cimon* 17). It is not known when Themistocles was subjected to the same treatment (Thucydides 1.135). Miltiades (Cimon's father) seems to have been impeached on a capital charge in 489 (the pit was at one time the place of execution for those branded enemies of the demos: Xenophon, *Hellenica* 1.7.20). He was traditionally supposed to have played an important part the year before in securing the decision to oppose the invading Persians, who were subsequently defeated by Athenian forces in a remarkable victory at Marathon.

it is – either with being a charioteer or in any other activity. Or do you think it is?

CALLICLES: No, I don't.

SOCRATES: In which case our claim just now was true, apparently.[110] We don't know anyone in this city who has been a good man when it comes to politics. You yourself agreed that none of the present lot is any good, though you thought some of those in the past were, and these were the men you chose. But they've been shown to be on a par with the present lot, which means that if they *were* orators, they were making use neither of the true rhetoric – since if they had used it they would not have been overthrown – nor of the flattering rhetoric.

CALLICLES: All the same, Socrates, nobody nowadays has ever come anywhere near achieving the kinds of things those people – take any of them you like – have achieved.

SOCRATES: Bless you, I'm not finding fault with them either, as servants of the city. I think they were much better servants than the people now, and more capable of providing the city with the things it wanted. But that's not what I mean. If it's a question of changing desires rather than giving in to them, of coaxing and compelling in the direction which would lead to the citizens becoming better people, then there was effectively no difference between those people and these. And yet that is the sole function of a good citizen. As for ships and walls and dockyards and all those kinds of things, I too agree with you that those people were cleverer at providing them than the people now.

We're doing something rather absurd, you and I, in our discussion. All through the time our discussion has been going on, we've been unable to stop coming round to the same point every time, each unaware of what the other is saying. Or it's certainly my impression, at any rate, that you have several times agreed and recognised that the business of dealing both with the body and the soul has in some sense two sides to it: one consists in a form of service whereby it is possible to provide food if our bodies are hungry, drink if they are thirsty, clothing, bedding and shoes if they are cold, and the other things which bodies can have a desire for. I'm deliberately using the same pictures to make it easier for you to understand. And I thought you had agreed that the provider of these things was a tradesman or merchant or maker of one of these same things – a baker, a cook, a weaver, a leather

517

b

c

d

e

cutter, a tanner.[111] It is hardly surprising if someone who supplies these sorts of services is thought to be a practitioner of care for the body, both by himself and by everyone else – by anyone, in fact, who doesn't realise that quite apart from all of them there is an art or science of physical training and of medicine, which is the true care of the body, and which should by rights rule over all these arts and make use of their products, since it knows which among foods and drinks is good and which bad for the excellence of the body – something all these other arts have no idea about.   518

I thought you realised they were slavish, menial, unworthy of a free person, these other arts, while the art of physical training and the art of medicine are, if we look at what is just, their masters.[112] And that these same things are true of the soul – well, sometimes I think you understand when I say it, and you agree as if you know what I mean. But then a little later there you are saying there have been people who were fine b upstanding citizens in the city,[113] and when I ask who they were, then the suggestions you make about people in politics seem to me to be exactly as if I were to ask you, on the subject of physical training, which people have been or are good at caring for the body, and you were to tell me in all seriousness that Thearion the baker, Mithaecus who wrote *Sicilian Cookery*, and the tradesman Sarambus – that these were the ones who were wonderful at caring for the body – one producing wonderful loaves of bread, the second fine cuisine, and the third wine.[114]   c

It would probably annoy you if I said to you: 'Look, mister, you don't know the first thing about physical training. They're servants, the people you're telling me about, people who satisfy wants without having any fine or worthwhile knowledge about them. They will fill people's bodies, if that is how the mood takes them, fattening them up with their full approval, and will destroy even the flesh they started with. The ones on the receiving end will have too little experience to hold those who d are feasting them responsible for their illnesses and the loss of the flesh they started with. No, it's the people who happen to be around, advising them, at the point where their earlier excess catches up with them, at a

---

[111] Socrates must have the passage at 500d–501c in mind (cf. also 513d–e), although Callicles' assent was less than half-hearted, and the list of occupations seems to recapitulate his angry outburst at 491a (cf. 490b–e).
[112] Socrates turns Callicles' polarity on its head (see 483b, 483c–484a, 491c–492c).
[113] See 503c.
[114] Aristophanes refers to Thearion's bread shop, evidently a well-known institution, but there is no reliable trace of the other figures Socrates mentions.

much later date, bringing illness with it – not surprisingly, since it all happened without any regard for what health requires – these are the people they will hold responsible, and blame, and do some harm to, if they can, whereas those earlier people, the ones responsible for their ills, they will praise to the skies.

e   And here you are now, Callicles, doing just the same thing. You're praising to the skies people who have feasted the Athenians, giving them an abundance of what they desired. People say they made the city great.
519 They don't realise that the city is now a swollen, festering sore because of those figures in the past. They have filled the city with harbours and dockyards and walls and tribute and rubbish of that kind, without a thought for restraint or justice. And when the crisis of the infirmity comes, they will blame their current advisers, and praise Themistocles and Cimon and Pericles, the ones responsible for their ills. It may be they will seize upon you, if you're not careful,[115] and my friend Alcibiades, when they lose what they had to start with as well as the gains they have
b   made since – despite your not being responsible for their ills, though you have maybe contributed to them.

There's a piece of real stupidity I see happening nowadays, and hear of in relation to men in days gone by. When the city treats one of its politicians as a wrongdoer, I see them getting upset and complaining that they are being badly treated: they have done the city many favours – and now they are being unjustly destroyed by it. That is their story.
c   But it's a pack of lies. No leader of a city could ever be destroyed unjustly by that same city of which he is the leader. It looks as if it's the same with those who set up as politicians as it is with those who set up as sophists. Sophists, though wise in other ways, do one thing which is incongruous. They claim to be teachers of human goodness, but then often accuse their pupils of treating them unjustly by not paying their fees and being generally ungrateful for the benefits they have
d   received from them. What could be more unreasonable than this claim, that people who have become good and just, who have had the injustice in them removed by their teacher and who have acquired justice, should be acting unjustly on account of something which they do not have? Don't you think that's incongruous, my friend? See what a real

115 This looks like an indication that Callicles fell into disfavour with the demos, and met an untimely end during the later stages of the Peloponnesian War, where Athens' worsening position and final defeat are presumably the 'crisis' to which Socrates refers.

104

soap-box orator you've forced me to become, Callicles, by refusing to answer my questions!

CALLICLES: And wouldn't you be the one who's incapable of speaking without someone to answer your questions?

SOCRATES: Well, apparently I am capable. I'm certainly drawing out several of my speeches today, since you refuse to answer my questions. But be good enough to tell me, by the god of friendship, don't you think it's illogical for them to claim to have made somebody good, and then criticise that person because, after being made good and being good through their agency, he is then wicked?

CALLICLES: Yes, I do think that is illogical.

SOCRATES: And do you hear this kind of thing said by those who claim to educate people in human goodness?

CALLICLES: I do. But what is there to be said about people worth nothing at all?[116]

SOCRATES: What is there to be said about those who claim to be leaders of the city, concerned that it shall be as good as possible, who then turn round and accuse it, when the mood takes them, of being most wicked? Do you think these people are any different from the previous lot? Bless you, a sophist and an orator are the same thing, or as near as makes no difference, as I was saying to Polus. Your ignorance makes you regard one of them – rhetoric – as marvellous, while you view the other with contempt. In truth, however, the sophist's art is a finer thing than rhetoric to the same degree that the legislative art is finer than the judicial, and the physical trainer's art than the medical.[117] But I thought that political leaders and sophists were actually the only ones not in a position to criticise this creature of their own education for behaving badly towards them, without also in the same breath accusing themselves of bringing no benefit to the people they claim to be benefiting. Isn't that so?

CALLICLES: It certainly is.

SOCRATES: And they're probably the only people in a position to offer the benefit they offer for no fee, if the things I've been saying are true. Anyone receiving any other benefit – being turned into a fast runner by a trainer, for example – might possibly withhold payment if the trainer trusted him

---

[116] A clear indication that those who associated with Gorgias saw him as offering something very different from what a sophist like Protagoras claimed to teach (cf. also *Meno* 89d–92d). Socrates will argue in his reply that there is indeed a distinction, but not much difference.

[117] See 465c.

rather than agreeing a fee and collecting the money as nearly as possible at
d the same time as imparting the skill of running fast. It's not slowness, after
all, which makes people act unjustly. It's injustice, isn't it?

CALLICLES: Yes.

SOCRATES: So if this is the thing – injustice – which someone is removing, then for him there is no danger of ever being treated unjustly. For
him alone it is safe to offer this benefit free – that's if he really did have
the power to make people good. Isn't that right?

CALLICLES: So I maintain.

SOCRATES: And that looks like the reason why there's nothing to be
ashamed of in receiving payment for other sorts of advice – about building, for example, or the other arts and sciences.

e CALLICLES: Yes, it does look like the reason.

SOCRATES: Whereas for this activity – the way in which a person can be
as good as possible, and manage his own household or city as well as possible[118] – to refuse to give advice unless you are given payment has come to
be regarded as disgraceful, hasn't it?

CALLICLES: Yes.

SOCRATES: And the reason is clear. It's because among the arts that con-
fer a benefit this is the only one which makes the person who is well
treated want to do good in return. So it's a good sign if someone who does
good by conferring this benefit is well treated in return, and not a good
sign if he isn't. Is that the situation?

521 CALLICLES: Yes, it is.

SOCRATES: So which way of caring for the city are you urging upon me?
Make that distinction for me: the one which involves battling with the
Athenians to make them as good as possible, like a doctor – or the one
which involves becoming their servant and trying to please them in my
dealings with them? Tell me the truth, Callicles. You began by speaking
your mind to me, so you ought by rights to go on saying what you think.
This is the moment for goodness and nobility, so speak up.

CALLICLES: I say the one which involves becoming their servant.

b SOCRATES: Nobly spoken! So you invite me to become a sycophant – a
flatterer!

CALLICLES: If you really want to use the F—word Socrates, yes.
Otherwise...

---

[118] This formulation is couched in terms very similar to the educational prospectus issued by
Protagoras in the *Protagoras* (318e–319a).

SOCRATES: Don't tell me what you've told me over and over again[119] –
that anybody who wants to will put me to death. I don't want to have to
say again that it will be a question of an evil man putting to death a good
man. And don't say he will confiscate whatever I possess. That will save
me saying: 'Well, when he's confiscated it he won't have any good use for
it. Just as he confiscated it from me unjustly, so, once he has taken it, he
will use it unjustly. And if unjustly, then disgracefully. And if disgrace- c
fully, then badly.'
CALLICLES: You really do seem confident, Socrates, that none of these
things will happen to you. As if living a quiet life means you couldn't
be dragged off to court, probably by someone utterly worthless and
contemptible.
SOCRATES: Then I really am an idiot, Callicles, if I don't realise that in
this city anything can happen to anybody. One thing I do know, and that
is that if I go to court, to face one of these dangers you are talking about, d
the one bringing me there will be an evil man – no decent person would
take somebody who was not acting unjustly to court – and it would be no
great surprise if I were put to death. Do you want me to tell you why that
is what I expect?
CALLICLES: Yes, I do. Very much.
SOCRATES: I think that in company with a few Athenians – I don't want
to say I'm the only one – I am attempting the true science of politics,
and I think I am the only one practising politics among people today.
And because I say the things I say on any occasion not out of any desire
to please, but with a view to what is best rather than what is most pleasant, refusing to go in for 'those subtleties' you recommend,[120] I won't e
have anything to say in court. The same analogy occurs to me that I used
when talking to Polus.[121] I shall be like a doctor on trial before a jury of
children, with a chef as prosecutor. Ask yourself what defence such a
person could make in that situation. Suppose the prosecutor said something like this: 'Children, this man here has done you many injuries – he
is the ruin of you yourselves, and in particular the youngest of you, with
the cuts and burns he inflicts; he reduces you to a state of paralysis by 522
starving and choking you, making you take the bitterest of drinks, and
forcing hunger and thirst upon you. Not at all like me, who feasted you

[119] See 486b; also 511a–b.
[120] Socrates echoes Callicles' quotation from Euripides at 486c (where they were not being
recommended), but applies the words to rhetoric, not dialectic.
[121] See 464d–e.

on all sorts of delicious things.' What do you think the doctor, caught in this predicament, would have to say? Suppose he told the truth: 'I did all these things, children, in the interests of health.' What uproar would this provoke among a jury of this nature, do you think? Pretty substantial, surely?

CALLICLES: Possibly.

SOCRATES: One has to think so. And don't you think he would be completely at a loss what to say?

b

CALLICLES: Indeed I do.

SOCRATES: The same kind of thing would happen to me, too, I am well aware, if I were to go court. I shan't be able to tell them about pleasures I have provided for them, which they regard as benefits and acts of assistance, though for my part I envy neither those who provide them nor those for whom they are provided. And if anyone says I am ruining the young by reducing them to a state of paralysis, or that I offend those who are older by the bitter taste of the things I say either in private or in public, I shall neither be able to tell the truth – 'I am quite justified in saying and doing all these things,' and then your favourite phrase, 'men of the jury' – nor be able to tell them anything else. As a result I shall probably have to put up with whatever happens to me.

c

CALLICLES: Do you think it is a good thing, Socrates, for a person in the city to be in that position, and have no power to protect himself?

SOCRATES: Yes, Callicles, provided he has the one thing which you have often agreed he should have – provided he has already protected himself by not saying or doing anything unjust in his dealings either with men or with gods. This we have several times agreed to be the most powerful form of protection he can have. Now, if someone were to prove me wrong, and show that I do not have this form of protection available to protect myself or anyone else, then I would be ashamed to be proved wrong, whether before a large group of people or a small group, or face-to-face with one person. And if I were put to death because of this inability, I would be very distressed. But if I met my end for want of sycophantic rhetoric, I have no doubt you would see me enduring death quite cheerfully. After all, being put to death is not something anyone fears in itself, unless he is utterly irrational and cowardly; what he does fear is acting unjustly. Arriving in Hades with a soul weighed down by countless unjust deeds is the worst of all evils. And to show that this is so, if it's all right with you, I'd like to tell you a tale.

d

e

CALLICLES: Well, you've worked your way through the rest of the discussion, so you'd better work your way through this too.

SOCRATES: Give ear, then, as they say, to a very fine tale. I expect you 523 will regard it as a story, but I regard it as an exposition, since the things I'm about to tell you I shall tell you in the belief that they are true. Homer tells us that Zeus, Poseidon and Pluto divided the dominion they inherited from their father.[122] Now in the time of Cronos it was traditional belief among mankind – as it is, now and always, among the gods – that any member of the human race who has passed his life in a just and holy manner should depart, when he dies, to the islands of the blessed and live b in all happiness, free from evils. Anyone who has lived an unjust and godless life should go to the prison of retribution and judgment, which they call Tartarus. Their judges in the time of Cronos, and still when Zeus first assumed power, were the living sitting in judgment on the living on the day when they were going to die. And as a result their judgments were not arrived at in a good way. So Pluto and the overseers of the islands of the blessed came to Zeus and told him they were getting people coming to both places who didn't deserve to be there. And Zeus said: 'Leave it to c me. I will stop this happening. At the moment judgments are not being arrived at in a good way. Those being judged are judged fully clothed, because they are judged while still alive. As a result,' he said, 'many who have wicked souls have clothed themselves in fine bodies, good family, and wealth, and when the judging takes place, many witnesses come forward on their behalf to testify that they have lived justly. The judges are confused by these people, and at the same time they too are passing judg- d ment clothed, their own soul cloaked by eyes and ears and their whole body. All these things get in the way – both their own clothing and that of the people being judged.

'So first of all,' he said, 'we must stop them knowing about their death in advance, since at present they do know. Prometheus has already been

---

[122] See Homer, *Iliad* 15.187–93. The division – following the overthrow of Cronos by his son Zeus – is between sky, sea, and underworld. Here at the outset of his account and at the end, too (526d), Socrates appeals to Homer's authority. But Plato adapts traditional material from Homer and elsewhere to his own purposes. In particular, his version of a last judgment, while doubtless owing its basic inspiration to Pythagorean and Orphic teaching, is presented as Socrates' own interpretation of the myth (524a–b), and worked out in terms which recapitulate ideas introduced earlier in the dialogue – notably its distinction between soul and body, its assessment of tyranny, and its conception of punishment.

e   given instructions to deprive them of this faculty.[123] Secondly, they must
be judged stripped of all these things; they should be judged when they
are dead. The judge too should be stripped, and dead, looking with the
soul itself at the soul itself, immediately on the death of each person,
when he is deprived of all kinsmen and leaves all those trappings on
earth behind, that the judging may be just. I realised all this before you
did, and have made my own sons judges – two from Asia, Minos and
524   Rhadamanthys, and one, Aeacus, from Europe. These, when they die,
will act as judges in the meadow, at the fork in the road from which the
two roads lead, one to the islands of the blessed, the other to Tartarus.
Rhadamanthys will judge those from Asia, Aeacus those from Europe. To
Minos, as a mark of seniority, I will give the final say in cases where the
other two are in any doubt, so that the judging about people's destination
may be as just as possible.'

These are the things I have heard, Callicles, and I am confident they are
b   true. What follows from this account, by my reckoning, is something like
this. Death is in fact, as I see it, simply the separation from one another
of two things, the soul and the body. And when they are separated from
one another, each of them retains pretty much its own state as it was when
the person was alive. The body retains its own nature, the care that has
been taken of it, the things that have happened to it, all plain to see. For
c   example, if someone's body while he was alive was large, either by nature
or upbringing or both, then when he dies this person's dead body will
also be large; or if stout, then his dead body, when he dies, will be stout
as well, and so on. Or again, if he was in the habit of having his hair long,
then his dead body will have long hair as well. In the case of some hard-
ened criminal, who when he was alive had the marks of blows as scars on
his body – whether from whips or other injuries – the body of the dead
man too can be seen bearing the same marks. And if someone's limbs
were broken or twisted while he was alive, these same characteristics will
d   be plain to see when he is dead. In a word, whatever state he had got his
body into while he was alive, all or most of these characteristics will also
be evident for a time after he is dead.

I think the same things are true of the soul, Callicles. Once it is
stripped of the body, everything in the soul is plain to see – both its

[123] The function attributed to the Titan Prometheus here is one which in the *Prometheus
Bound* attributed to Aeschylus he claims to have conceived for himself, and to have
achieved by making humans succumb to 'blind hopes' (248–53). Prometheus will figure
again, in the *Protagoras* (*Prot.* 320d–322a).

110

natural characteristics and the things which have happened to it, the things the person had in his soul as a result of his approach to all his activities. Anyway, when they come to the judges – those from Asia to e Rhadamanthys – Rhadamanthys halts them, and takes a look at the soul of each, not knowing whose it is. And often he fastens upon the Great King, or some other king or potentate, and sees nothing healthy in his soul, but finds it whip-marked and full of scars from the perjuries and 525 injustice imprinted on his soul by his every action – everything mis-shapen from falsehood and boasting, and nothing straight – the result of an upbringing devoid of truth. He sees a soul filled with asymmetry and ugliness as a result of its licence, luxury, insolence and lack of con-trol over its actions; and when he sees it, he sends it away in disgrace, straight to prison. When it gets there, it will have to endure the things which are appropriate for it.

What is appropriate for anyone undergoing punishment, and being b justly punished by someone else, is either to be made better and helped, or to be made an example to the rest, so that others may be frightened by seeing him suffer the things he suffers, and so be made better. The ones who are helped by gods and men, and pay a just penalty, are those whose faults are curable. Yet it is through pain and distress that their help comes, both here and in Hades, since it is not possible to be rid of injustice in any other way. The ones who commit the most extreme injustice, and who on account of such unjust deeds make themselves c incurable – these are the ones who are made an example of. They them-selves can no longer derive any benefit, since they are incurable; never-theless others are benefited – those who see them undergoing, for their faults, the greatest, most painful and most fearsome sufferings for the whole of time, just hanging there in the prison in Hades as an example – a spectacle and instruction for those among the unjust who are arriv-ing at any particular moment. And of these, I maintain, Archelaus will d be one, if what Polus says is true, along with anyone else who is a tyrant of that kind.[124]

In fact, I think the majority of these examples will come from tyrants and kings and potentates and those who have engaged in political life. They are the ones who have the opportunity to commit the greatest and most unholy crimes. Homer is evidence for this, representing those who are being punished in Hades for the whole of time as kings and potentates

[124] See 470d–471d.

e – Tantalus, Sisyphus, Tityus. Nobody has represented Thersites,[125] or any other private individual who was wicked, as being an incurable, held fast in the grip of severe punishments – he didn't have the opportunity, I suppose, which is why he was more fortunate than those who did. No,
526 Callicles, it is among the powerful that the really wicked people are to be found – though even among them there is nothing to stop good men coming into being, and they are entitled to great admiration when they do. After all, Callicles, it is hard for someone who is born with great opportunities for acting unjustly to live his life justly; he is entitled to great credit. But people like this rarely do come into being. Here and elsewhere there have been, and no doubt will be, fine upstanding people
b with this virtue of dealing justly with whatever is entrusted to them. One in particular, Aristides the son of Lysimachus, has become very famous all over Greece.[126] But, with all due respect, the majority of those who exercise power turn out bad.

Anyway, as I was saying, when Rhadamanthys takes someone of that sort, he knows nothing about him – who he is, what family he comes from – beyond the fact that he is evil. And when he sees this, he sends him off to Tartarus, with a mark to show whether he thinks he is curable
c or incurable. And he for his part suffers what is appropriate when he gets there. And sometimes there's a soul which has lived a holy life, in company with truth, a soul belonging to some private individual, or somebody of that sort, or most likely, as I maintain, Callicles, the soul of a philosopher who has minded his own business in life, and not poked his nose into the affairs of others. When he catches sight of one of these, he is filled with wonder, and sends him off to the islands of the blessed. Aeacus does the same, each of them holding a staff. Minos presides over them, seated, and
d he alone has a golden sceptre, as Homer's Odysseus says he saw him,

With golden sceptre judging all the dead.[127]

Well, for my part, Callicles, I am convinced by these accounts, and my concern is how I can present my soul to the judge in as healthy a state as possible. So I shall say goodbye to the honours most people are interested

[125] For the three principal sinners, see Homer, *Od.* 11.576–600. Thersites is the common soldier who criticises Agamemnon's generalship in the *Iliad*, and is beaten for his pains by Odysseus: *Il.* 2.211–77.
[126] But although celebrated for his justice (e.g. Herodotus 8.79), Aristides too was ostracised (in 483 BC: Aristotle, *Athenian Constitution* 22.7; Plutarch, *Aristides* 7) – which has earlier been taken as proof of failure by a statesman to improve the demos (515c–516c).
[127] See Homer, *Od.* 11.569.

in, and in the practice of truth try both to live and, when I die, to die as
truly the best person I have it in my power to be. And so far as lies in my   e
power I invite the whole of the rest of mankind – and you in particular,
returning your invitation – to this life and this struggle, which I maintain
is more important than all our struggles here. My criticism of you is that
you will not be able to protect yourself when you meet the judgment and
verdict I've just been describing.[128] You will go before that judge, the son
of Aegina, when he seizes hold of you and brings you before him, and you   527
will go dizzy and stand there gawping, you in that place no less than I in
this. Who knows, you may be given a knuckle sandwich and be well and
truly trampled on.

Of course, you may regard all this as a story, an old wives' tale, and treat
it with contempt. And there'd be nothing so very surprising about treating
it with contempt if we had somewhere else to turn in our search for better and truer answers. But as it is, you can see that you three – you, Polus
and Gorgias – who are the wisest of Greeks alive today, are not able to
demonstrate that we should lead some other life than the one which is so   b
clearly in our best interest in the world beyond also. Among so many arguments, while the others are proved wrong, this argument[129] alone stands
its ground – that we should more beware of acting unjustly than of being
treated unjustly, and that more than anything, what a man should practise,
both in private life and public life, is not seeming to be good, but being
good. And that if someone turns out badly in some respect, he should be
punished. This is the second good, after being just – becoming just, and   c
paying the penalty by being punished. All sycophancy, whether directed
at one's self or at others, at few or many, is to be avoided. That is how rhetoric should be employed – aiming always at the just – as should any other
activity.

Listen to me, then, and follow to that destination where, when you
arrive, you will be happy both while you live and after you die, as the
argument clearly indicates. Allow people to treat you with contempt, as a
fool, to trample all over you, if they choose – and heavens, yes, even welcome the striking of that shameful blow. Nothing terrible will happen to   d

---

[128] Socrates turns Callicles' critique of the helplessness of philosophy (483a, 486b–c) into
a prediction of what he will experience himself at the last judgment. Aegina is here the
nymph after whom the island was traditionally supposed to have been named, and mother
of Aeacus in consequence of one of Zeus's many sexual adventures.

[129] Socrates now recapitulates the central arguments of the dialogue, originally articulated in
the conversation with Polus.

you if you really are a fine, upstanding person who practises virtue. And when we have practised it together, only then, if we think we should, will we turn our hands to politics. That will be the time for us to contribute whatever views we have by way of counsel, when we are better at counsel than we are now. It's a disgrace for people in the state we now appear to be in to go swaggering around as if we were somebody, when we never hold the same opinions about the same things – even about things of the

c greatest importance, to such a depth of uneducated ignorance have we sunk. Let us therefore take as our guide the argument which has been made clear to us. It indicates that this is the best way of life – to live and die practising justice and the rest of virtue. This argument, then, let us follow, and invite everyone else to join us, not the one which you so confidently invite me to follow, but which is of no value, Callicles.

Menexenus

Dramatis personae

MENEXENUS With his cousin Ctesippus became a member of Socrates' intimate circle, to judge from their presence in the prison on the day the hemlock was administered (*Phaedo* 59b). In the *Lysis* Menexenus (again in Ctesippus's company) and his friend Lysis are boys of twelve or thirteen. In the *Menexenus* he is evidently a few years older. Socrates suggests that he came from a prominent political family – but history has left no clues enabling us to identify the public figures Plato might have had in mind.

SOCRATES (469–399) Sustains throughout the dialogue the teasing pretence that he is currently a student of rhetoric, with Pericles' mistress Aspasia for his teacher. What purpose Plato had in representing him in this alien and improbable guise is discussed in the Introduction.

Analysis

234a–236d – Introductory conversation
236d–249c – Speech of Aspasia
  236b–237b Introduction
  237b–238b Good birth and upbringing: Athenian autochthony and how it shapes the life of the population
  238b–239a Good upbringing: the Athenian political system
  239a–246b Noble exploits: Athenian history
- *239b–c:* Athens' very earliest military exploits – the subject of poetry
- *239c–240e:* The rise of Persian imperialism; the Athenian victory at Marathon, and what it taught the Greeks
- *240e–241c:* The Athenian naval victories at Salamis and Artemisium – further lessons for the Greeks
- *241c–e:* Further victories over the Persians instil fear in the Great King
- *241e–242c:* Peace with Persia followed by a Greek backlash against the Athenians – war between Greeks
- *242c–e:* The Athenians victorious in the Peloponnesian War (to 421)
- *242e–243d:* Resumption of the war – the Sicilian expedition, the battle of Arginusae, final self-inflicted defeat
- *243d–244b:* Reconciliation following the civil war of 404–03
- *244b–d:* Athens quiet and resentful at her treatment by the other Greeks; Spartan imperialistic ambitions
- *244d–245b:* Athenian resurgence and magnanimity towards former enemies – the Corinthian War
- *245b–246a:* Athenian resistance to Persia leaves her again Greece's sole defence against the barbarian, emerging from conflict intact

  246b–249a Encouragement and consolation
- *246b–247c:* For the children of the fallen
- *247c–248d:* For the parents of the fallen
- *248d–249c:* For the citizens

249d–e: Concluding conversation

Menexenus

SOCRATES: So where has Menexenus been? The agora?   234
MENEXENUS: Yes, Socrates, the agora. The council-chamber.[1]
SOCRATES: You, going to the council-chamber? Why, in particular?
No, don't tell me, you think you've reached the end of education and
philosophy, and you're planning to move on to greater things, fully
equipped as you now are. Your aim is to hold high office among us (can
you believe it – at your age!), despite our seniority. You don't want a time
ever to come when your family is not providing someone to keep an eye b
on us.[2]
MENEXENUS: That's up to you, Socrates. With your permission and
guidance I shall be very glad to hold high office. Otherwise not. But that
wasn't why I went to the council-chamber today. I went because I'd heard
the council was going to choose somebody to make the speech in honour
of those who have been killed.[3] You know they are planning the funeral.
SOCRATES: Indeed I do. Who did they choose?
MENEXENUS: No-one. They put it off till tomorrow. If you ask me,
though, Archinus or Dion will be chosen.[4]
SOCRATES: Well, Menexenus, there are certainly plenty of reasons why c
being killed in battle looks like a good move. You get a fine, imposing
funeral, even if you die a pauper; you get praised, even if you're a nobody,
by wise men speaking not just off the cuff, but after lengthy preparation
of what they are to say. So fulsome is their praise – invariably credit-
ing you both with qualities you do possess and with qualities you don't
possess, and using the finest language to embellish it all – that they cast 235
a spell over our souls, heaping all manner of approval on the city, and

---

[1] See note on *Gorgias* 447a. The council chamber was in the Metrôon sanctuary, on elevated
ground to the south of the agora.
[2] Socrates' teasing here makes sense only if Menexenus is no more than a teenager. Readers
of the *Gorgias* may be put in mind of Callicles' views on philosophy as apposite education
for boys, but activity ridiculous and demeaning in a grown man.
[3] This was an Athenian tradition of long standing. The most famous example, surviving to
us in Thucydides' version (2.35–46), was Pericles' speech of 431 BC, celebrating those who
had fallen in the first year of the Peloponnesian War.
[4] There is no other trace in the historical record of the Dion Menexenus mentions, but
Archinus was for a short while at least a leading Athenian politician, prominent in the
party which helped restore democracy in 403 BC, and over the next two years one of those
most active in trying to establish the security of the new regime. We are naturally led to
assume that the encounter between Socrates and Menexenus is imagined as occurring at
just this time.

singing the praises of those who have died in the war, of all our ancestors from times past, and of us who are still alive. The effect of their
praise on me, Menexenus, is to fill me with feelings of my own nobility. I
b stand there entranced each time, as I listen, and feel that I have suddenly
become taller, more noble, and more good-looking. I tend always to have
some foreigners with me, keeping me company and listening with me,
and in their eyes too I suddenly become more impressive, since the effect
on them seems to me to be exactly the same, extending not only to me but
to the whole city as well: carried away by the speaker, they regard the city
with greater admiration than they did before. And this aura of impress-
c iveness doesn't just last until the day after tomorrow; the speech, and the
voice of the speaker, so take me over that it's not until three or four days
later that I come to my senses and realise where I actually am – up to that
point I have regarded myself, to all intents and purposes, as inhabiting
the islands of the blessed,[5] such is the skill of our orators.

MENEXENUS: You're always making fun of orators, Socrates.[6] This time,
though, if you ask me, the person chosen is not going to find it easy. It's
very much on the spur of the moment, this choice, so the person speaking
will probably have no option but to make it up as he goes along.

d SOCRATES: Don't you believe it! They've got speeches ready-made,
every one of them[7] – quite apart from which, that kind of stuff is hardly a
problem anyway, even if you do have to make it up as you go along. If they
had to speak well of the Athenians before an audience of Peloponnesians,
or the Peloponnesians before an audience of Athenians, then it would
take a good orator to carry conviction and win approval. But when someone is performing in front of the same people he is praising, then making
a good impression is no great achievement.

MENEXENUS: You think not, Socrates?

---

[5] On the islands of the blessed, see *Gorgias* 523c. Socrates seems here and in what precedes
to echo the comically ecstatic reaction to rhetoric that Aristophanes puts in the mouth of
the chorus in the *Wasps* (636–41): 'He has gone into everything and left nothing out, so that
I grew bigger as I heard it, and thought myself a judge in the islands of the blessed, in my
pleasure with the speaker.'

[6] Readers of the *Gorgias* will think primarily of that dialogue.

[7] An extract survives from a funeral speech by Gorgias, a rhetorical exercise prepared as
though for an Athenian audience in his usual highly studied, artificial style (Fr.6). Elsewhere
Plato has Socrates satirise the speechwriter Lysias's similar compositions, and the way his
admirers might themselves try to learn them by heart (*Phaedrus* 227c–228e). A funeral oration attributed to Lysias survives, very likely also a rhetorical exercise. If authentic (as most
scholars think), it will have been a very recent example of the genre, perhaps dating from
393 or 392, since it commemorates Athenians who had died fighting at Corinth, where the
major engagement was the battle of the Nemea River in the winter of 394.

SOCRATES: No, certainly not.

MENEXENUS: Do you think *you* would be capable of making the speech,   e if you had to – if the council chose you?

SOCRATES: Well, in my case, Menexenus, it's no great surprise if I am capable of making the speech, since my teacher was in fact a woman of some ability where rhetoric is concerned. She created many fine orators; and one of them in particular – Pericles the son of Xanthippus – was the finest speaker in Greece.

MENEXENUS: Who was she? No, don't tell me, you mean Aspasia?[8]

SOCRATES: I do. Together with Connos, son of Metrobios. Those two are my teachers – Connos in music and poetry, Aspasia in rhetoric. And 236 if a man has that kind of upbringing, it's not so very remarkable if he's a clever speaker. But even someone with a less good education than I had – taught poetry and music by Lampros, and rhetoric by Antiphon of Rhamnus – even he, if it was a question of praising the Athenians in front of the Athenians, would be able to win approval.[9]

MENEXENUS: So what would you find to say, if you did have to speak?

SOCRATES: Well, if you mean me, my own ideas, not very much, maybe. But I heard Aspasia, only the other day, giving a complete funeral speech b in honour of precisely these people. She'd heard the things you've been telling me – that the Athenians were going to choose someone to make the speech. So the next thing, she was going over for me the kind of speech which needed to be made, partly impromptu, and partly using stuff she had prepared in the past, when she was composing the funeral speech given by Pericles, I imagine – pasting together discarded fragments from that.

MENEXENUS: And would you be able to recall the things Aspasia said?

SOCRATES: Yes, unless I'm much mistaken, I would. I did my best to learn it off by heart from her. I was lucky not to get a beating when I c couldn't remember.

MENEXENUS: Why not recite it, then?

---

[8] Aspasia was a courtesan, and Pericles' mistress. The suggestion that she taught Socrates or anyone else oratory is all part of the elaborate fictional game Plato – following Aeschines of Sphettos – is playing in the *Menexenus*. What she was expert in, no doubt, was the giving of pleasure: a main complaint about rhetoric in the *Gorgias*.

[9] Whether this too is a pretence or not, Socrates mentions Connos as his teacher on the *kithara* elsewhere: *Euthydemus* 272c, 295d. As Méridier points out (*Ménexène*, p.79), the implication that Lampros and Antiphon were inferior teachers is another joke: Lampros was Sophocles' instructor, and Thucydides rates Antiphon of Rhamnus as the finest Athenian orator of his time (Thuc. 8.68).

SOCRATES: I'm a bit worried my teacher will be annoyed with me if I make her speech public.

MENEXENUS: Nonsense, Socrates. No, make the speech, and I'll be eternally grateful. I don't care if it's Aspasia's speech you want to deliver, or whose – just make the speech.[10]

SOCRATES: I dare say you'll laugh at me – playing the fool at my age, you'll think.

MENEXENUS: Nonsense, Socrates. Just make the speech. I insist.

SOCRATES: Well, you're not somebody I can say no to.[11] If you told me to
d strip and dance, I'm not sure I wouldn't say yes, seeing that there's only the two of us here. Hear it, then. She began her speech, I think I'm right in saying, by talking about the dead themselves. These were her words:

   'By what we have just done we have paid these men the tribute due to them. Secure in its possession, they now travel their appointed road, conveyed in solemn procession publicly by the whole city, and privately by their own families. Words are the honour it now remains to pay them.[12]
e The law requires it, and we should do it. Noble deeds call for fine words well delivered, since they become the memorial and adornment, in the ears of those who hear them, of those who did the deeds. What is needed is the kind of speech which will do justice to the merits of those who have died, while gently encouraging the living: if they are children or brothers, urging them to show the same courage, and if they are fathers, mothers, or any other older relatives still living – then offering them consolation.

237   'What must a speech of this kind be like, we ask ourselves. Where should we properly begin in praising good men who in their lives gladdened the hearts of their friends by their courage, and whose death was the price they paid for the security of those yet living? Just as there was a natural order to their goodness, so I think we should observe the same order in our praise of them. Why were they good? Because they were born of good ancestry. Let us therefore pay tribute first to their noble
b birth, and secondly to their upbringing and education. After that let us

---

[10] Plato makes Menexenus nudge us into scepticism about the real authorship of the speech Socrates is about to deliver.

[11] The vocabulary of sexual banter here (the verb *charizesthai*, literally 'gratify') recalls the erotic themes of Menexenus's conversation with Socrates in the *Lysis*. It is perhaps echoed in the repetition of *charis*, 'gratitude', at the end of the dialogue (249d–e).

[12] Thucydides' Pericles likewise begins his funeral oration with a contrast between words and deeds (one of the most frequent tropes of all formal Greek prose), similarly followed by reflection on what will make the speech appropriate to the occasion (2.35).

highlight the fine things they did and the way they showed themselves worthy of their ancestors.[13]

'Their noble birth? Let's start with the origin of their ancestors. They were not immigrants; they did not themselves come from anywhere else; they presented these their descendants to the world not as foreigners resident in this land, but as an indigenous people living and dwelling in what is truly their native country, and brought up not (as some are) by a stepmother, but by a true mother, the land in which they lived.[14] And now that they have died, they lie in their own familiar corners of the land c which bore them and raised them, and which has now received them. So it is above all just that we should begin by celebrating their mother in her own right, since in this way what we shall be doing is celebrating also the noble birth of these her sons.

'Our country truly merits the praise of the whole of mankind, not just of ourselves. This is for many reasons, of which the first and greatest is that she is loved by the gods. For this claim our evidence is the strife between the two gods who quarrelled over her, and the way it was resolved.[15] She whom the gods praised – how is she not entitled to be d praised by the whole of mankind? But praise is rightfully hers also – and this is the second reason – because at the time when the whole earth was yielding up and bringing forth all manner of living things, both wild and domestic, that was the moment for our land to show herself pure, bearing no wild beasts at all; of animals she selected for herself and bore only mankind, superior to the rest in intelligence, and the only one to acknowledge justice and the gods.

'There is strong evidence for the claim that this land of ours actually e gave birth to the ancestors they share with us: everything which gives

---

[13] The topics here listed (and throughout) are standard items in funeral orations, but 'Aspasia's' speech is unusual in announcing sequence and transitions so explicitly. This rhetorical mannerism is caricatured in Agathon's speech in the *Symposium* (194c–195a).

[14] The Athenians made much of this theme in drama as well as oratory. All surviving Attic examples of funeral speech refer to it (Thucydides 2.36.1, Lysias 2.17, Demosthenes 60.4, Hyperides, *Epitaphios* 8), but only this version in the *Menexenus* develops the topic at length and in such exaggeratedly literal-minded detail (compare the *Republic*'s Noble Lie, received with polite disbelief by Glaucon: *Rep.* 3.414b–415b). 'Aspasia' returns to it with renewed emphasis at 245c–d, which helps her to bring the first part of her speech to a resounding conclusion.

[15] 'Aspasia' refers to the tale that Athena and Poseidon disputed which of them should be the city's presiding deity. The gods decided that the olive (Athena's gift) was more valuable than the salt-water spring on the Acropolis (Poseidon's).

birth has a supply of nourishment adapted to its offspring; this is how a woman is known to be the real mother or not – if she does not have a source of nourishment for the child she bears. And this land and mother of ours offers us ample evidence that she gave birth to human beings, since she alone at that time was the first to produce nourishment for humans – the harvest of wheat and barley, from which the human race gets its finest and best nourishment; and this shows that it was she herself who truly gave birth to this creature. And when applied to the land, this kind of evidence carries greater weight than when applied to a woman, since in conception and giving birth it is not the land which imitates woman, but woman the land.

238

'Nor was she grudging of this harvest. She bestowed it on everybody else, and later brought forth, for their descendants, that cure for all hardship, the olive. And when she had brought the people up, and seen them grow to adulthood, she introduced gods as their rulers and teachers. Today is not the moment for naming them; we know them already. They furnished us with our livelihood – both in our day-to-day living, giving us the first education in the arts and sciences, and also in the defence of our land, instructing us in the possession and use of weapons.

b

'Thus equipped by birth and education, the ancestors of these men lived under a political system which deserves some brief mention. For human beings, a political system is their nurse: a good nurse produces people who are good; her opposite, people who are bad. I must now demonstrate, therefore, that those who went before us were raised under a good political system, which made good citizens of them, and which still today makes good citizens – among whom these who have died are to be numbered. After all, it was the same political system then as now, the system under which we live today and have lived, for the most part, ever since those days. Some call it democracy, others give it some other name, as they fancy. What it is, in truth, is aristocracy tempered by the approval of the masses.[16] Kings? Yes, we always have those – at one time hereditary, at another by election.[17] But the control of the city lies for the most part

c

d

---

[16] The subtle complexity of the Athenian political system is a major topic of Pericles' funeral speech, and is characterised in comparable terms (Thuc. 2.37). Lysias's (2.18–19) stresses that the Athenians only achieved democracy by expelling ruling élites (an echo here, perhaps, of its restoration after the defeat of the junta of Thirty Tyrants in 403 BC), whereas 'Aspasia' contrives to give the impression that it is their natural birthright, which they have exercised almost throughout.

[17] 'Aspasia' plays down the significance of Athens' mostly legendary early period of hereditary kingship (Euripides interestingly makes Theseus – much the most famous of their kings – an eloquent advocate of democracy: *Suppliant Women* 399–441). In historical times

with the masses; it is they who give office and power to those they regard, at any particular time, as the best. No-one is disqualified by weakness or poverty or obscurity of birth, nor appointed because of their opposites. No, there is one sole criterion: he who is thought to be wise and good, he it is who holds power and rules.

'And the reason for this political system we have? Equality of e birth. Other cities have populations which are diverse and dispro-portionate, resulting in political systems which are correspondingly disproportionate – tyrannies and oligarchies, where some of the inhabit-ants regard the others as slaves, and the others look on them as masters. By contrast, we and our countrymen, brethren all, born of one mother, do not think it right to be either slaves or masters of one another. Instead 239 our natural equality of birth drives us to seek equality of rights in accor-dance with law. Only when it comes to reputation for goodness and wis-dom do we acknowledge one another's superiority.

'Being thus raised in total freedom, and well born, the fathers of these men, and our fathers, and these men themselves, performed many fine deeds, for all the world to see, both in their private lives and in public life, in the belief that freedom was worth fighting for, whether for Greeks b against Greeks or for Greece as a whole against barbarians. As for how they defended themselves when Eumolpos and the Amazons, and others before them, invaded their land, how they defended the Argives against the descendants of Cadmus, or the Heracleidae against the Argives – well, time is too short to do justice to the story; and besides, fine poets have celebrated their courage in song, making it well enough known to the whole world. If we try to embellish the same deeds using unadorned c prose, I suspect we would come off a clear second-best, and so I think it best to say no more on the subject. Their deeds have the recognition they deserve. But the deeds for which no poet has yet given deserved credit to those who deserve it, and which lie still in virgin state[18] – these I think I *should* mention, praising them and proposing to others that they make them the subject of odes or other kinds of poetry in a style which does justice to their doers. The deeds of which I speak are chiefly these.[19]

the title *basileus*, 'king', was accorded to a high official (*archón*) primarily concerned with religious matters; Socrates was tried and sentenced in his court.

[18] 'in virgin state' translates the reading of the best manuscripts, *mnêsteiai*, rather than *amnês-tiai* ('forgotten'), adopted by Burnet in the Oxford Classical Text.

[19] Having done no more than mention episodes in the legendary phase of the Athenian past, 'Aspasia' now proceeds to eulogise Athenian achievements in historical times. This long section of the speech continues as far as 246a. The narrative initially builds up to the

d 'When the Persians were the leading power in Asia, and starting to
enslave Europe, it was the descendants of this land of ours – our own
parents – who kept them at bay. It is right to start – in fact, it is our duty –
by recalling and celebrating their courage. And the way to look at their
courage, if you want to celebrate it properly, is to think yourself back
into the time when the whole of Asia was in slavery to the third of the
Great Kings. Cyrus, the first of them, liberated his own fellow-citizens
the Persians by his own sound judgment, at the same time making their
e masters the Medes his slaves; he made himself ruler of the whole of Asia
as far as Egypt. His son was the ruler of as much of Egypt and Libya as
is not desert; and the third, Darius, pushed the boundaries of his rule by
land as far as Scythia, while with his navy he was master of the sea and
240 the islands; no-one so much as dreamt of challenging him. The minds of
all mankind had been enslaved, so many, so great and so warlike were the
races the Persian empire had now reduced to slavery.

'Then came an accusation against us and the Eretrians from Darius,
who alleged that we had been implicated in the revolt against Sardis.[20] He
sent an expedition of half a million men in merchant ships and warships,
together with a battle-fleet of 300 ships, under the command of Datis.
He told Datis, if he wanted to keep his head on his shoulders, to come
b back with the Eretrians and Athenians. Datis sailed to Eretria, against
men who were among the most renowned in war of the Greeks at that
time, and not few in number, and in three days overwhelmed them. He
combed the entire land, to make sure no-one escaped, and this is how
he did it: his soldiers went to the borders of Eretrian territory, forming
a line from coast to coast, at equal intervals. Then joining hands, they
c swept the whole land, so that they could tell the Great King that no-
one had escaped them. It was with the same intention that they set sail
from Eretria and put in at Marathon. They thought there was nothing to
stop them carrying off the Athenians into slavery as well, using the same
coercion they had used with the Eretrians.

moment when the Athenians overcame the massive forces of the Persians at Marathon
(490). Then follows the sequel at Artemisium, Salamis, and Plataea, when the Persians
invaded unsuccessfully a second time (480–479). Finally 'Aspasia' goes on to operations
against them in subsequent decades near the river Eurymedon on the southern coast of
Turkey (perhaps 469), and in Cyprus and Egypt (perhaps 459).
[20] A reference to the ultimately unsuccessful Ionian revolt of 497, in which many of the
Greek cities under Persian rule on what is now the Turkish coast (and indeed further afield
in the eastern Mediterranean) participated.

'While all this was either achieved or in the process of being attempted, none of the Greeks came to the assistance of the Eretrians or the Athenians apart from the Spartans – and they arrived on the day after the battle. The rest all kept their heads down, scared stiff and clinging on to their safety while it lasted. That is the situation you have to think yourself into d if you want to grasp what kind of people they really were who met the onslaught of the barbarians at Marathon, who punished the arrogance of the whole of Asia, and who were the first to set up memorials commem- orating victory over the barbarians. They acted as guides and teachers to the rest of Greece, the lesson being that the power of the Persians was not irresistible, that all the numbers in the world, and all the wealth in the world, are no match for courage. For my part, therefore, I maintain that those men are not merely our fathers in a physical sense, but also fathered e freedom both for us and for everybody in mainland Greece. That was the action to which the Greeks looked when they screwed up their courage to take their chance in the later battles for their freedom. They were pupils of the heroes of Marathon.

'First prize, then, to them my speech must award – and second to those who fought the sea battles of Salamis and Artemisium, and were victor- 241 ious. Of these men there are many tales you could tell – the onslaughts they had to face both by land and by sea, and how they fought them off. But what strikes me as their finest achievement – this I *will* mention – is that they completed the task bequeathed to them by the heroes of Marathon. Those who fought at Marathon made it clear to the Greeks that it was possible for them, though few against many, to fight off the barbarians by land. No more than that. When it came to ships, things b were still uncertain; the Persians had the reputation of being irresistible by sea – alike because of their numbers, their wealth, their expertise and their strength. So a good reason for praising the men who fought those battles at sea is that they released the Greeks from the grip of fear, stopped them being afraid of sheer numbers of ships and men. What they brought about, these two groups – those who fought at Marathon and those who fought the sea battle at Salamis – was the education of c the other Greeks, who learnt from them the lesson of not fearing the barbarians, in the one case on land, and in the other at sea, and made not fearing them a habit.

'Third among actions which saved Greece, both in numerical order and in terms of courage, I put the one at Plataea – a joint action this time between the Spartans and the Athenians.

'Those men, all of them, fought off the greatest and most deadly danger. For their courage they are praised by us today, and in the future
d will be praised by those who come after us. But after Plataea there were still many Greek cities on the side of the barbarian, and the Great King himself, it was reported, was planning to make another attempt against the Greeks. So it is right for us also to remember those who crowned the work of their predecessors, and made our security complete by sweeping the seas clean and removing all trace of the barbarian. These were the
e ones who fought the sea battle at the Eurymedon, who carried out the expedition to Cyprus, who sailed to Egypt and many other places. We should remember them and be grateful to them. They made the Great King fear for his own safety, forcing him to concentrate on that and stop planning the destruction of Greece.

'That war was fought from start to finish by the entire city, fighting
242 for themselves and those who shared their language, against the barbarians. In the peace which followed our city was highly regarded, but then encountered the usual human response to those who are successful – first rivalry, and after rivalry, resentment.[21] This involved our city, against its will, in a war against Greeks. And what happened then, when war started, was that they met the Spartans at Tanagra, and fought for
b the liberation of Boeotia. The battle was indecisive, but what followed was not. The Spartans withdrew and went home, abandoning the people they had come to help, while our side won a victory at Oenophyta two days later, and with justice on their side restored those who had been unjustly sent into exile.[22] These people were the first since the Persian war – though this time coming to the help of Greeks against Greeks, in
c the cause of freedom – to show themselves brave men, liberating the people they had come to help, and the first the city honoured with burial in this tomb.

'After this war became general, and the whole of Greece marched against us and laid waste our land – a poor way of showing their gratitude to our city. Our people defeated them in a sea-battle, and took their

---

[21] Lysias too makes the origin of 'Greek war' envy and resentment against Athens (2.48).

[22] According to Thucydides (1.108.1), the Spartans were victorious at the battle of Tanagra in Boeotia (457), but with huge loss of life on both sides. Rather more believably than 'Aspasia', he puts the decisive Athenian victory at Oenophyta sixty two (not two) days later (Thuc. 1.108.2–3). In 'Aspasia's' telling, this episode marks the beginning of the Peloponnesian War, or rather of war not now against the barbarians, but against other Greeks.

leaders the Spartans prisoner at Sphagia. They could have killed them, but instead they spared them, returned them, and made peace, in the d belief that against their own race they should make war only up to the point of victory, and not destroy the unity of the Greeks in the pursuit of one single city's vendetta, whereas against barbarians the aim should be to destroy them.[23]

'Such are the men who fought that war and now lie here. It is right for us to praise them. What they showed was that if anyone after all that claimed that in the earlier war against the barbarians there was anybody better than the Athenians, his claim was false. They showed this at that time by their military success when Greece was at war with itself, when e they got the better of the leaders of the rest of Greece, and all on their own defeated the people with whom they had once jointly defeated the barbarians.

'Following this period of peace there was a third war, appalling and unexpected, in which many brave men died.[24] They are buried here. Many of them set up victory memorials all over Sicily, fighting for the liberation of Leontini; they had sailed to that region to help them, fulfill- 243 ing pledges of alliance, but the length of the voyage put Athens at a disad-vantage, and without the capacity to keep them adequately supplied. So they had to give up, and came to grief. Yet for their discipline and courage they receive more praise from their enemies and those who fought against them than most people receive from their friends. And then there were all

---

[23] 'Aspasia' compresses the entire first phase of what Thucydides takes to be the Peloponnesian War (431–421) into little more than a brief account of perhaps its most famous military episode, the blockade and eventual capture by the Athenians of a Spartan garrison on Sphacteria (or Sphagia, as it is called here), an island protecting the harbour at Pylos in the south western Peloponnese. Although she portrays the Athenians as plucky victims of aggression deserted by all the other Greeks, Athens in fact controlled a huge empire throughout the period, which it taxed heavily and governed (as the Thucydidean Pericles puts it) as a 'tyranny' (2.63.2). It is true, however, that Athenian territory was invaded and devastated each summer by Spartan land forces. The war was in truth inconclusive overall, with victories and defeats and above all exhaustion on both sides.

[24] For the second and final phase of the Peloponnesian War 'Aspasia' develops the plucky victim theme, and emphasises again that the Athenian agenda was liberation of the oppressed. She refers in turn to the Sicilian expedition of 415–413 (putting the best gloss she can on what was in truth an entirely miscalculated imperialistic adventure ending in disaster); to naval battles at Cynossema (411), and at Cyzicus (410), when the Peloponnesian fleet was annihilated; and to the successful relief of Mytilene at the battle of Arginusae (406), where, however, failure to pick up the Athenian wounded and dead caused outrage back in the city.

those who fought the sea battles in the Hellespont, when they captured
b an entire enemy fleet in one day, and won many other victories besides.

'When I speak of the appalling and unexpected character of this war,
what I am referring to is the antagonism of the rest of Greece towards
our city, which reached a level where they could bring themselves to
make overtures to their worst enemy, and invite the Great King, whom
they and we had jointly driven out of Greece, back into Greece – a barbarian attacking Greeks – for their own selfish reasons, assembling the
entire Greek and barbarian world against our city.[25] That was when the
c strength and courage of our city truly shone forth. She had been fought
to a standstill, it was thought; her ships were cut off at Mytilene; yet
the Athenians came to their relief with sixty ships, manning the ships
themselves, and by defeating their enemies and bringing deliverance to
those who were friendly to them, showed themselves, beyond dispute,
men of the highest courage. But they were not rewarded with the fortune they deserved. They were not picked up from the water, and they
do not lie here.

'We should remember them and praise them for evermore, since it was
d their courage that carried the day for us not only in that sea battle but in
the rest of the war as well. It was they who gave the city its reputation
for invincibility, though the whole world should come against it. And a
justified reputation too: we were not destroyed by others, but were rather
the agents of our own destruction. Defeat we ourselves have inflicted on
ourselves, and have been that way overcome. Where our enemies are concerned, we remain undefeated to this day.[26]

e 'After that there was a lull, and peace with everybody, and we had our
own war here. But the way it was fought – well, if people were fated to
have a civil war, anyone would pray for his city to be afflicted in the way
ours was. Look how willingly and closely the citizens – those from the
Piraeus and those from the city – combined with one another and (surprisingly) with the other Greeks! See what restraint they showed in their
244 handling of the war against the party at Eleusis! And the reason for all

---

[25] In 412 the Spartans and their allies made a treaty with the Great King which marked
the beginning of a period of increasing intervention in Greek affairs on the part of the
Persians.

[26] Thucydides (2.65.12) had already judged that what brought about eventual Athenian
defeat in the Peloponnesian War was internal dissension. This is trumped by 'Aspasia's'
claim here.

this? Simply the true kinship which produces, not just in theory but in actual practice, a firm friendship based on shared nationality.[27]

'These people, too, those who died at one another's hands in this war, deserve mention. We have to reconcile them in whatever way we can in such a situation, using prayer and sacrifice, praying to those who have power over them, now that we ourselves have been reconciled. It was bad luck which set them against one another – not wickedness or malice. We who are still living are ourselves the evidence for this. We are of the same b race as they, and we have forgiven one another for the things we did and the things we had done to us.

'After this we were completely at peace, and the city had a period of inactivity. She forgave the barbarians their strong retaliation for the harm she did them, but she was angry with the Greeks when she remembered the good she had done them, and how they showed their gratitude – making common cause with the barbarians, stripping us of those ships c which had once been their salvation, and destroying our walls as a way of thanking us for saving theirs from being pulled down. Deciding in future not to defend Greeks who were being enslaved – either by one another or by the barbarians – our city lived accordingly.[28] And profiting by this decision of ours the Spartans decided that the champions of liberty had been brought low – meaning us – and that it was now their job to enslave everybody else. Which is what they then started to do. d

'Why prolong the story? It's not a long time ago, what happened next, not the story of people a long time ago, if I were to tell you about it.[29] We have seen with our own eyes the leaders of the Greek world – the Argives, the Boeotians, the Corinthians – coming to our city in fear of their lives

[27] 'Aspasia' refers first to the amnesty of 403 that followed the civil war in which the Thirty Tyrants were defeated. The democratic party had been based in Piraeus, with those who sympathised with the regime or had decided to put up with it remaining in the city. The terms of the settlement provided that Eleusis (less than ten miles west of Athens) should function as an independent city accommodating the remnant of the oligarchic party. But after a couple of years – as Plato fails to mention but doubtless wants us to remember – the Athenians attacked (apparently with allies), and reincorporated it into their own territory, torturing and executing the Eleusinian commanders.

[28] In 404 the Spartan king Lysander caused the long walls (see note on *Gorgias* 455c) to be dismantled and the boat sheds that housed the Athenian war triremes destroyed. The vast majority of the ships themselves had to be handed over to him. Any Athenian 'decision' not to pursue its previous 'liberation' agenda was in truth necessitated by the city's reduced circumstances as in effect a demilitarised Spartan vassal state.

[29] Socrates died in 399. The part of the narrative that follows relates to the years after that. The flagrant anachronism suggests that Plato wanted to highlight continuing delusion about Athens' motives, role and standing as an actor on the international stage.

to ask for help; and most astonishing of all, the Great King reduced to
such helplessness that his only remaining hope of survival lay with the
c city he had been so keen to destroy. Indeed, if you wanted to accuse our
city and have justice on your side, the only thing you could properly say
in accusation would be that she is always too inclined to compassion, too
caring where the weak are concerned.

'On this occasion too she was unable to go through with it and stick
to her decision, if any of those who had treated her unjustly was being
245 enslaved, to refuse them help. She buckled, and did help them: in the case
of the Greeks, she acted herself, helping them and releasing them from
slavery – with the result that they were free until they themselves once
again enslaved one another. As for the Great King, she could not bring
herself to assist him herself; she had too much respect for the memorials commemorating the victories of Marathon, Salamis and Plataea. But
merely by allowing exiles and volunteers to help him, she saved him, as is
generally agreed. Then she fortified the city, built a fleet, undertook the
b war which had been forced upon her, and made war on the Spartans in
defence of the people of Paros.[30]

'Once he saw the Spartans giving up on the war at sea, the Great King
started to fear our city. He wanted to withdraw from the alliance, and so
he asked for the Greeks on the mainland of Asia – whom the Spartans
had previously handed over to him – as the price for his continued alliance with us and his other allies. He thought we would refuse, and that
c this would give him an excuse to withdraw from it. He was wrong about
his other allies: the Corinthians, the Argives, the Boeotians and the rest
of the allies were quite happy to hand them over to him; they came to an
agreement, and swore oaths, that they would hand over the Greeks on the
mainland to him if he was prepared to pay them a cash sum. We were the
only ones who could not bring ourselves to hand them over or swear the

[30] The events recounted here belong to the years 395–393. Since the end of the Peloponnesian
War, Sparta had become by far the major Greek power, increasingly feared by her allies
in that war, and had been engaging in effective operations of various kinds against the
Persians. Athens – whether as a major or minor partner – joined with the Argives,
Boeotians, and Corinthians in resisting Spartan aggression on the Greek mainland. At
the same time (summer of 394) the Athenian admiral Conon, commanding a large fleet of
Persian warships in the eastern Aegean, inflicted a crushing defeat on the Spartan fleet at
the battle of Cnidos. Following further naval operations the following year against Spartan
territory itself, Conon persuaded the Persians to transfer a substantial part of the fleet to
Athenian control, chased the Spartans from the Cyclades (this may explain the reference
to Paros), and with Persian financial assistance put completion of the rebuilding of the
long walls and the Piraeus in hand.

oaths.[31] So firm and robust was our city's attachment to nobility and freedom, so instinctively anti-barbarian – the result of our being pure Greeks d
with no barbarian admixture. We have none of those Pelopses, Cadmuses,
Aegyptuses or Danauses dwelling among us – none of those others whom
convention calls Greeks, but who are really barbarians. We live as out-
and-out Greeks – not a drop of barbarian blood in us – which is why our
city has this pure, ingrained hatred of anything essentially foreign.

'Despite everything, therefore, we were once again left on our own, thanks
to our refusal to perform the disgraceful and unholy act of handing Greeks e
over to barbarians. This put us in the same position we had been in before,
when we were overwhelmed, only this time, with god's help, we brought
hostilities to a more satisfactory conclusion. We finished the war still in possession of our ships, our walls and our colonies,[32] so eager were our enemies
to finish it. All the same, we lost brave men in that war too – those who found
themselves fighting on impossible ground at Corinth, or those who were
betrayed at Lechaeum.[33] Brave, too, were those who liberated the Great King,
and drove the Spartans from the seas. With men such as these, it is my task to 246
bring them to your attention. What you have to do is help me praise them and
celebrate them.

'So much for the actions of the men who are buried here, and of the
others who have died for the city.[34] There are the many fine deeds I have

---

[31] Were the negotiations 'Aspasia' refers to here those that took place in 392–391 (on Spartan
rather than Persian initiative), or those of 387–386 that resulted in what is nowadays called
the King's Peace? Certainly the late 390s was a time when for the Spartans the war at sea
was lost, whereas by the time of the King's Peace a naval victory over the Athenians in the
north eastern Aegean was to leave the Spartan admiral Antalcidas 'master of the sea' and
the Athenians desperate for peace (Xenophon, *Hellenica* 5.1.13–29). On the other hand an
admittedly confused fragment of the historian Philochorus (*FGrH* 328 F149a) connects the
Athenian position of refusal to accede to Persian rule over the Greeks in Asia with the King's
Peace (or as the Greeks called it, the peace of Antalcidas) of 387–386. For further historical
details consult P.J. Rhodes, *A History of the Classical Greek World* 478–323 BC, pp.192–3.

[32] In the terms of settlement debated in 392–391 the Persians made no objection to Athens'
retention of the north Aegean islands of Lemnos, Imbros and Scyros. The same was to be
true of the subsequent King's Peace.

[33] The probability is that 'Aspasia' is referring to Athenian losses at the battle between the
Spartans and the allied forces at the Nemea River (394; see *Hellenica* 4.2.14–23, although no
mention is made there of 'impossible ground'), and to fighting involving the anti-Spartan
coalition (including Athenian mercenaries under Iphicrates) at or near the Corinthian port
of Lechaeum (392), where there was what an Athenian patriot might regard as 'betrayal'
of the allied fortified position by Corinthian dissidents (*Hellenica* 4.4.1–12). 'Aspasia' then
refers once more to Conon's naval exploits against the Spartans (397–394).

[34] 'Aspasia' now concludes the oration in something approximating the traditional manner,
with words of encouragement and consolation to those still living (as does Thucydides'

described, but many more and finer are those I have omitted. It would
b take me many days and nights if I was going to list them all, and even then
it would not be enough. Let us remember them, therefore, and let each
man among us urge their descendants, as we would in time of war, not to
break ranks with their forefathers, not to give way to cowardice and turn
tail. For my part I urge you now, you children of brave men, and no mat-
c ter where I come across you in the future I will remind and instruct you
to set your hearts on being as brave as you possibly can. Today, however,
it is right for me to give you the message which your fathers, when they
were about to risk their lives, ordered us to give to those who were left
behind, should anything happen to them. What I am going to say to you
will be what I actually heard from their own lips, and also the kind of
thing they would want to say to you now if they could, judging by what
they did say then. You must regard the message you hear from me as
being spoken by them in person. What they said was this.[35]

d ' "Children, that you are born of brave fathers, the present occasion
of itself makes clear. We could have gone on living, without honour, but
instead we have chosen to die with honour. We do not want to bring
reproach upon you and upon those who come after you; we do not want
to shame our own fathers and all our kin who went before us. For the person who brings shame on his own family, we think, life is not worth living; such a person has no friend – neither among mankind nor among the
gods, neither on earth nor under the earth when he is dead. Remember
our words, therefore, and whatever occupation you pursue, be sure to
e pursue it with courage, in the knowledge that without that all possessions
and activities are shameful and evil. Wealth with cowardice adds no lustre
to him who has it – the wealth of someone like that benefits another, not
himself – and physical strength and good looks are clearly not becoming,
are in fact positively unbecoming, when found in one who is cowardly

Pericles: Thuc. 2.42–5; see also Lysias 2.67–81). The language employed in the opening
section (246a–c) is reminiscent of that used by Socrates in his speech to the jurors in the
Apology, when describing his attitude to death (28d–29a) and the imperative about living
the good life he feels obliged to impress on everyone he meets (29d–30a; 'no matter where
I come across you', 246b6–c1, almost exactly echoes a similar phrase at *Apol.* 29d6).
[35] Plato likes writing hypothetical speeches of this kind. Parallels are (again) the harangue the
Socrates of the *Apology* imagines himself delivering to whatever Athenians he runs into
(29d–30c), and the address by the laws of Athens in the *Crito* (50a–54d). 'Aspasia' speaks
first and at some length to the children of the departed, something left to the very end by
Thucydides' Pericles, and then given just two short sentences (Thuc. 2.45.1; in Lysias
only half a sentence: Lys. 2.72).

and base. They draw attention to their possessor, and advertise his cowardice – just as all knowledge, when divorced from justice and the rest of moral goodness, is clearly not wisdom but unscrupulous opportunism.[36]

' "For these reasons your aim must be to devote your energy – first, last, and at all times and in all ways your entire energy – ideally to outdoing us and those before us in glory; failing that, then be aware that if we are victorious in our contest of courage with you, victory brings with it disgrace, whereas defeat, if we are defeated, brings happiness. And the best way for us to be defeated and you to be victorious is for you not to treat the reputation of your ancestors as something you can draw upon for day-to-day spending. You must realise that to a man who has any opinion of himself at all nothing is more shameful than presenting himself to the world as an object of distinction not because of anything *he* has done, but because of the fame of his ancestors. For children, the distinction of their parents is a fine and imposing treasure. But to use up a treasure – be it in money or distinction – and not leave it to your children, because you have no personal wealth or reputation of your own, is shameful and unmanly.

' "Do as we say, and when your own fate brings you here, you will arrive among us as friends among friends. Disregard our advice – play the coward – and you will not be welcome at all. To our children, then, let that be all we have to say.

' "Some of us have fathers and mothers still living.[37] You must encourage them always to bear their misfortune, if that is indeed what it is, as lightly as they can, and not join in a general outpouring of grief. They have no need of something which will upset them further – what has happened already will be quite capable of doing that. No, you must heal and soften their hurt by reminding them that the gods have listened to the most important of their prayers. They did not pray for children who were immortal, but children who were courageous and of great renown. And that is what they have got – no small blessing. And for all in his life to turn out in accordance with his wishes is, for a mortal man, no easy matter.

247

b

c

d

---

[36] Cicero appropriates this sentiment (which could be construed as a version of the doctrine of the unity of the virtues), acknowledging its Platonic provenance, in his *On Duties* (1.63).

[37] Now 'Aspasia' turns to comfort for the parents of the departed. Both the Thucydidean Pericles (Thuc. 2.44) and Lysias (who waxes eloquent at this point: Lys. 2.72–8) see the parents' situation as intrinsically miserable, though Lysias takes a starker and more fatalist line than Pericles. 'Aspasia's' tone is much more positive, perhaps at root because her advice incorporates the Socratic idea that our happiness depends on ourselves and our virtues, not on others and their fortunes (247c–248a; compare for example *Apol.* 41c–d: no harm can come to a good man).

' "Also, if they bear their misfortunes bravely, they will be recognised as the true fathers of brave sons, who possess the same quality themselves.
e If they give way to their misfortunes, they will arouse the suspicion either that they are not our fathers, or that the people singing our praises are liars. They should not let either of those things happen; instead they should be the ones who most praise us – by their actions – thus showing themselves to be, clearly and in truth, men and the fathers of men. We think the old saying 'Nothing in excess' was well said, and in truth it *is* a good saying. A man whose prospects of happiness depend in their entirety just on him,
248 give or take a little, not on other people whose success or failure necessarily brings a fluctuation in his fortunes as well – this is the person who is best equipped for life; he is the one with self-control, brave and wise. And if first he comes by money or children and then loses them, he more than anyone will give ear to that maxim. He will not make a great parade either of his joy or his grief, because he puts his trust in himself.
b ' "That is how we think our families should be, how we would like them to be and what we say of them, just as we ourselves show the same qualities in not being unduly upset or frightened if this is the time for us to die. We appeal to our fathers and mothers to adopt the same resolve as they live out the rest of their lives. Let them be aware that it will give us no great pleasure if they mourn us and grieve for us. Indeed, if the
c dead have any perception of the living, then that is what would give us least pleasure. It would be bad for them, and make it hard for them to bear their misfortunes, whereas bearing them easily and with restraint would please us most. For us, after all, things are about to come to what is, for mankind, the finest of conclusions – a reason for celebrating, not mourning. The best way for them to forget their misfortunes, and live a life which is finer, truer and more pleasing to us, is to turn their atten-
d tion to the care and upbringing of our wives and children.
' "That is all the message our families need from us. To the city we would urge that they take care of our fathers and sons for us. Educate our sons properly, and look after our fathers in their old age, as they deserve – though we are well aware that it will take good care of them even without our urging."
'To you, children and parents of those who have died, that is the mes-
e sage which they have commanded us to convey.[38] And I for my part am

---

[38] For the rest of her speech 'Aspasia' reflects on the responsibilities of the city itself to the dead, their children, and their parents, modulating from the fictive voice of the fallen

conveying it with all the seriousness I can command. Here in person, speaking for them, I ask their families to follow their example, if they are sons, and to feel no anxiety on their own behalf, if they are parents, since we, individually and collectively, will take care of you in your old age and look after you, wherever any single one of us comes across any single one from their families. As for the city, you are yourselves no doubt well aware of the provisions she makes. She has provided by law for the children and parents of those killed in war, and has instructed 249 those who hold the highest office to watch over them above all the other citizens, to make sure the fathers and mothers of these people are not treated unjustly.

'When it comes to the children, the city herself takes a hand in their upbringing: in her determination that they should have as little awareness as possible of being fatherless, she herself fills the position of father to them for as long as they remain children; and when they reach manhood, she fits them out with full military equipment and sends them to claim what is theirs; in this way she highlights and recalls the achievements of the fathers by giving the sons the tools of the fathers' noble occupation, while at the same time ensuring that the possession of weapons gives b them an auspicious start on their journey to their ancestral hearth, where they will need strength to rule.[39]

'As for the dead themselves, the city never stops honouring them: each year she herself pays all of them publicly the same observance as is paid to each individual privately; on top of that, she holds competitions in athletics and riding, and in every branch of music and poetry. Quite simply, to those who have died she acts as son and heir; to their sons, as father; c and to parents and other relatives, as protector. In this way she takes every possible care of every one of them, every day of their lives. You must keep these things in mind, and that will help you bear your misfortune more lightly; in that way you will best show your affection both to those who have died and to those who yet live; and you will most easily care and be cared for.

---

soldiers to her own. Lysias has nothing comparable, although Pericles has a great deal to say of a rather different kind about the way of life fostered by the city, and ends by remarking on the responsibilities towards the children that it recognises (Thuc. 2.46.1).

[39] Before the performance of tragedies at the Great Dionysia festival, sons of citizens killed in war were on reaching adulthood presented to the people and clothed in hoplite armour. This marked their formal entry into the duties of head of household.

'And now, since you – along with everyone else here – have completed the public mourning for the dead in accordance with the law, go your ways.'[40]

d   There you are, Menexenus – the speech of Aspasia of Miletus.

MENEXENUS: Heavens, Socrates, how gifted you make Aspasia out to be. Fancy a woman being able to compose a speech as good as that.

SOCRATES: If you don't believe me, come with me now. You can hear her speaking for herself.

MENEXENUS: No, I've met Aspasia, Socrates. Lots of times. I know what she is capable of.

SOCRATES: Don't you think she is wonderful? Aren't you now grateful to her for her speech?

MENEXENUS: Yes, Socrates. I am extremely grateful for the speech –
e   and to the woman or man who recited it.[41] And I'm grateful to the speaker for many other things as well.

SOCRATES: I'm glad to hear it. But mind you don't betray me, so that I can bring you many more of the fine speeches she writes for political purposes.

MENEXENUS: Don't worry, I won't betray you. Just keep bringing them.

SOCRATES: You can count on it.

---

[40] 'Aspasia's' final words echo Pericles' at the end of his funeral speech in Thucydides (2.46.2). Both may be using the same traditional concluding formula.

[41] Menexenus implies that he takes Socrates, not Aspasia, to be the real author.

Protagoras

Dramatis personae

Dates of birth and death given below are conjectural, except for Socrates and for the deaths of Alcibiades and Critias.

ALCIBIADES (451–404) Flamboyant Athenian aristocratic politician, brought up in Pericles' household as his ward. An associate
of Socrates from an early age: Socrates' erotic interest in him is
explored in the *Symposium*, and alluded to in both the *Gorgias* and
the *Protagoras*. He was the main advocate and initially commander
of the Sicilian expedition (415–413), but was indicted in connection
with religious scandals and recalled from his command. After intri-
guing first with the Spartans and then the Persians, he subsequently
led the Athenian fleet to victory over the Spartans at Cyzicus in the
Bosphorus (410). After further personal vicissitudes, he was mur-
dered by Persian agents in Phrygia (modern Asiatic Turkey).

CALLIAS (450–365) His father Hipponicus was an Athenian aristocrat reputed to be the richest man in Greece and still active in the
420s (he served as general in 426/5). The family were connected to
Pericles' family by marriage. Following the precedent of Eupolis's
comedy *Sycophants* (421), Plato here imagines Callias as a mature
man who has recently inherited the principal family house (315d)
and is lavishing his wealth on sophists (see further *Apology* 20d). We
hear of Callias as a public figure in his later years (general, 391; diplomatic envoy, 371). The money (derived largely from the Laurium

silver mines) seems to have run out fairly quickly, and in comedy of the early fourth century his name had become a byword for penury.

CRITIAS (460–403) A distant cousin of Plato, who seems to have associated at one point quite closely with Socrates – something which may have helped precipitate the latter's trial in 399. Critias was a considerable intellectual. Quite a number of extracts from his published writings survive, notably from his two works on the Spartan constitution (one in prose, the other in elegiac verse), which clearly evoked his admiration. His authorship of *Sisyphus* – a play from which a rationalistic account of the origins of belief in the gods is preserved – is disputed (Euripides is the other claimant). Like Alcibiades Critias was accused of participation in religious outrage in 415 (but was subsequently released from custody). He came to political prominence as a main leader of the regime of the Thirty in 404–403, and was regarded as the mainspring of some of its most oppressive and murderous acts. He was killed fighting against the forces of the democratic party at Munychia (near Piraeus) in spring 403.

HIPPIAS A sophist from Elis in the north western Peloponnese, who served as ambassador for his city on several occasions (according to *Hippias Major* 281a–b). The *Protagoras* makes him considerably younger than Protagoras himself (we should perhaps suppose he is roughly the same age as Socrates), and he seems to have lived on into the fourth century. The dialogue represents him as a polymath, with astronomy and mathematics figuring prominently among the subjects in which he undertook to give instruction (but he is probably not the Hippias Proclus named as author of an early technical discovery in geometry). In attempting to trace affiliations between the ideas of philosophers and their poetic predecessors (as suggested by his Fr.6), such as those suggested at *Symposium* 178a–c, he was probably a pioneer. He plays a leading role in two dialogues in the Platonic corpus named after him, known for convenience as *Hippias Major* and *Hippias Minor*.

HIPPOCRATES Socrates' young Athenian friend, introduced as someone 'from a powerful and prosperous family' (316b), with great natural ability, and no less political ambition. But we hear no more of him from any other source, nor is anything known about his father Apollodorus.

PRODICUS From Iulis on Ceos (the most northerly of the western string of Cycladic islands in the Aegean), which he represented on various official delegations (according to *Hippias Major* 281c). He seems to have been a good deal younger than Protagoras, and like Hippias he is mentioned by Socrates in the *Apology* (19e) as still practising as a sophist at the time of his trial (399). Teasingly or otherwise, Socrates several times refers to him as teacher or friend. The Suda (an early medieval Byzantine encyclopedia) makes him a contemporary of Democritus and Gorgias. He was perhaps the best known of the sophists in the Athens of the Peloponnesian War; his is the name Aristophanes mentions when he wants to get a laugh at their expense in plays of 423 (*Clouds* 361) and 414 (*Birds* 692). Apart from the passion for 'correctness of names' emphasised in the *Protagoras*, he appears to have had a wide range of intellectual interests, with our best information relating to his naturalistic theory of religion, which he related particularly to humans' concern for their own wellbeing and the development of agriculture.

PROTAGORAS (490–420) Born in Abdera, a city on the northern Aegean seaboard, like his younger contemporary Democritus. He visited Athens on several occasions, and was also resident in Sicily for a time. He is said to have drawn up laws for the South Italian colony of Thurii (founded in 443). He was the oldest of the figures in the sophistic movement known to us, portrayed in the *Protagoras* as rather august, and elsewhere described as a practitioner of his profession – which he appears to have dominated – for forty years (*Meno* 91e). The book of his known as *Truth* contained the famous thesis: 'Man is the measure of all things'. There also survives a fragment announcing agnosticism about the existence and attributes of gods.

SOCRATES (469–399) Viewed as a promising sophist of a younger generation by the Platonic Protagoras (*Prot.* 361d–e) at the imagined date of the meeting recounted in the dialogue (probably around 433–432). Indeed Plato here makes him no less competitive than the sophists with whom he is in discussion. Readers have often sympathised with Protagoras's unease at Socrates' dialectical tactics. How far we are supposed to take him as genuinely committed to the arguments he uses, or to the positions he advances (notably the hedonism articulated at 353–8), has been much debated.

Analysis

309a–310a – Frame conversation

310a–311a – Hippocrates visits Socrates

311b–314b – 'What is a sophist?' Socrates' discussion with Hippocrates

314b–316a – The assembly of the sophists in Callias's house

316a–319a – Protagoras explains the nature of his profession

319a–320c – Socrates: can human goodness be taught?

320c–328d – Protagoras's great speech

- *320c–323c:* The myth of Prometheus and Epimetheus, with commentary on its meaning
- *323c–324c:* The practice of punishment reveals a general belief that goodness can be taught
- *324cd–328a:* The relevant forms of teaching are not a matter for a specialised art or science
- *328a–d:* Protagoras reformulates his manifesto, and summarises the case he has made

328d–334c – Socrates questions Protagoras

- *328d–330b:* Does human goodness have parts and, if so, of what kind?
- *330b–332a:* Justice and holiness: what is their relationship?
- *332a–333b:* Wisdom and prudence: their relationship is examined
- *333b–334c:* Justice and prudence: abortive examination of their relationship

334c–338e – Interlude on procedure

338e–348a – Criticism of the poets

- *338e–339d:* Protagoras criticises a poem of Simonides
- *339d–342a:* Socrates' response: linguistic distinctions
- *342a–343c:* Socrates' response: Spartan philosophy and the seven sages
- *343c–345c:* Socrates' exposition: being and becoming good
- *345c–347a:* Socrates' exposition: nobody does wrong willingly
- *347a–348a:* Discussion of poetry abandoned

348a–349d – Socrates re-engages with Protagoras on goodness

349d–360e – Final sequence of argument with Protagoras

- *349e–351b:* Wisdom and courage: Protagoras's view is examined
- *351b–e:* Hedonism: views of Protagoras and the majority
- *352a–353b:* The power of knowledge

- *353b–355b:* Hedonism: proof that the majority are committed to views that entail hedonism
- *355b–e:* Given the truth of hedonism, the idea that pleasure could overcome knowledge is absurd
- *355e–357b:* Measuring pleasures and pains
- *357b–e:* Mistakes in choice of pleasures and pains are due to ignorance
- *358a–d:* The sophists concede
- *358d–360e:* Discussion of wisdom and courage resumed and concluded

360e–361c – Resumé: reversal of positions of Socrates and Protagoras
361c–362a – Concluding exchange

Protagoras

FRIEND:[1] Where have you sprung from, Socrates? Or – no prizes for guessing – out hunting? Out after the lovely young Alcibiades? I saw him the other day. Still as handsome a man as ever, I thought – man being the operative word, Socrates, between you and me, with just the beginnings of a little beard.

SOCRATES: And what of that? You're not going to quarrel with Homer, are you, when he says the most appealing age is puberty – the age Alcibiades is now?[2]

FRIEND: Well, what's the news? Is that where you've sprung from? Is the young man giving you any encouragement?

SOCRATES: Yes, I thought so – particularly today. He was supporting me, and spoke up for me several times. And I *have* just come from him. But the funny thing is, I don't mind telling you, that although he was there, I didn't take much notice of him. In fact, I kept forgetting all about him.

FRIEND: How come? For you two, that's serious stuff. You can't have met somebody more handsome, surely? Not in Athens, anyway.

SOCRATES: Yes, I have. Much more handsome.

FRIEND: Really? An Athenian, or a foreigner?

SOCRATES: A foreigner.

FRIEND: Where from?

SOCRATES: Abdera.[3]

FRIEND: And he struck you as so handsome, this foreigner, that you found him more handsome than the son of Cleinias?

SOCRATES: Bless you, aren't we always going to find what is wisest more handsome?

FRIEND: Ah, so it's some wise man you've been spending time with, have you, Socrates? And now here you are.

[1] Unusually in a Socratic dialogue, this character is not named (the best parallel is in the *Symposium*, which similarly frames its main narrative with a short dialogue between the narrator and an unnamed friend). The friend serves only to enable Socrates to introduce himself as *philosophos* – 'lover of wisdom', as what is most truly handsome or beautiful (*kalon*) – and to offer an ironic characterisation of Protagoras as someone who has actually achieved wisdom. Thus the affinity with the *Symposium*, Plato's classic treatment of philosophy as a sublimation of erotic love, is more than formal.

[2] On Alcibiades son of Cleinias (and other key figures who appear in the dialogue), see Dramatis personae.

[3] On the coast of Thrace in northern Greece; the birthplace of the philosopher Democritus, as well as Protagoras.

d SOCRATES: The wisest alive – if you think the wisest is Protagoras.

FRIEND: What? Protagoras staying here in Athens?

SOCRATES: Yes. He arrived two days ago.

FRIEND: And you've just been with him?

310 SOCRATES: Yes, I had a long conversation with him.

FRIEND: Come on, then, tell us about the meeting – unless there's something else you should be doing. Sit down here. Get the boy here to stand up and make room for you.

SOCRATES: By all means. You'll be doing me a favour by listening.

FRIEND: And you will be doing us one by speaking.

SOCRATES: Two favours for the price of one, then. All right, listen. This very morning, before it was light, Hippocrates the son of Apollodorus,

b Phason's brother, came hammering at my door with his stick. And when they opened it, he came rushing in, shouting: 'Socrates, are you awake or asleep?'[4]

I recognised his voice. 'That's Hippocrates,' I said. 'Has something happened?'

'No, nothing's happened,' he said. 'Or only something good.'

'You'd better tell me,' I said. 'What's up? What brings you here so early?'

He came and stood by me. 'Protagoras has arrived,' he said.

'The day before yesterday,' I said. 'Have you only just heard?'

c 'Why, yes,' he said. 'Yesterday evening.' Saying this he felt for the bed,[5] sat down by my feet, and said: 'Yes, in the evening. I got back from Oenoe really late. My slave Satyrus ran away. I meant to tell you I was going after him, but something happened, and I forgot. I got back, and we'd had dinner and were just about to go to bed when my brother said that Protagoras had arrived. Even then I was all set to come straight round to see you,

d until I realised how late it was. But as soon as I had slept off my exhaustion, I got straight out of bed and came round here, as you can see.'

Seeing Hippocrates so determined and excitable, I said: 'And what's your interest in this? He's not wronging you in any way, Protagoras, is he?' He laughed. 'Oh yes he is, Socrates. He keeps his wisdom to himself,

---

[4] In Hippocrates' assault on Socrates' door before dawn has broken, there is an echo of comic drama. It is a sort of reversal of the scene at the beginning of Aristophanes' *Clouds*, where the elderly Strepsiades wakes up his son Pheidippides at this same time of day, to get him to become a student in *Socrates'* philosophical school.

[5] The word is *skimpous*, apparently a sort of camp-bed. Socrates' invitation to Strepsiades to sit on 'the sacred camp-bed' angles for a laugh at *Clouds* 254.

instead of making me wise too.' 'For heaven's sake,' I said. 'Give him some money and talk nicely to him, and of course he'll make you wise as well.'

'If only it were that simple,' he said. 'God knows I'd spend every penny ⲉ I possess – and every penny my friends possess as well. But that's why I've come to you now – so you can put in a word for me with him. Whereas I – well, I'm too young, for one thing. And anyway, I've never even seen Protagoras, never heard him. I was a child the last time he came to Athens. You must, Socrates. Everybody says how wonderful the man is, what a clever speaker he is. Why don't we walk round there and catch him at home? He's 311 staying with Callias the son of Hipponicus, I gather. Do let's go.'

And I said: 'Hang on, there's a good lad. It's very early. There's no point in going yet. Let's get up and go into the courtyard here. We can walk around there for a bit until it gets light, and then we can go. Don't worry, Protagoras spends most of his time at home, so in all probability we shall find him in.'

Then we got up, went into the courtyard and started walking around. I wanted to try Hippocrates' strength, so I started examining him and b asking him questions. 'Tell me something, Hippocrates,' I said. 'You're off to visit Protagoras, and make him a cash payment for his services. What sort of person do you think you will be consulting, and what do you think you will become? I mean, imagine you'd been planning to go to your namesake Hippocrates of Cos,[6] of the medical fraternity, and make him a cash payment for his services, and someone asked you: "Tell me, Hippocrates, here you are, about to pay Hippocrates a fee; what do you take him to be?" What would your answer have been?' ⲥ

'I'd have said "A doctor." '

' "And what do you expect to become?" '

'A doctor,' he said.

'And if you'd been planning to go to Polyclitus the Argive or Phidias the Athenian,[7] and make cash payment to them, and someone said to you: "It's your intention to make this cash payment to Polyclitus and Phidias; what do you take them to be?" What would your answer have been?'

' "Sculptors", I'd have said.'

---

[6] Hippocrates of Cos, in the south-western Aegean, was (as the Oxford Classical Dictionary puts it) 'the most famous physician of antiquity and one of the least known'. He was perhaps roughly contemporary with Socrates. It is doubtful whether he was himself the author of any of the extensive collection of medical treatises associated with his name.

[7] Phidias and Polyclitus were the most famous of all Greek sculptors. Both were active in the fifth century; Phidias was notable particularly for the statues of Athena in the Parthenon and Zeus at Olympia.

' "With a view to becoming what yourself?" '

'A sculptor, obviously.'

d   'Very well,' I said. 'Here we are – you and I – off to see Protagoras. And we're going to be all prepared to make him a cash payment for his services, if our money will stretch that far and we can persuade him. Failing that, we're going to spend our friends' money as well. We're raring to go, in fact. Now, suppose someone asked us: "Tell me, Socrates and Hippocrates, here you are planning to pay money to Protagoras; what do you take him to be?" What answer would we give him? What else do we

e   hear him being called apart from Protagoras? We hear Phidias being called a sculptor, and Homer a poet. What description of that sort do we hear applied to Protagoras?'

'Sophist, Socrates,' he said. 'Well, that's certainly what they call the man.'[8]

'So it's because we think he's a sophist that we're setting off to pay him some money?'

'Absolutely.'

'And suppose someone asked you the further question: "And you?

312   What do you expect to become if you go to Protagoras?" '

He blushed – it was getting a bit light by now, and I could see him clearly – and said: 'If this is at all like the other examples, I'm clearly expecting to become a sophist.'

'Good god!' I exclaimed. 'You! Wouldn't you be embarrassed to present yourself to the world as a sophist?'

'Heavens, yes, Socrates – if you want my real opinion, I would.'

'But then maybe you imagine, Hippocrates, that the teaching you get from Protagoras will not be like that – more like the teaching you got

b   from your schoolteacher or music teacher[9] or physical trainer? You learnt all those things not as a professional skill, with a view to being a practitioner, but as part of your education – what's expected of a private citizen[10] and a free man.'

'Yes,' he said, 'I think Protagoras' teaching is much more like that.'

---

[8] The connotations of the word 'sophist', and the associated topic of cash payment, are discussed in the Introduction, p.x.

[9] Literally, 'exponents of the *kithara*' or lyre, the stringed instrument famously associated with Apollo, which would be taught to boys of aristocratic family.

[10] Here 'private citizen' (*idiôtês*) contrasts not with 'politician', but as often with 'professional', 'someone who advertises his expertise'. By virtue of his study with the professional, the *idiôtês* might well come to command a degree of expertise. But he would remain a 'layman' (another possible translation), because as a free person living out his freedom

'And do you realise what you're going to do?' I asked. 'Or do you not realise?'

'Do? About what?'

'You're going to entrust the care of your own soul to a man who is, by your own admission, a sophist. Exactly what a sophist is, I'd be surprised if you have any idea. And yet if you don't know that, then neither do you know what you are handing your soul over to – you don't even know if it's a good thing or a bad thing.'

'I *think* I know,' he said.

'All right, then. What do you think a sophist is?'

'Well, in *my* view he is, as the name suggests, a person who has knowledge of wise things.'[11]

'You could say that about painters and carpenters,' I said. 'You could say they are people who have knowledge of wise things. And if someone asked us what wise things painters had knowledge of, I imagine we'd tell him it was wise things to do with the creation of images – and the same with the others. But if someone asked the question: "And the sophist? What wise things is he knowledgeable about?" What answer would we give him? Of what activity is he the master?'

'What would we call him, Socrates? How about "master of making people clever at speaking"?'

'We might well be right,' I said. 'Not right enough, though, since our answer prompts the further question: "What does the sophist make them clever at speaking *about*?" – in the way the teacher of the kithara, I take it, makes people clever at speaking about the thing which he also gives them knowledge of, which is playing the kithara. Isn't that so?'

'Yes.'

'All right. And the sophist – what does he make people clever at speaking about? Obviously, the thing he also makes them know about.'

'Probably.'[12]

'But what is it, this thing about which the sophist himself has knowledge and also gives his pupils knowledge?'

---

he would wish to retain the independence of action those who practise or teach for money cannot (on Plato's aristocratic assumptions) claim for themselves.

[11] Hippocrates appeals to a false etymology, whereby *sophistēs* is derived from the roots *soph-* ('wise') and *ist-* ('know'). *istēs* is in fact simply an agent-forming suffix, generating words meaning 'practitioner of ...'.

[12] Editors disagree over who says what here. Burnet's OCT allocates 'Obviously...about' to Hippocrates, and 'Probably' as well as 'But what is it ...' to Socrates. We follow Heindorf's alternative, and his insertion of *ē* before *dēlon*.

'Help!' he said. 'I give up.'

313   At which point I said: 'What? Do you have any idea of the kind of risk you will be running if you gamble with your soul? If it had been a question of entrusting your body to somebody, with no certainty whether it would end up in a good or bad state, you'd have thought very carefully about entrusting it to him or not – you'd bring your friends and family into the discusson, and spend some days thinking about it. But something you regard as more important than your body – your soul – something on which your entire wellbeing depends, according as it ends up in a good or bad state – when it comes to that, you haven't consulted your
b   father or your brother, or any of us who are your friends, about whether or not you should entrust your soul to this foreigner who has just arrived. You hear about it in the evening, you say, and here you are, first thing in the morning, all set to spend your own and your friends' money, without any discussion or advice on whether you should entrust yourself to him or not, as if you've already made up your mind that you positively must be with Protagoras, when you admit you don't know him and have never
c   spoken to him, and when you call him a sophist, though just what this sophist thing is to which you propose to entrust yourself, you clearly have no idea.'

He heard me out, then: 'That seems to be about the size of it, Socrates,' he said, 'judging by what you say.'

'Well, Hippocrates, isn't the sophist in fact a kind of trader or stallholder dealing in the commodities by which the soul is nourished? That's pretty much what he seems to me to be.'

'And what is a soul nourished by, Socrates?'

'The subjects it is taught,' I said. 'And we have to be careful, my friend, that the sophist doesn't deceive us by talking up what he sells, in the same
d   way as those who provide food for the body – the trader or stallholder. These people don't themselves know, I think it's fair to say, which of the commodities they deal in is good or bad for the body, though they talk them all up as they sell them. And with the possible exception of someone who is in fact a trainer or a doctor, the people who buy from them don't know either. That's how it is with the people who hawk the subjects they teach round the cities, selling and bargaining with whoever happens to be interested at any particular moment. They talk up everything they sell, and yet it may be, my fine friend, that some of them, too, don't know which of the things
e   they sell is good or bad for the soul. And the same goes for the people who buy from them, unless again you get someone with a doctor's knowledge

of the soul. So in your case, if you really are knowledgeable about which of these things is good or bad for you, then it's safe for you to buy from Protagoras or from anyone else the things he teaches. Otherwise, as you value your happiness, don't gamble and take chances with what is most pre- 314 cious. Buying things people teach is, after all, a much riskier business than buying food. If you buy food and drink from a trader or stallholder, there's nothing to stop you carrying it away in its own containers; and before you allow it into your body by drinking it or eating it, you can store it away at home and take advice – call in someone who is an authority on what can be eaten and drunk and what can't, in what quantities, and when. So there's no great danger in buying it. But with things people teach there's no carrying b them away in their own containers. You have no choice, once you've paid for them, but to take the things you've learnt into your very soul, and go away in a worse or better condition as a result of having learnt them. So this is a matter I suggest we consider with those who are older than us, since we are still young to be making such an important decision.

'Anyway, let's stick to our original plan, and go and hear the man. Then when we've heard him, we can discuss it with others. He's not here on his own, Protagoras. Hippias of Elis is here as well, and I think Prodicus of c Ceos.[13] And plenty of other wise people.'

That seemed a good idea, so we set off. And when we reached the doorway, we stood there discussing some subject we'd started along the way. We wanted to finish it and then go in, rather than leave it incomplete, so we stood in the doorway discussing it until we had reached agreement.[14] I think the doorkeeper, a eunuch, must have heard us. And because of all the sophists he was probably fed up with people coming to d the house.[15] Anyway, when we knocked at the door, he opened it, took one look at us. 'Ugh! Sophists!' he said. 'He's busy.' At the same time he slammed the door with both hands as hard as he could. We knocked some more, and his answer came, with the door still closed: 'Hey! Are you deaf? I said he's busy.'

---

[13] Two other leading sophists, who will have roles to play in the philosophical drama that unfolds. For more information, see Dramatis personae.
[14] The pause in the doorway to complete the discussion parallels Socrates' delayed arrival at Agathon's party in the *Symposium*: there he has been standing preoccupied in thought in a neighbour's doorway (*Symp.* 174d–175d).
[15] The surly doorkeeper as an obstacle to be negotiated is another trope of Aristophanic comedy: see *Acharnians* 393–409, *Clouds* 131–3, 220–1.

'Don't worry, my dear fellow,' I said. 'We haven't come to see Callias.
e And we're not sophists. It's Protagoras we've come to see. Kindly
announce us.'

Well, finally, with a bad grace, the fellow did open the door to us. And
when we got inside, we found Protagoras walking up and down in the colonnade. And with him, walking up and down in formation, were on the
one side Callias the son of Hipponicus, his half-brother Paralus the son of
315 Pericles, and Charmides the son of Glaucon, and on the other side Pericles'
other son Xanthippus, Philippides the son of Philomelus, and Antimoerus
of Mende, who has the best reputation among Protagoras' pupils, and is
studying with him professionally, because he wants to be a sophist.[16]

Of those who were following behind, listening to what was being said,
the majority were evidently foreigners. Protagoras collects them from all
the cities he passes through; he puts a spell on them with his voice, like
b Orpheus, and they follow the voice, spellbound. But there were some
Athenians in the chorus as well.[17] This chorus I found a delight to watch,
such care did they take never to be in front of Protagoras and get in his
way. When he and his group turned, then this retinue parted on either
side, this way and that, in a nice orderly fashion, came round in a circle,
and each time took up station again to the rear. Perfect.

'Then next I sighted' – that's Homer speaking[18] – Hippias of Elis,
c sitting on a raised chair in the colonnade opposite. Round him, sitting
on benches, were Eryximachus the son of Acumenus, Phaedrus of
Myrrhinus, Andron the son of Androtion – and among the foreigners,
compatriots of Hippias and some others.[19] They seemed to be questioning Hippias on natural science, particularly points of astronomy, and he

[16] Plato assembles here the *jeunesse dorée* of the Athenian aristocracy: we are put in mind of
its wealth (Callias) and power (Pericles) – and of his own family connections (Charmides,
uncle on his mother's side, and associated with the junta of 'Thirty Tyrants' in 404).
Despite his promising reputation, Antimoerus has otherwise vanished from the historical
record.

[17] The reference to Orpheus suggests a chorus of initiates (his name became associated with
mystery religion); but the choreography perhaps more specifically a dramatic chorus. One
thinks of the chorus of the initiates in Aristophanes' *Frogs* encountered by Dionysus and
Xanthias on their arrival in the underworld (see next note).

[18] Socrates quotes Odysseus's words in the *Odyssey* (*Od.*11.601) on sighting the last of the
heroes he encounters following the descent he makes to Hades.

[19] Eryximachus and Phaedrus are also in the company gathered at the party described
in Plato's *Symposium*. Both were among the aristocrats accused (like Alcibiades and
Adeimantus son of Leucolophides) of religious violations in 415. For Andron, see note on
Gorgias 487d.

was sitting there on his chair, pronouncing judgment on all their questions and carefully explaining his answers.

'There Tantalus too I saw'[20] – Prodicus of Ceos being here in Athens
as well. He was in a room which Hipponicus had always used as a store- d
room, but because of the number of people staying Callias had cleared this
as well and turned it into accommodation for guests. Prodicus was still
in bed, buried under a heap of sheepskins and blankets, by the looks of
it. Sitting by him on the nearby couches were Pausanias from Cerameis,
and with Pausanias a youngster, just a lad still – but of a fine, upstanding
character, I would say, and as for his looks, well, quite something. I got e
the impression his name was Agathon, and it wouldn't surprise me if
he was in fact Pausanias' boyfriend. So there was this young lad, and
the two Adeimantuses, both of them, the son of Cepis and the son of
Leucolophides, and a few others were in evidence, too. What they were
talking about I couldn't hear from outside, desperate though I was to hear
Prodicus. I think the man's inspired – a genius. But the deepness of his 316
voice created a kind of resonance in the room which made it impossible
to hear what he said.

We'd only just got inside when right behind us in came the handsome
Alcibiades – as you call him, and I see no reason to disagree – with
Critias the son of Callaeschrus.[21] Anyway, once we were in, we waited
a few moments, taking in the scene. Then we went up to Protagoras,
and I said: 'Protagoras, it's you that Hippocrates here and I have come b
to see.'

'Do you want to have a talk with me in private?' he said. 'Or with
everybody there?'

'We don't mind,' I said. 'Listen to what we have come for, and then you
can consider the question.'

'Very well,' he said. 'And what *have* you come for?'

---

[20] The quotation is from the same passage of the Odyssey (*Od*.11.582). Tantalus is there represented as up to his chin in a pool of standing water, in distress as food and drink perpetu-
ally just elude him. No doubt (like Prodicus) he might also have caught a chill. Prodicus's
indistinct booming contrasts amusingly with the exactness of the verbal distinctions he
will make later in the dialogue (e.g. 337a–c).

[21] With the arrival of Alcibiades and Critias Plato couples together two figures who were to
become the most reviled Athenian politicians of the next generation – both closely and
indelibly associated in public memory with Socrates himself. Alcibiades also completes a
cast which supplies the speakers in the *Symposium*: Phaedrus with his lover Eryximachus,
Agathon with his lover Pausanias, and Socrates himself – all except Aristophanes, who is
of course a presiding spirit (see e.g. notes on 310a–b, 310c, 314d, 315b).

'Hippocrates here is an Athenian, the son of Apollodorus, from a powerful and prosperous family; in himself I'd say he's a match, in nat-
c ural ability, for anybody his age. His ambition, I think, is to make his mark in politics, and this he believes would be most easily brought about by being your pupil. So it's for you to consider: are those things you think should be discussed in private, or with other people there?'

'Thank you, Socrates,' he said, 'for being cautious on my behalf. If a man is a foreigner, and visits great cities, and persuades the best of their young men to give up spending time with anybody else, be they family or non-family, older or younger, and spend time with him in the belief that being with him will make them better people – well, anybody
d who does that has to be careful. It can give rise to great resentment and various forms of hostility and intrigue.[22] I maintain that the sophist's art is an ancient one, but that its practitioners among men of old, afraid of the odium attaching to it, put up a screen. Some veiled it with poetry – Homer, Hesiod and Simonides, for example – some with ritual and prophecy – the followers of Orpheus and Musaeus.[23] Some even with physical training, I have heard: Iccus of Tarentum, for example, and – still alive today, and a sophist second to none – Herodicus of
e Selymbria, formerly of Megara. Your countryman Agathocles, a great sophist, employed music as a cover, as did Pythoclides of Ceos and many others.[24] All of them, as I say, used these arts and skills as a screen, because they were afraid of arousing envy.

317 'That is where I part company with all of them. I do not think they were very successful in their aim. They did not fool those who hold power

[22] Throughout the dialogue Protagoras is represented as highly self-conscious about the way anything he says will be perceived. Socrates elsewhere comments on the good reputation he enjoyed throughout the whole time – forty years – that he practised his expertise (*Men.* 91c).
[23] Protagoras's representation of the poets as closet sophists is his idiosyncratic variation on the common Greek conception of poets as teachers. For example, Hesiod was regarded as an authority on theology (in his *Theogony*) and agriculture (*Works and Days*). Mystery cults had for some time appropriated the name of Orpheus (as of the more obscure Musaeus) not just as 'author' of the theological poetry they produced, but also as an authority on religious practice, above all avoidance of animal sacrifice. The appearance of Simonides' name in this awesome company is perhaps a little surprising. But Protagoras has evidently taken a special interest in him, subsequently revealed (339a–d).
[24] Herodicus was supposedly one of the teachers of the physician Hippocrates (for whom see note on 311b), Iccus a famous wrestler: both were celebrated for the austerity of their respective regimes. Agathocles is elsewhere described as teacher to one of Pericles' closest associates, the music theorist Damon (*Laches* 180d), and Pythoclides is said to have been Pericles' own teacher (*Alcibiades* 118c).

in the cities – who were the ones for whose benefit these disguises were adopted, since most of the population are blind to practically everything, and simply repeat the things the people in power tell them. And if you are going to run away, but not actually get away, merely draw attention to yourself, then it is the height of folly even to try, and must inevitably make b people more hostile towards you. They think someone like that, whatever else he may be, is certainly a crook. That is why I have gone down completely the opposite road from them. I admit I am a sophist, and that I teach people, and I think this precaution – acknowledgment rather than denial – is better than the other. I have taken other precautions as well, so that – touch wood – no harm has come to me from admitting I am a sophist, though I have been in the business a fair number of years now, c being a good age myself – I could be father to any of you lot. So I would much prefer, if you want to talk about these things, to have our discussion in front of all the people in here.'

I suspected that he wanted to show off in front of Prodicus and Hippias, and make a bit of a display of the fact that we had turned up as his admirers.

'In that case,' I said, 'why don't we ask Prodicus and Hippias and the d people with them to come and listen to us?'

'By all means,' Protagoras said.

'Would you like us to arrange some seating,' Callias suggested, 'so you can have your discussion sitting down?'

That seemed a good idea. Delighted at the prospect of listening to wise men, we all took hold of the benches and couches ourselves, and arranged them near Hippias, since that was where the benches were to start with. Meanwhile Callias and Alcibiades came, the two of them bringing Prodicus – they'd got him out of bed – and the people with e Prodicus.

When we were all sitting down together, Protagoras said: 'Now, this is your chance, Socrates, now that we have got all these people here as well, to say the things you mentioned to me a few moments ago, speaking on your young friend's behalf.' And I said: 'I'll begin the same way I did 318 then, Protagoras – with my reason for coming. Hippocrates here is really very keen on spending some time with you. And he says he'd very much like to know what he will get out of it if he does spend his time with you. That's as much as we've said so far.'

And Protagoras said in reply: 'Well, young man, what you will get if you spend your time with me is this: the day you join me, you will return home better than when you came. Likewise the second day. Each day you will make progress towards what is better.'

b   'That's not so very remarkable, Protagoras,' was my reaction. 'I dare say even you, for all your years and wise as you are, would become better if someone taught you something you didn't in fact know already. Don't give us that sort of answer. Suppose, rather, that Hippocrates here suddenly changed his mind, and wanted to be a pupil of this young man who's just come to live in Athens, Zeuxippus of Heraclea.[25] Suppose

c   he went to him, as he is now coming to you, and heard from him exactly what he has heard from you, that each day he spent with him he would become better and make progress. If he asked him the further question: "Better at what, are you saying? Progress in what?" Zeuxippus would say to him: "In painting." And if he became the pupil of Orthagoras the Theban, and heard from him exactly what he has heard from you, and asked him the further question, what he would be better at each day if he became his pupil, Orthagoras would say: "At playing the reed pipe."[26] That's what we want you to tell this young man – and me, since

d   I am asking questions on his behalf. If Hippocrates here becomes the pupil of Protagoras, then on the day he starts being his pupil he will go home better than when he came, and on each succeeding day he will make the same sort of progress – towards what, Protagoras? In what subject?'

Protagoras heard me out. Then 'Your strength, Socrates,' he said, 'is asking the right question. Mine is that I enjoy giving an answer to people who ask the right question. What will happen to Hippocrates, if he comes to me, is not what would have happened to him if he had become the pupil of any of the other sophists. Other sophists treat young people dis-

e   gracefully. The young come to them to get away from school subjects, and what do they do? Take them and plunge them, against their will, straight back into those subjects again. They teach them arithmetic and astronomy and geometry and music' – here he glanced at Hippias – 'whereas if he comes to me he will learn only what he came to learn. And what I teach is good judgment in his own affairs – the ability to manage his own

---

[25] For Zeuxippus see note on *Gorgias* 453c.

[26] 'Reed pipe' translates *aulos*, in many variant forms the other main type of instrument favoured by the Greeks besides the lyre. It was popular at parties, in the theatre, at weddings, and in religious cult, but disapproved of by Plato and Aristotle for use by citizens. Not much is known about Orthagoras, who is said to have taught the instrument to the distinguished Theban general Epaminondas, at the height of his power in the 360s BC.

household in the best way – and in public life how best to exercise polit- 319
ical power, whether acting or speaking.'[27]

'Do I follow you correctly?' I asked. 'You seem to me to be talking about the art of politics, and promising to turn men into good citizens.'

'That, Socrates,' he said, 'is precisely the claim I make.'

'That's certainly a fine skill to have acquired,' I said, 'if indeed you have acquired it – since to you of all people I intend to say exactly what I think. My own view, Protagoras, was that this was not something that could be taught. If you say it can, then I have to believe you. But I'm b entitled to say why I think it is not teachable, and why it cannot be passed on by one person to another. You see, I maintain, along with the rest of Greece, that the Athenians are a clever lot. And when we gather together in the assembly,[28] then if the city has some business relating to a building project, I notice it's the builders they send for to advise on the building works. And if it's a question of shipbuilding, then the shipbuilders, and the same with all the other things which are thought capable of being c learnt and taught.

'If anyone else tries to advise them, and they don't recognise him as a specialist, then no matter how handsome or wealthy he may be, or how distinguished his family, they still won't put up with it. They jeer and make an uproar until either the person trying to speak is shouted down and gives up of his own accord, or the archers drag him away or remove him on the orders of the presiding committee. So when they think it's a question of technical expertise, that's how they act. But when they have to make some decision on a question relating to the government of the city, then the person who stands up to advise them on this may equally d well be a carpenter, a metal-worker, a leather-cutter, a merchant or ship-owner, rich or poor, of high or low birth. With these speakers nobody raises the objection they raised in my earlier example – that they haven't studied anywhere, that they have no teacher, and yet here they are trying to act as advisers. And the reason, obviously, is that they don't think it can be taught.

---

[27] A pivotal moment in the dialogue: Protagoras sets out the manifesto which at once distinguishes him from other sophists (as he claims), and prompts Socrates' line of questioning about goodness and its teachability that will be pursued throughout the rest of the conversation.

[28] All male citizens over eighteen were entitled to attend meetings of this body, which took all major decisions on matters of public policy.

'And it's not just where the common interest of the city is concerned.
e In our private lives as well the wisest and best of the citizens are unable to pass on this goodness of theirs to other people. Take Pericles, the father of these young men here – he gave them an admirable education in the things that can be got from teachers. But when it comes to his own wisdom, he
320 neither educates them himself nor sends them to anyone else.[29] Instead they wander around on their own, like sacred cattle, grazing on human goodness as and when they stumble on it left to themselves. Or if you prefer, take Cleinias, younger brother to Alcibiades here. The same man, Pericles, is his guardian, and because he was worried about him, in case he might be led astray – can you believe – by Alcibiades, he took him away from Alcibiades, installed him safely in Ariphron's[30] house, and started to have him brought up there. Before six months were out he gave him back
b to Alcibiades. He had no idea how to cope with him. And there are plenty of others I could quote you: people who are good themselves but who never made anyone else – whether their own relatives or anyone else – any better. As for me, Protagoras, when I look at these facts I do not believe human goodness is something that can be taught. But when I hear you saying what you've just said, then I change direction and think there must be something in what you say. I believe you to be a person of great experience – someone who has learned much from others and made discoveries of his own. So if you are in a position to demonstrate more clearly to
c us that human goodness *is* teachable, give us your demonstration. Don't keep it to yourself.'

'No, Socrates,' he said, 'I will not keep it to myself. But shall I demonstrate it by telling you a story, as the old do when they talk to the young, or by giving you a reasoned explanation?'

A number of the people who were sitting nearby encouraged him to give his explanation in whichever way he preferred.

'In that case,' he said, 'I think it will be more appealing to tell you a story.[31] Once upon a time there were gods, but no mortal species.

[29] Pericles' inability to teach his sons 'his own wisdom' is a theme on which Plato's Socrates expatiates elsewhere (and applies to other leading public figures, too): see *Meno* 93a–94c.
[30] Pericles' brother, according to Plutarch (*Alcibiades* 1) co-guardian of the young Alcibiades – but he may be extrapolating from this very passage.
[31] Protagoras's tale of the Titans Prometheus and Epimetheus (their names signify 'fore-thought' and 'afterthought') employs a traditional story form, couched in elevated language notable for studied antitheses and some innovative technical vocabulary. Plato adapts Hesiod's version of the Prometheus myth (*Theogony* 507–616, *Works and Days* 42–105) for his own allegorical purposes, in what is probably a pastiche of something written by

And when their time came, the time appointed for their creation, the d
gods formed them within the earth from a mixture of earth and fire and
the elements that are compounds of fire and earth. When they were about
to bring them into the light of day, they commanded Prometheus and
Epimetheus to equip them and assign to each species the powers appropriate to it. And Epimetheus asked Prometheus to let him do the job by
himself. "When I have done it," he said, "you can check it." He got his
way, and set about assigning powers. His way of assigning them was to
bestow strength but not speed on some, and to equip the weaker ones e
with speed. To some he gave weapons, or if he gave them an unarmed
nature, then he devised some other mechanism for their safety. Some of
them he clothed in smallness, but gave them winged flight or a dwelling
under ground. Others he made larger, making this their salvation in itself. In the same way he assigned the remaining powers, keeping a balance 321
between them.

'His chief concern in all these provisions was that no species should be
exterminated; and when he had given them means of escape from mutual
destruction, the next thing he devised was protection against the elements, clothing them in thick hair and tough hides, sufficient to keep out
the winter cold and yet at the same time able to resist scorching heat – and
such that when they went to sleep, this same hair and hide should also
provide its own natural bedding for each. On their feet he gave some of b
them hooves, and others hard, bloodless skin. Next he provided different
creatures with different food – the earth's pasture for some, fruit from
the trees for others, roots for yet others. And to some he gave the flesh of
other living things as their food. To these he gave few offspring, while to
those who were preyed on by them he gave many offspring, so preserving
the species.

'Now, Epimetheus was not without shortcomings in wisdom, and he
used up all the powers on the non-rational creatures without realising c
what he was doing. So he was left with the race of men unprovided
for, and no idea what to do with them. So there he is, without ideas,
when Prometheus comes upon him, wanting to inspect the assignment
of powers, and sees that while the other creatures are suitably provided
for in every way, man is naked, unshod, without bedding or weapons.
And already it was the appointed day on which man was to come out

Protagoras himself (though some scholars have thought it original Protagorean material
incorporated by Plato into his text).

from the earth, into the light of day. So Prometheus, with no idea what
d means of survival he can find for man, steals knowledge of the arts from
Hephaestus and Athene, and with it fire, since without fire it was not possible for the knowledge to be acquired by anyone or be any use to them.[32]
And this is his gift to man.

'That, then, is how man gained the knowledge needed to stay alive,
but political knowledge he still did not have. That was in Zeus's keeping. There had been no time for Prometheus to enter the citadel, Zeus's
dwelling-place – and besides, Zeus's guards[33] were fearsome. But he does
e manage, without being seen, to get into the dwelling shared by Athene
and Hephaestus, where the two of them practised their arts, and steals
Hephaestus' skill with fire, and the rest of the arts, which belonged to
Athene – and gives them to man; this provides man with the means of life
322 in abundance. As for Prometheus, the punishment for his theft caught up
with him later, so it is said[34] – and all on account of Epimetheus.

'Since man shared in the divine apportionment, then in the first place,
because of his divine kinship, he alone among living creatures acknowledged the gods, and began setting up altars and images of the gods. He
also soon used his skill to develop articulate speech and words for things,
and found himself housing, clothing, footwear, bedding, and food from
b the earth. Thus provided for, humans began by living in scattered units;
there were no cities. So they began to be destroyed by wild beasts, because
they were altogether weaker than them. Their skill at making things gave
them adequate protection when it came to providing food, but not when
it came to warfare against wild beasts, since they did not yet have the art
of politics, of which the art of warfare is a part. So then they sought to
group themselves together, and protect themselves by founding cities.
And when they were grouped together, they started treating each other
unjustly – lacking the art of politics as they did – and consequently split
up again and went on being destroyed.

[32] In older versions of the story Prometheus steals fire from Zeus, not Athene and Hephaestus. But they were the gods associated with crafts and technology, and Protagoras wants to make political knowledge the special province of Zeus as ruler of gods and humans.
[33] Power and Violence: see Hesiod, *Theogony* 383–403 (cf. Aeschylus, *Prometheus Bound* 12).
[34] In the traditional version (Hesiod, *Theogony* 521–5): 'Prometheus fertile in schemes he [i.e. Zeus] bound ineluctably with cruel bonds, and drove a stake through the middle. And he set an eagle with long wingspan upon him, which ate away at his immortal liver – but during the night it grew all over an amount equal to whatever the long-winged bird ate over the day as a whole.'

'And so Zeus, fearing that our species might be destroyed in its en- c
tirety, sends Hermes[35] to mankind, to bring them respect and justice,[36]
that there might be order in cities and the bond of friendship to hold
men together. And Hermes asks Zeus in what manner he should give
justice and respect to mankind. "Am I to apportion these too in the way
the arts have been apportioned? The way *they* have been apportioned is
this: one person with medical knowledge does for many ordinary people,
and the same with other experts. Is that how I am to allocate justice and
respect among mankind, or should I make a distribution among them d
all?" "Make a distribution to all," said Zeus. "Let all have a share. There
could be no cities if only a few of them had a share, as with the other arts.
And lay it down as law, on my authority, that if anyone is unable to share
in respect and justice, he should be regarded as a plague upon the city,
and put to death."

'In this way, Socrates, and for these reasons, when it is a question of
what is best in carpentry or some other area of expertise, people in general, and the Athenians in particular, think that only a few people should
contribute advice. If someone other than these few offers advice, they e
do not allow it, as you point out. And rightly so, as I say. But when they
want advice calling for good citizenship – a process of deliberation which
has to be conducted entirely on the basis of justice and prudence – then 323
they allow anyone to speak, in the not unreasonable belief that this is an
excellence in which everyone must share, or else there could be no cities.
That is the reason, Socrates.

'To reassure you that the whole world really does think everyone has a
share in justice, and good citizenship generally, here is another proof for
you. When it comes to other areas of excellence, then as you say, if somebody claims to be a good player of the reed pipe when he is not – or to
possess some other skill – they either laugh at him or get angry with him.
His family come and tell him off, treat him as if he were mad. But with b
justice and good citizenship generally, even if they know somebody to
be unjust, if the person actually admits it himself in public, and tells the

---

[35] In Greek religion Hermes is Zeus's ambassador to gods and humans, and guides human
souls to the underworld after death.
[36] In speaking of respect (*aidôs*) and justice (*dikê*), Protagoras uses Hesiod's by now archaic
diction (*Works and Days* 192). In his subsequent commentary on the morals to be drawn
from the story (323a–c), he substitutes contemporary vocabulary. Justice is now *dikaiosunê*,
and instead of *aidôs* we have *sôphrosunê*, a word with a large and elusive semantic range,
whose core meaning is 'soundness of mind' or 'good sense', but then in different contexts
'self-control', 'moderation', 'prudence' (adopted in this translation).

truth, then the thing which up to now they regarded as prudence – namely telling the truth – they now regard as madness. They say everybody should claim to be just, whether they are or not, and that the person who does not
c put up some sort of show of justice is mad, since everyone must necessarily have some sort of share in it, or not be counted as human.

'So much for it being reasonable for them to accept any man as an adviser on goodness of this kind, in the belief that everybody has a share in it. That they believe it to be teachable, not innate or spontaneous, and something which is acquired, when it *is* acquired, by hard work – this is the second thing I will try to make clear to you. Where people believe one
d another's failings to be the result of nature or chance, no-one gets angry with those who have these failings; they do not reprove them or try and teach them, or punish them to stop them being like that. No, they pity them. Who, after all, is foolish enough to try and do any of those things to people who are ugly, or small, or weak? They are well aware, if you ask me, that with these things – whether admirable or the opposite of admirable – it is by nature or by chance that people possess them. By contrast, the goods which they think people possess as a result of hard work, study
e and teaching – if somebody is without those, and has the bad qualities which are their opposites, those surely are the people who incur anger and punishment and reproof. Injustice is one of these qualities, as is impiety and in general everything which is the opposite of good citizenship.
324 That is where anybody will get angry with anybody, and tell them off, clearly in the belief that it can be acquired by hard work and learning.

'Think about punishment, Socrates, if you will – what exactly its effect is on those who do wrong – and that will show you that people do think goodness can be acquired. Nobody punishes wrongdoers simply for doing wrong – that is not what they have in mind, not the real reason,
b unless it is just mindless retaliation, like a wild animal. No, the person who sets about punishing in a rational way is not exacting retribution for the past wrongdoing – after all, what is done cannot be undone – so much as thinking about the future, to prevent any further wrongdoing either by the man himself or by anyone else who sees his punishment. And if this is what he thinks, he must also think goodness can be acquired by education. Certainly he punishes as a deterrent. This is the universally held opinion of those who
c exact retribution in either a private or a public capacity. People – and in particular the Athenians, your countrymen – exact retribution from those they think are doing wrong, and punish them. So on this argument the Athenians too are among those who think that goodness can be passed on and taught.

'Well, I think that is sufficient demonstration for you, Socrates, that your countrymen are right to listen to a smith or leather cutter[37] giving advice about political questions, and that goodness can be taught and passed on.　　　　　　　　　　　　　　　　　　　　　　　　　d

'That leaves the difficulty you raise about men who are good – why it is that men who are good teach their own sons and make them expert in the things which can be got from teachers, but when it comes to the goodness which they themselves have, they make them no better than anyone else. For this question, Socrates, I am going to switch from story to argument. Think about it this way. Is there, or is there not, some one thing which it is essential that all the citizens have a share of if there is to be a city? Here, if anywhere, is where the solution of your difficulty is to　e be found. If there is, and if this one thing is not carpentry or metalwork or pottery, but rather justice, prudence and what is holy – human good-　325 ness, to give it a single name – if this is what all must share in, what every man must act with, whatever else he may choose to learn or do, or without it not act at all; and if the person who does not have a share in it – child, man or woman – must be taught and punished until they become better by being punished, and if those who do not respond to punishment or teaching must be regarded as incurable and banished from the cities or　b put to death – if this is how things are, and if in this situation good men have their sons taught other things but not this, think what extraordinary people good men must be. That they think it can be taught, after all, both privately and in the public sphere, is something we have demonstrated. So given that it can be taught and developed, do they therefore have their sons taught all those other things, where death is not the penalty if they do not know them, but where death and exile *are* the penalty for their children if they do not learn and are not educated into goodness – and not　c only death, but confiscation of property and virtually the wholesale ruin of their households – do they then not have them taught these things, not take all possible pains with them? We have to suppose they do, Socrates.

'Throughout their lives, starting from earliest childhood, they do teach them and instruct them. The minute a child can understand what is said to him, the one thing his nurse, his mother, his tutor and his father himself strive for is that the child should be as good as possible.　d They are teaching him, pointing out, whatever he does or says, that one thing is just and another unjust, that this is good and that bad, this

---

[37] Leather cutters were important above all as shoemakers.

holy and that unholy; "do this", "don't do that". And it may be he listens to them readily. But if not, then they straighten him out, like a twisted, bent piece of wood, using threats and beatings. After that they send him to school, with instructions that greater attention be paid to

c the children's behaviour than to their letters or music. The teachers do pay attention to this, and when the children learn their letters, and, as with speech before, are now ready to understand things that are written, they put before them, at their benches, the works of good poets to read,

326 compelling them to learn them. These works contain many pieces of advice, many narratives in praise and celebration of good men in history, so that the child may be inspired to imitate them and strive to become like them.

'Then there are the music teachers, doing the same kind of thing. They concentrate on discipline, to make sure the young do not go to the bad in any way. On top of this, when they learn to play the kithara,[38] they duly teach them the poems of other good poets, song-writers, setting them to the

b kithara. They drill the rhythms and harmonies[39] into the children's souls, to make them more civilised, and so that, as they gain in rhythm and harmony, they may be effective in speech and action – all human life being in need of rhythm and harmony. Then again, on top of all this, they send their children to a physical fitness trainer as well, so that when the mind is formed they can enlist a better body in its service, and not be compelled by

c physical weakness to play the coward in war or other activities.

'These things are done most by those most able to do them, and those most able to do them are the richest. Their sons begin going to school at the earliest age, and leave at the latest. And when they leave, then the city in its turn compels them to learn the laws and model their lives on

d them, so that they will not be left to themselves to act haphazardly, but rather, just as teachers of writing use the stylus to draw the outlines of the letters for those of the children who are still not much good at writing, then give them the slate and get them to write following the outlines of the letters – well, in just the same way the city draws the outline of the laws, the discovery of great lawgivers in the past, and requires people to rule and be ruled in accordance with them. It punishes anyone who steps

---

[38] On the *kithara* see note on 312b.

[39] Harmony here (as generally in Greek) signifies the attunement of an instrument for performance of music in the scalar system of one of a number of particular modes (or melodic forms), as in Handel's 'harmonious blacksmith'. Greek music was primarily a matter of melody, not what is nowadays generally meant by harmony.

outside them, and the name of this punishment, both with you and in many other places, is correction, since what the legal process does is to c correct.[40] Given that so much attention is paid to human goodness, both privately and in the public sphere, are you surprised, Socrates – does it puzzle you – if goodness is something which can be taught? It ought not to. In fact, you should be much more surprised if it were something which could *not* be taught.

'Why then do so many sons of good fathers turn out good-for-nothing? Well, I have an answer to that too. It is what you would expect, if I was right in what I said earlier about this thing human goodness – that if there is to be a city at all, there must be nobody who is a layman at it.[41] 327 And if what I say really is true – and believe me, it is – then take any other activity or subject, and think about that. Suppose it were impossible for there to be a city unless we were all players of the reed pipe, at whatever level each was capable.[42] Suppose this was what everybody taught everybody else, both privately and in the public sphere, rebuking anyone who played badly, and not keeping their knowledge to themselves – just as at present nobody keeps his knowledge of what is just and lawful to himself, or keeps it secret in the way they do in many skilled occupations. I think b it is because justice and goodness towards one another is in our interest. That is why everyone is more than ready to tell everyone else, and teach them, what is just and what is lawful. Well, as I say, if it were the case with playing the reed pipe that we were all eagerness to teach one another, with no attempt to keep our skill to ourselves, do you think, Socrates,' he said, 'that the sons of good players would turn into good players any more than the sons of bad players? I think not. No, it would be a question of whose son had the greatest natural talent for the reed pipe. He would be the one to prosper and become famous. The son with no talent would c remain in obscurity. You would often get a useless son of a good player, often a good son of a useless player. What is certain is that they would all

---

[40] The word Protagoras comments on is *euthunai*, which in Athens was standardly applied to the public scrutiny officials were required to undergo on termination of their period of office. His suggestion that it is a term applied more generally to punishment of lawbreakers by a city through its courts might have been correct for 'other places', but perhaps shows that he hasn't understood Attic usage, visitor that he is.

[41] Literally 'nobody must be a layman (*idiôteuein*)'. Protagoras refers back to what he said at 323c.

[42] Plato himself thoroughly disapproved of performance on the reed pipe (see for example *Republic* 3.399d), so it is hard not to suspect a sardonic undertone in his having Protagoras select this for his example, counterfactual though it is.

be pretty reasonable players compared with non-musicians who do not know the first thing about playing.

'It is the same with what we are discussing. You have to consider that the person who, of all those brought up among laws and among human beings, strikes you as the most unjust – this person *is* just, a paragon of
d justice, in comparison with people who have no education, no law courts, no laws, nothing to compel them to pay constant attention to human goodness – savages of some kind, like the ones the poet Pherecrates portrayed last year at the Lenaea.[43] If you found yourself among them, as the haters of humanity in that chorus did, you would be only too delighted to run into Eurybatus or Phrynondas.[44] You would really miss the wicked-
e ness of people here. As it is, you are spoilt for choice, Socrates – you are surrounded by people teaching goodness to the best of their ability, and you cannot see any of them.

328 'It is like asking who is a teacher of the Greek language. You would not find one – any more, I imagine, than if you asked who could teach the sons of our skilled workers that skill which they have in fact been taught by their fathers, to the best of their ability, and by their father's friends in the trade. If you went on asking who could teach them – well, I do not think it is a simple matter, Socrates, for a teacher of these people to be found, though finding teachers for beginners is the easiest thing in the world – and it is the same with human goodness and everything else. No,
b if there is anyone among us who is even a little bit better at advancing people on the road to goodness, that is something to be thankful for. And it is my belief that I am one of them, that I am better than other people at helping to turn out fine, upstanding citizens, and well worth the fee I charge. More, in fact – ask my pupils. That is why I have adopted the method of charging fees I have adopted. When people study with me, they have paid the fee I charge in advance, if it suits them. Otherwise they
c can go to a temple, swear on oath what they think the teaching is worth, and pay me that.

'There you are, Socrates. That is my story and argument showing that goodness *is* something which can be taught, that the Athenians regard it as such, and that it is no surprise if there are good-for-nothing sons of

[43] Pherecrates was a comic playwright – a slightly older contemporary of Aristophanes – whose work survives only in fragments. His *Savages* was produced in 420 BC. The Lenaean festival was the occasion when contests for the best comedy of the year took place.
[44] Eurybatus and Phrynondas (both apparently historical figures) had become bywords for criminality.

good fathers and good sons of good-for-nothing fathers. Even the sons of Polyclitus, who are the age of Paralus and Xanthippus here,[45] are nothing compared with their father, and the same is true of the sons of other craftsmen. Though it is early days to be accusing these two. They are still d young, and full of promise.'

With this tremendous display of eloquence, Protagoras brought his speech to a close.[46] I was entranced, and for a long time I sat there looking at him in the hope that he had something more to say. I didn't want to miss anything. When I realised he had indeed finished, I managed to pull myself together somehow or other. Turning to Hippocrates: 'Thank you, son of Apollodorus,' I said, 'for getting me to come here. I think the things Protagoras has been talking about are of great importance. e I have always thought, up to now, that there was no human subject of study which makes good people good. Now I'm convinced there is one. Mind you, I do have one small difficulty, which I'm sure Protagoras will easily clear up for me, having made so many things clear already. You could spend time discussing these very topics with any of our leading orators, and you might hear just that kind of thing said by Pericles or 329 some other able speaker. But ask one of them some further question – well, you might as well ask a book. They can't give you an answer, nor can they ask a question of their own. Ask them even a trivial question about what has been said, and it's like banging a gong – if nobody puts a hand on it, it just goes on and on reverberating. That's how it is with orators. One small question, and they're away and into their stride. b Whereas Protagoras here is perfectly capable of giving us a fine, long speech – as we have just heard for ourselves – but equally capable of giving a short answer to a question, or asking a question and then waiting for the answer and listening to it – an accomplishment not shared by many people.

---

[45] Here Plato tacitly marks the fragility of the glittering aristocratic world he has recreated: Paralus and Xanthippus were soon to predecease their father Pericles, victims of the plague that ravaged Athens early in the Peloponnesian War (430–429 BC).
[46] The performance or display set piece (*epideixis*), such as Protagoras has just delivered, was a standard item in a sophist's repertoire. Prodicus gives the company a miniature example at 337a–c: a disquisition on correct linguistic usage, one of his favourite themes, in the guise of a contribution to discussion on procedure. His 'Choice of Heracles' was celebrated; Xenophon paraphrases it in his *Reminiscences of Socrates* (*Mem.*2.1). Hippias offers a display piece of his own on Simonides' poem (347b), but Alcibiades succeeds in deflecting him.

'So – just one small additional question, Protagoras.[47] Answer me that, and that's all I need. You say human goodness is something which can be taught, and I would sooner believe you than anybody else in the world.

c The thing which surprised me in what you said – do you think you could just fill me in on that? You said Zeus sent justice and respect to mankind, but then, at various points in your speech, justice, prudence, holiness and all those things were referred to as if, taken all together, they were one single thing, which is human goodness. That's the point I'd like you to explain, please, in a precise and systematic way. Is goodness one single thing, and are justice and prudence and holiness parts of it? Or are the

d things I was listing just now all names for the same one thing? That's what I'm still missing.'

'That is an easy enough question to answer, Socrates,' he said. 'Goodness is one single thing, and the things you are asking about are parts of it.'

'Parts like parts of the face?' I asked. 'Mouth, nose, eyes, ears – or like parts of a piece of gold where the parts are no different either from one another or – except in being large or small – from the whole?'

e 'The first, I think, Socrates. Like the parts of a face in relation to the face as a whole.'

'And how,' I asked, 'are these parts of goodness distributed among mankind? Do some people have one and some another? Or does the acquisition of one necessarily entail the possession of all?'

'By no means,' he said. 'There are plenty of people who are courageous but unjust. Or just but not wise.'

'Are those also parts of human goodness, then?' I asked. 'Wisdom and
330 courage?'

'They certainly are,' he said. 'Wisdom is the most important of the parts.'

'And is each of them,' I asked, 'different from the others?'

'Yes.'

'Does each of them also have its own specific function? With the parts of the face, for example, the eye is not like the ears, nor is its function the same. And with the other parts, none is like any other, either in its function or in any other way. Is that how it is with the parts of goodness

---

[47] Socrates' 'small additional question' marks a turning point. It in fact introduces the major philosophical issue which will require the strenuous dialectical argumentation that will occupy much of the rest of the discussion.

as well? Is no one like any other, either in itself or in its function? Surely   b
that's obviously how it is, if the comparison is to hold good?'

'Yes, that is how it is, Socrates,' he said.

And I said: 'So none of the other parts of goodness is like knowledge,
or like justice, or like courage, or like prudence, or like holiness.'

'No,' he said.

'Very well,' I said, 'let's examine together what kind of a thing each of
them is. First question – is justice a thing, or not a thing?[48] I think it is a   c
thing. How about you?'

'Yes, I think it is too,' he said.

'All right. Next question. Suppose somebody asked you and me: "Tell
me, the two of you, Protagoras and Socrates – this thing you've just given
a name to, justice, is it in itself just or unjust?" The answer I would give
him is that it is just. How would you cast your vote? The same way as me?
Or differently?'

'The same,' he said.

' "In which case, it is the nature of justice to be something just" would
be my answer to the question. Yours too, presumably?'   d

'Yes,' he said.[49]

'Suppose he went on to ask: "And do you say there is such a thing as
holiness?" We would say there was, I imagine.'

'Yes,' he said.

' "And are you saying that too is a thing?" We'd say yes, wouldn't we?'

He agreed to this too.

' "And this same thing, do you say its nature is such as to be unholy
or such as to be holy?" I don't know about you, but that question would
annoy me. I'd say: "Watch your tongue, mister. It's hard to see how anything could be holy if holiness itself is not to be something holy." How   e
about you? Wouldn't that be your answer?'[50]

---

[48] Socrates often launches a line of questioning by asking whether the topic of conversation
exists or not. It is never made explicit what exactly is at stake, or what those who answer in
the affirmative might be committing themselves to. But the parties to the discussion seem
to proceed as if a positive answer is what they need if they are to be entitled to explore further what else it might be true to say about the topic – as they do here.

[49] It is unclear what Socrates means when he asks whether justice (*dikaiosunē*) as an ingredient
in human goodness is just. Perhaps his thought is that justice must be what is *essentially* just
(as in the *Symposium* the Form of the Beautiful is itself beautiful: *Symp.* 210c–211b).

[50] Holiness is nowadays conceived of as a quality possessed only by exceptionally saintly persons notable for religious devotion, where indeed the notion of it survives at all. Greeks
of the fifth century were in no doubt that there were many human actions – that might
be performed by any of us – sanctioned or required by divine ordinance: the sphere of *to*

'It certainly would,' he said.

'And suppose the next thing he asked us was: "What was it you were saying, then, a few moments ago? Did I not hear you correctly? What I thought you said was that the relationship to one another of the parts of human goodness was such that one was not like another." I would say: "For the most part you did hear correctly – but not if you think I was the one who said it. It was Protagoras here who gave that answer. I was the one asking the questions." He might then say: "Is it true, Protagoras, what he says? Is it you who say that no part of human goodness is like any other part? Are you the one putting forward this view?" What answer would you give him?'

'I would have no choice, Socrates. I would have to agree.'

'And after agreeing these points, Protagoras, what answer will we give him if he goes on to ask us: "Does that mean holiness is not such as to be a thing which is just, and that justice is not such as to be a thing which is holy? Is it such as to be not holy? Is holiness such as to be something not just – something unjust, in fact? Is justice something unholy?" What answer shall we give him? Speaking purely for myself, I would say that justice was something holy and that holiness was something just; and that's the answer I'd make for you, if you allowed me to, that justness is either the same thing as holiness or as like it as makes no difference, and that justice is extraordinarily like holiness – as is holiness like justice. See if you want to stop me giving that answer, or if you too agree with me.'[51]

'I do not think it is quite that simple, Socrates,' he said. 'I cannot agree that justice is something holy, and holiness something just. I do think there is a difference. But what does it matter?' he said. 'By all means let us say, if you like, that justice is something holy and holiness is something just.'

'No, thanks,' I said. 'It isn't this "if you like" and "if that's how you feel" I want tested. It's you and me. And by "you and me" I mean I think the argument would be best tested by taking the "if" out of it.'

331

b

c

d

---

hosion, the holy. Socrates asks a question parallel to the one he asked about justice: whether holiness itself (*hosiotês*) – a settled disposition to perform such actions – is something holy.

[51] Plato would doubtless have expected most readers to agree with Socrates. Many passages elsewhere in his dialogues (and in other writers) treat 'neither just nor holy' almost as a hendiadys. Much religion was civic religion, its practices designed to supplicate or celebrate the protection of the city by its presiding deities. The spheres of the just and the holy were interpenetrating.

'Well of course,' he said, 'justice does resemble holiness to a certain extent.[52] Anything you care to name resembles anything else you care to name in some way or other. There is *some* resemblance, after all, between white and black, hard and soft, and other things which we regard as complete opposites. The things we said earlier had different functions and were not like one another – the parts of the face – do still resemble one another, and the one is like the other, in some way or other. Using this method of argument you could prove, if you wanted, that all of them are like one another as well. But it is not right to call things which have some similarity similar, if the similarity is very small, any more than to call things which have some dissimilarity dissimilar.'

I found this surprising. 'Is that really how the just and the holy are related, in your view?' I asked. 'Is there just some small similarity between them?'

'No, not exactly' he said. 'But then again, not exactly the way you seem to think it is either.'

'Well,' I said, 'you don't seem very happy with this approach, so let's forget about that and look at something else you said. Is there something you call folly?'[53]

He said there was.

'Isn't it something whose complete opposite is wisdom?'

'Yes, I think so,' he said.

'And when people act in a way which is correct and to their advantage, do you then regard them as being prudent in acting like this, or the opposite?'

'Being prudent,' he said.

'And is it by means of prudence that they are prudent?'

'Necessarily.'

'And those who do not act correctly act foolishly, and are not prudent when they act like this?'

'I agree,' he said.

'In which case, is acting foolishly the opposite of acting prudently?'

He said it was.

---

[52] In the distinctions he draws in the rest of this discussion of justice and holiness Protagoras demonstrates considerable dexterity and acuteness, and may well have the better of the argument.

[53] 'Folly' translates *aphrosunê*, with the prefix a- privative: so 'mind*less*ness', '*un*wisdom'. As its morphology indicates, the word can serves as an antonym to *sôphrosunê* ('*sound*mindedness', 'prudence') as well as to *sophia*, 'wisdom'. And so *mutatis mutandis* with the adverbs *aphronôs*, 'foolishly', and *sôphronôs*, 'prudently'.

'And are things which are done foolishly done with folly, and things which are done prudently done with prudence?'

He agreed.

'And if something is done with strength, is it done strongly, and if with weakness, weakly?'

He thought so.

'And if with swiftness, then swiftly; and if with slowness, then slowly?'

He said yes.

c 'In fact, if something is done in the same way, is it done by means of the same thing, and if in the opposite way, then by means of the opposite thing?'

He agreed.

'Well now,' I said, 'is there such a thing as being beautiful?'

He agreed there was.

'Does it have any opposite apart from the ugly?'

'No, it does not.'

'How about being good? Is there such a thing as that?'

'Yes, there is.'

'Does it have any opposite apart from the bad?'

'No, it does not.'

'What about high pitch – of sounds?'

He said yes.

'There's surely no opposite to that apart from low pitch?'

He said there was not.

'So for each one of the opposites,' I said, 'is there just one opposite, and not a number of them?'

He agreed with this.

d 'Come on then,' I said, 'let's take stock of what has been agreed between us. We've agreed that one thing has just one opposite, and no more.'

'We have.'

'And that what is done in opposite ways is done by means of opposites?'

He said yes.

'Have we agreed that what is done foolishly is done in the opposite way to what is done prudently?'

He said we had.

'And that what is done prudently is done with prudence, and what is done foolishly is done with folly?'

He agreed.

'And if done in the opposite way, then it would be done with its e opposite?'

'Yes.'

'And one is done with prudence, the other with folly?'

'Yes.'

'In an opposite way?'

'Absolutely.'

'With things that are opposite, then?'

'Yes.'

'In which case, is folly the opposite of prudence?'

'Apparently.'

'And do you remember it being agreed between us, earlier on, that folly was the opposite to wisdom?'

He agreed it had been.

'And that one thing can have only one opposite?'

'Yes.'

'Which of our claims, in that case, Protagoras, are we to give up? The 333 claim that one thing can have only one opposite, or the one in which it was said that wisdom was something different from prudence, that each was a part of human goodness, and that in addition to being different they are unlike both in themselves and in their functions, like the parts of the face? Which are we to give up? These two claims seem somewhat discordant. They are not in tune, not in harmony with one another. How could they be in tune, if one thing must necessarily have only one opposite and no more, b and then again if folly, which is one thing, seems to have wisdom and prudence as its opposites? Is that the position, Protagoras?' I asked, 'Or what?'

He agreed, very reluctantly, that it was.

'In which case, would prudence and wisdom be one single thing, just as a little while ago it became clear to us that justice and holiness were pretty much the same thing?

'Come on, Protagoras,' I said, 'we mustn't weaken. Let's carry out the rest of our enquiry. Do you think somebody doing wrong is being c prudent in doing wrong?'

'Well, speaking for myself, I would be embarrassed to agree to that, Socrates,' he said, 'though a large part of mankind does say it.'

'In which case, shall I address the argument to them,' I asked, 'or to you?'

'If it is all the same to you,' he said, 'why not have a discussion of the majority view first?'

'Well, I don't mind which. I just want you to give me the answers – whether you agree with them or not. All I really want is to test the argument, though it can happen that both I who ask the questions and the person answering them are tested as well.'

d   Well, to start with Protagoras went all bashful on us, saying the discussion was not to his taste. But then he did agree to answer. 'Come on, then,' I said, 'answer my questions from the beginning. Do you think some people are being prudent in acting unjustly?'

'Let us say they are.'

'And by being prudent, do you mean being sensible?'

He said he did.

'And by being sensible do you mean planning their unjust action well?'

'Let us say so.'

'Is that if their unjust action turns out well,' I asked, 'or if it turns out badly?'

'If it turns out well.'

'And do you say some things are good?'

'I do.'

'And are good things,' I asked, 'the ones which are beneficial to people?'

e   'Yes, dammit,' he said. 'Though even if they are not beneficial to people, I personally may still call them good.'

I got the impression Protagoras had taken offence, that he was taking up the cudgels, ready to do battle with his answers. Seeing his reaction, I started picking my words with care, and asked him gently: 'Protagoras,

334   do you mean things which are not beneficial to any human being, or things which are not beneficial at all? Are those the kinds of things you are calling good?'

'Not at all,' he said. 'Speaking for myself, I know plenty of things which are harmful to people – food, drink, drugs, any number of things – and plenty which are beneficial. And then there are things which are neither, as far as humans are concerned, but which are beneficial for horses. Or only for cattle, or dogs. And things which are not beneficial for any of these, though they are for trees. Or good for the roots of trees, but harm-

b   ful for the young shoots – manure, for example, which is a good thing for all growing plants if spread on the roots, but disastrous if you took it into your head to put it on the shoots and new branches. Then there is olive oil, which is extremely bad for all plants, and has a very harmful effect on the hair of all living creatures apart from man, though for human hair it can be a help, and for the rest of the body. So varied and diverse a thing is the good that in this example it can be good for the human body applied externally, and yet the same thing can be extremely bad taken internally. c That is why all doctors forbid those who are ill to use olive oil, apart from a very small quantity in the things they are going to eat – just enough to counteract their distaste for the smell of food and cooking.'

Well, the people there thought this was a fine speech, and when he had finished speaking they burst into applause. 'Protagoras,' I said, 'I really have a terrible memory. I find if somebody makes a long speech, I forget what it is that's being talked about. Now, if my failing were deafness, d you'd realise you had to speak louder than usual if you were going to have a conversation with me. In just the same way now, since you're stuck with someone who can't remember, please cut down your answers and make them shorter, if you want me to follow you.'[54]

'What do you mean, give short answers? Am I to give shorter answers,' he asked, 'than are needed?'

'Of course not.'

'As long as are needed, then?'   e

'Yes,' I said.

'As long as I think are needed? Is that how long my answers should be? Or as long as you think?'

'Well,' I said, 'I've heard that you have the ability yourself, and can teach others, either to speak at length on a given subject, if you choose, without ever running dry, or again to speak with such brevity that nobody 335 can be briefer than you. If you're going to have a conversation with me, you'll have to use the second method – speaking briefly.'

'Socrates,' he said, 'I have had a number of opponents in argument, in my time. If I did what you are telling me to do – conducted the discussion in the way my opponent told me to conduct it – I would not be perceived as any better than anyone else, and Protagoras would not have become a name in the Greek world.'

I realised he was dissatisfied with the answers he'd been giving, and that left to himself he wouldn't choose to engage in discussion as the one b answering the questions, so I decided my part in the gathering was at an

---

[54] Socrates' characteristic expression of his habitual aversion to long speeches (instead of proper conversation) precipitates a crisis for the discussion, resolved by an entertaining debate on procedure which allows the other leading characters to show their mettle.

end. 'Well, Protagoras,' I said, 'I have no desire at all for this gathering of ours to continue in a way you don't approve of. When you're willing to discuss in a way I can follow, then I'll engage in discussion with you. You, after all – this is what they say about you, and the claim you make yourself – are capable of conducting a discussion using either long speeches or short speeches. You're clever enough to do that. Whereas I can't cope
c with these long speeches – I wish I could. No, you're the one who can cope with both, so it was up to you to make us some concession, if you wanted there to be a discussion. As it is, you're not prepared to, and I've got things to do and wouldn't have time to hang around while you drag out these long speeches – there's somewhere I have to be – so I'll be off. Though I dare say I'd quite enjoy listening even to the long speeches.'

With these words I got up to go. But as I was getting up Callias seized
d my hand with his right hand, and grasped this cloak I'm wearing with his left, and said: 'We're not going to let you go, Socrates. Our discussion won't be the same without you. Stay, I beg you. Personally, I can't think of anything I'd rather listen to than a discussion between you and Protagoras. Please – as a favour to all of us.'

And I said – standing up now, ready to go – 'Son of Hipponicus, I've always been impressed by your passion for wisdom, and now in particular I'm full of approval and admiration. I really would like to do you a favour,
e if what you're asking were within my power. As it is, it's like asking me to keep up with the sprinter Criso of Himera in his prime, or take on one of the long-distance runners or all-day runners, and keep up with them. I'd
336 say to you: "I'm every bit as keen as you are that I should run with them, but I simply can't. No, if you have some desire to see Criso[55] and me running in the same race, you must ask him to make some allowance for me. I can't run fast, but he can run slowly." And if you're keen to listen to Protagoras and me, you must ask him now to go on giving me answers like the ones he gave me at the beginning – short, and answering the question.
b Otherwise what kind of discussion can we have? It's always been *my* view that spending time together in discussion and making a public speech were two different things.'

---

[55] Criso was a sprinter, victorious in three successive Olympics in the 440s BC. The most famous all-day runner was Phidippides, the courier who in 490 ran all the way from Athens to Sparta, arriving the day after he set out, on a mission to raise reinforcements for the battle against the Persians which was to take place at Marathon.

174

'But can't you see, Socrates, Protagoras' claim to be allowed to discuss things in the way he wants seems perfectly legitimate – just as yours to discuss them in the way you want.'

That's where Alcibiades interrupted: 'No, you're wrong, Callias. Socrates here admits he has no gift for long speeches. He agrees Protagoras has the better of him there. But when it comes to discussing, c and understanding how to present an argument or have one presented to him, I'd be surprised if anyone in the world has the better of him. So if Protagoras in his turn admits that he is inferior to Socrates at discussion, that's all Socrates wants. If he is challenging Socrates, let him take part in the discussion by asking and answering questions, instead of drawing out a long speech in reply to every question, keeping the argument at arm's length, refusing to explain himself, and just rambling on until most of the people listening have forgotten what the question d was about. Though Socrates won't forget, I'll lay money on it, for all his jokes about his memory. Anyway, if you want my opinion, Socrates has the better case. It's up to each of us, after all, to make it clear what he thinks.'

The next person to speak after Alcibiades, if I remember rightly, was Critias. 'How do you feel, Prodicus and Hippias? Callias seems to me to be firmly on Protagoras' side, and Alcibiades is being his usual com- e bative self. But for us there's no need to take sides, either with Socrates or Protagoras. What we should be doing is getting together to ask both of them not to break off the meeting half-way through.'

Hearing this, Prodicus said: 'I think you are right, Critias. People 337 who are present at a discussion of this kind should listen to both the two speakers alike – though not equally, which is not the same thing – they should listen to both alike, not giving equal weight to each, but rather giving more weight to the wiser and less to to the less wise. My own personal view, Protagoras and Socrates, is that you should jointly resolve to dis- agree with one another, but not to quarrel – disagreeing is what friends b do, on good terms, whereas a quarrel is between enemies, people who are at odds with one another. That would give us the best kind of meeting. You speakers can win approval from us, your audience – approval, not praise, since approval exists, free from deception, in the souls of those who hear, whereas praise is often a matter of lying words, contrary to the true opinion of those who utter them – while we, the audience, would c in our turn gain the greatest satisfaction – though not pleasure, since satisfaction comes from learning something, using the mind alone to take part in intellectual activity, whereas pleasure comes from eating or some other pleasurable bodily experience.'

These remarks of Prodicus found favour with most of the audience. And Prodicus was followed by Hippias the wise: 'Gentlemen here present,' he said, 'I count you all kinsmen, friends and fellow-citizens – by

d nature, though not by convention. In nature like is akin to like, whereas convention, lording it over mankind, imposes many things forcibly in defiance of nature.[56] We who know the nature of things, and are the wisest of the Greeks, which is precisely why we have assembled here in Athens, Greece's holy of holies for wisdom, in this, the greatest and most flourishing house in that city – we should be ashamed of ourselves if we can-

e not put on a display worthy of this reputation, but start squabbling like a bunch of nobodies. So I make a personal appeal to you, Protagoras and Socrates. I advise you to come to an agreement, find some middle ground. Regard us as arbitrators bringing you together. Socrates, there

338 is no need for you to be too set on this very precise form of argument, with its insistence on brevity, if Protagoras finds it distasteful. Make some concessions, give the argument its head. That way it will be more impressive and more attractive to us. Then again Protagoras, no piling on all sail and running before the wind, disappearing out of sight of land on a sea of words. Strike a middle course, both of you. That is what you must do, and – take my advice – choose a referee, a chairman, a president, who can

b check that the length of speeches on either side is reasonable.'

The people present thought this was a good idea, and they all applauded. Callias said he wouldn't allow me to go, and they asked me to choose a president. I said I thought choosing an umpire for our discussion was insulting. If the person chosen was our inferior, then it wouldn't be right for an inferior to be presiding over his betters, and if he was our equal, then that wouldn't be right either. An equal would do as we did, so it would be

c pointless choosing him. Choose someone better than us, then? Truth to tell, it's impossible, in my view, for you to choose anyone wiser than Protagoras here. And if you choose someone who is no better, and claim he is better, that too is an insult to Protagoras – this is not a nonentity you are choosing someone to preside over. For my part, it's neither here nor there.

---

[56] Hippias here appropriates a famous phrase of the poet Pindar: '*Nomos*, king of all the mortals and immortals', quoted by Plato's Callicles at *Gorgias* 484b. By *nomos* Pindar probably meant 'law' rather than 'convention', and Hippias substitutes 'tyrant' for 'king', hence our translation '*lording it over* mankind'.

'What I am prepared to do, so that the thing you want – this meeting and discussion – can take place, is this. If Protagoras doesn't want to be the one answering the questions, let him be the one asking them, and I will answer. While I'm at it I can try and show him how I maintain the d person answering should answer. When I've answered any questions he wants to ask, let him in his turn give an account of himself in the same way. Then if he doesn't seem too keen on answering what is actually being asked, you and I will join forces to ask him, as you asked me, not to spoil our meeting. We won't need one president for this, since you will all be e joint presidents.'

Everybody thought that was what we should do. Protagoras was opposed to the idea, but he was compelled to say he would be the questioner, and when he had had enough of asking questions, give an account of himself in his turn, answering briefly.

He began his questions something like this: 'It is my belief, Socrates, that for a man the most important part of his education is a knowledge of poetry – that is to say, being able to understand which among the things 339 said by the poets are well written and which are not, knowing how to distinguish between them, and accounting for one's view when questioned.[57] In this particular case, my question is going to be about the same thing you and I are now discussing – namely, human goodness – the only difference being that it is translated into the realm of poetry. Addressing Scopas, the son of Creon the Thessalian, Simonides says, if I am not mistaken:

> Truly becoming good is hard for a man,   b
> Standing four-square with hands and feet and mind,
> Fashioned beyond reproach.

Are you familiar with the poem, or would you like me to go through the whole thing with you?'

And I said: 'No, there's no need for that. I am familiar with it. In fact, I've made something of a study of the poem.'

'Good,' he said. 'And do you think it is a fine poem – well written – or not?'

'A very fine poem,' I said. 'Very well written.'

'Do you think it is a fine poem if the poet contradicts himself?'

'No,' I said, 'I don't.'

---

[57] Poetic criticism was another speciality of the sophists' teaching. Protagoras himself famously took Homer to task for using the imperative in the first line of the *Iliad* ('Sing, goddess'), as the mood appropriate to instruction, not prayer (see Aristotle, *Poetics* 19.1456b15–18).

'Well then,' he said, 'take a closer look at it.'

c 'I've studied it all I need, thank you very much.'

'Are you aware, then,' he asked, 'that a bit later in the poem he says:

> It strikes a wrong note,
> That saying of Pittacus – though wise the man
> Who spoke it – "Being good," he said, "is hard."

You realise it is the same person talking here as in the earlier passage?'

'Yes, I'm aware of that,' I said.

'And in your view,' he said, does this second passage agree with the first?'

'Yes, I think so' – though as I said it I rather feared he might have a point. 'Don't you think so too,' I asked.

d 'How could I think he is being consistent when he says both these things? First he himself lays it down that truly it is hard for a man to become good, but then a little further on in the poem he has forgotten he said it, and criticises Pittacus for saying exactly the same thing *he* said – that it is difficult to be good.[58] He refuses to accept it, though Pittacus is saying exactly the same as he said. But in criticising the person who says exactly the same thing he says, he is clearly criticising himself as well. So either the first thing he says or the second is incorrect.'

This brought a buzz of approval from many of those present. As for me,

e for a moment it was like being hit by a top-class boxer. Things went black, and I was reeling from the effects of his words and everybody applauding. I turned to Prodicus – playing for time, to be honest, so I could think about what the poet meant – and appealed to him: 'Prodicus,' I said, 'Wasn't Simonides a fellow-countryman of yours? You're the right person to come

340 to the man's assistance, which is why I have now decided to call upon you. Homer describes Scamander, beset by Achilles, calling upon Simois:

> Let two of us, dear brother, stay the man.[59]

---

[58] This passage constitutes the only surviving evidence for Simonides' poem. Its original meaning has been much debated. Many scholars subscribe to the view that in criticising Pittacus, the poet does not so much contradict what he himself asserts about human goodness in his opening lines, as begin upon the task of showing why nonetheless the ideal it articulates is inappropriate to the human condition. A partial reconstruction of the poem, based on the extracts Socrates quotes, is presented in the appendix; Denyer's edition (*Plato: Protagoras*, p.142) advocates an alternative reorganisation.

[59] Socrates quotes from *Iliad* 21.308–9, a book largely devoted to Achilles' struggle against the river Scamander.

In the same way I too call upon you. We don't want Protagoras utterly demolishing our Simonides. To justify Simonides, we need that art of yours which enables you to distinguish wanting and desiring as two diff- b erent things, and all those other fine things you said just now. Now, see if you agree with me, since I don't think Simonides *is* contradicting himself. I want you, Prodicus, to reveal your opinion first. Do you think becoming and being are the same thing, or are they different?'

'Different, of course,' said Prodicus.

'In which case,' I said, 'didn't Simonides reveal his real opinion in the first passage, when he said truly it was hard for a man to become good?'

'Yes, you're right,' said Prodicus. c

'And he criticises Pittacus,' I said, 'not, as Protagoras imagines, for saying the same thing he said himself, but for something else. That wasn't what Pittacus said – that it was hard to *become* good. He said it was hard to *be* good. They're not at all the same thing, Protagoras, being and becoming, as Prodicus here will tell you.[60] But if being is not the same thing as becoming, then Simonides is not contradicting himself. Maybe Prodicus here, and many others, might say with Hesiod that to become good is hard, since: d

> The gods demand we climb by sweat alone
> The path to goodness; then, the summit reached,
> The prize so hardly won, is held with ease.'[61]

Well, Prodicus congratulated me on my explanation. But Protagoras said: 'Socrates, the error in your justification is worse than the error you are trying to justify.'

And I said: 'I don't seem to have done very well, in that case, Protagoras. I'd be a bit of a joke as a doctor – my cure is worse than the disease.' e

'Well, it is true,' he said.

'Please explain,' I said.

'It would be complete idiocy on the part of the poet,' he said, 'to say the possession of goodness is a simple matter when the rest of the world thinks it is the hardest thing of all.'

And I said: 'My goodness, it's a bit of luck having Prodicus here as a party to our discussion. I'm inclined to think, Protagoras, that Prodicus'

[60] Socrates' ingenious attempt to find a significant difference between 'being' and 'becoming' in Simonides' verses is only the first instalment in a tour de force of misinterpretation that outdoes the sophists at their own game: Socrates' own 'exhibition' piece. In Simonides' Greek the words are used without emphasis, as in effect synonyms.
[61] This passage of Hesiod (from *Works and Days* 289–92) evidently appealed greatly to Plato. He cites it again at *Rep.* 2.364c and *Laws* 4.718e.

341 branch of knowledge has long been divinely inspired, going back to Simonides or even further. For all the other knowledge you have acquired, you seem to have no acquaintance with it. I have picked up a bit, because I'm a student of Prodicus here. And in this instance I don't think you've realised that maybe Simonides does not understand by this word "hard" what you understand by it. It's like the word "terrible". Prodicus here is for ever telling me off if I praise you or anybody else by saying: "Protagoras

b is a terribly clever man". "Aren't you ashamed," he asks, "to call things which are good terrible?" What is terrible, he says, is bad. At least, nobody ever talks about terrible riches, or terrible peace, or terrible good health. They talk about terrible illness, terrible war, or terrible poverty, clearly thinking that what is terrible is bad. Well, maybe the Ceans and Simonides take "hard" likewise to mean bad, or some other meaning you don't know about.[62] Let's ask Prodicus. He's the right person to ask about Simonides'

c dialect. What did Simonides mean by "hard", Prodicus?'

'Bad,' he said.

'Which would be why, Prodicus,' I said, 'he criticises Pittacus for saying it is hard to be good. It's as if he had heard him saying it was bad to be good.'

'Of course that is what Simonides means, Socrates,' he said. 'He is criticising Pittacus for not being able to distinguish the meanings of words properly. How could he, coming from Lesbos? Greek was not even his first language.'[63]

'Do you hear that, Protagoras,' I asked, 'what Prodicus here is saying?

d Do you have any answer to it?'

And Protagoras said: 'You are a long way wide of the mark, Prodicus. I am quite sure that by "hard" Simonides meant what the rest of us mean – not "bad", but "what is not easy, what takes a lot of trouble to bring about".'

'Yes, I think that's what Simonides means too, Protagoras,' I said, 'as Prodicus here well knows. I think he's joking, and has taken it into his head to test your ability to defend your position. The very next thing

---

[62] The suggestion that people from Ceos (an island in the Cyclades close to the mainland of Attica) such as Simonides and Prodicus used "hard" to mean bad is another piece of Socratic gamesmanship, with which Prodicus is made to connive – presumably because Plato wants to reinforce the impression that sophists invariably approached intellectual discussion in a competitive spirit.

[63] The suggestion that Lesbians are provincials who don't speak proper Greek – living far from the mainland, just off what is now the Turkish coast – is a familiar form of racist humour.

Simonides says strongly suggests that he doesn't mean "bad" when he
says "hard". He says:

> Only a god can have this privilege.

If this is what he means – that it is bad to be good – he can't possibly then
go on to say that only god can achieve this, that he awards this as a privilege
to god alone. In that case, Prodicus would be calling Simonides some sort
of criminal, disowning him as a Cean. I'd be happy to tell you what I think
Simonides is getting at in this poem, if you want to try out my ability with
poetry, as you put it. Or if you prefer, I'll listen to your opinion.'

Protagoras listened to this. 'If that is what you want, Socrates,' he said.
Prodicus and Hippias both urged me strongly to do so, as did the others.

'Very well then,' I said, 'here is my view of this poem, which I will
now try to explain to you. In Greece, philosophy in its earliest and
most widespread form is to be found in Crete and Sparta, and there
are more sophists there than anywhere on earth.[64] They don't own up
to it, however; any more than the sophists Protagoras was talking about.
They pretend to be stupid, because they don't want it known that it is
wisdom which makes them supreme among the Greeks. They allow it to
be thought their supremacy rests on fighting and courage, their reasoning being that if it were known what it really rested on – namely wisdom
– then everybody would start working at that. As it is, by keeping quiet
about it they have fooled the admirers of Sparta in the various cities.
Some give themselves cauliflower ears to be like them, bind up their
hands with thongs, do lots of physical training, and go around in short
cloaks, as if these were the things which made the Spartans masters of
Greece.[65] When the Spartans are fed up with consulting their sophists
in secret, and want to consult them openly, they have a wholesale expulsion of foreigners – all those admirers of Sparta and any other foreigners living in their country.[66] Then they consult their sophists without
foreigners knowing about it.

[64] There were apparently close affinities between the relatively closed social and political
systems at Sparta (or Lacedaemon, as it is actually referred to here and usually elsewhere
in Greek texts) and in Cretan cities; Plato frequently speaks of them in the same breath,
above all in his last dialogue, the *Laws*. The suggestion that philosophy flourished in Crete
and Sparta is an elaborate joke. There is no other evidence of philosophical activity there
in the classical period.

[65] A fashion popular with some Athenian aristocrats: see for example Aristophanes, *Birds*
1281; Demosthenes, *Against Conon* 34. See further note on *Gorgias* 515e.

[66] Periodic expulsion of foreigners was a Spartan practice often commented on by Athenians.
It should probably be interpreted as spasmodic xenophobia less calculating than Socrates

'For themselves, they don't allow any of their young men to travel
d abroad – any more than the Cretans do – to make sure they don't unlearn
the things they themselves are teaching them. These are cities where it's
not just men who pride themselves on their education – women do too.
And if you want to be sure I'm telling the truth, that the Spartans have had
the best education in philosophy and in speaking, then talk to a Spartan –
even one who's not up to much – and for most of the discussion you'll find
e he's pretty hopeless, but then suddenly he's like a sharpshooter. At some
point in the conversation he throws in some unforgettable remark, brief
and to the point, making the person he's talking to look like a mere child.

'There are today, and have been in the past, people who have understood this fact – that admiring Sparta has much more to do with love of
wisdom than love of physical exercise. They have realised that the ability
to produce utterances of this kind is the mark of a truly educated person.
343 Thales of Miletus was one of these people, as was Pittacus from Mytilene,
Bias of Priene, our own Solon, Cleobulus of Lindos, and Myson from
Chen. Seventh on the list, we are told, was a Spartan, Chilon.[67] All these
people were admirers, lovers and students of Spartan education. And
their own wisdom was of the same kind, as you can tell from the short,
memorable sayings each of them is known for. It was they who got to-
b gether to offer the first-fruits of their wisdom to Apollo at his temple in
Delphi, inscribing those words which are now household phrases: "Know
thyself" and "Nothing in excess".

'And the point of all this? Well, this was the style of the philosophy
of the ancients – a kind of Laconic brevity.[68] This saying of Pittacus' in
particular, "Being good is hard", circulated privately and met with strong
c approval among the wise. Simonides, who was out to make a name for
himself where wisdom was concerned, realised that if he could put
down this saying – like some famous athlete – and get the better of it, he
would win a reputation for himself among the people of his day. So it was
against this saying, and with this aim, wanting to cut it down to size, that
he composed the whole poem, if you ask me.

'Why don't we all examine the poem together, to see if what I am
saying is true? Take the very beginning of the poem. If all he wanted to

pretends (see Plutarch, *Lycurgus* 27.5).
[67] Socrates' version of the list of seven sages, venerated thinkers and statesmen of the seventh
and sixth centuries BC.
[68] 'Laconic' – whence of course 'laconic' – or 'Spartan': Laconia was the region of the
Peloponnese in which Sparta was situated.

say was that it was hard for a man to become good, it would be idiotic
to put the emphasis where he does.[69] The emphasis seems to have been d
added for absolutely no reason, unless you take Simonides to be quarrelling with what Pittacus said – Pittacus saying "Being good is hard",
and Simonides disagreeing, and saying "No, but to *become* good is hard
for a man, Pittacus, truly" – not "truly good", that's not what the word
"truly" applies to, as if some people were truly good, while others were e
good but not truly good. That would obviously be silly, and not something Simonides would say. We have to regard "truly" in the verse as
hyperbaton, and take Pittacus' saying first, rather as if we imagined
Pittacus actually speaking and Simonides answering him – Pittacus saying "Being good is hard, O mortal men", and then Simonides answering "No, Pittacus, you are wrong. It is not being good, but becoming 344
good, four-square with hands and feet and mind, fashioned beyond
reproach, which is hard for a man, truly." In that way the emphasis
which has been put on "become" clearly makes sense, and the "truly"
is rightly placed at the end.[70] Everything that follows supports this interpretation. The detail of the poem gives proof all through of skilful b
composition – it is a quite charming piece, and thoroughly well crafted
– but it would take too long to go through it in detail. Instead let us
concentrate on its general character and intention, the fact that it is first
and foremost, throughout the poem, a refutation of Pittacus' saying.

'A little further on after this he says, as if he were presenting a formal
argument, that while becoming a good man is truly hard, it is nonetheless
possible, at least for a time. But remaining in this state *after* becoming, and
actually *being* a good man – which is what you are talking about, Pittacus – c
is not humanly possible. Only a god can have this privilege, whereas:

> He cannot but be bad, a man, when once
> Helpless disaster brings him down.

'Now, in commanding a ship, who is brought down by helpless disaster?
Not the ordinary passenger, obviously, since the passenger has been down

---

[69] 'Emphasis' here substitutes for the particle *men* (in ancient Greek, use of particles was
the principal linguistic device for indicating emphasis). This particle standardly flags the
expectation of some kind of contrast between the clause to which it is attached and a balancing clause. So Socrates may well be right to think Simonides signals such a contrast here,
and more specifically with the clause introducing the saying of Pittacus.

[70] In the Greek 'truly' is in fact placed between 'good' and 'becoming'; Socrates' insistence
that grammatically it qualifies the whole clause, and so in effect gets postponed (by hyperbaton, as grammarians still say), thus going most closely with 'difficult' (the last word in
the Greek), is a far-fetched although not totally impossible reading.

all the time. It's like not being able to knock down somebody who is lying down. If they're standing up, you can knock them down and make them lie down, but if they're lying down already you can't. In just the same way helpless disaster might bring down the resouceful person, but not the person who is always helpless. If it's a helmsman, a great storm might fall upon him and render him helpless; for a farmer the onset of bad weather might make him helpless, and it's exactly the same for a doctor. It's the good man who can become bad, according to the testimony of another poet, who says:

> A good man is now bad, now good.

whereas the bad man can't become bad, but must necessarily always be bad. So when helpless disaster brings down the capable, wise and good person, "he cannot but be bad". You say, Pittacus, that "being good is hard", but in fact it is becoming good which is hard – though possible – whereas being good is impossible:

> For any man is good when things go well,
> But bad when they go ill.

345 'When it comes to writing, what counts as going well? What activity makes a man good at writing? Obviously, knowledge of the alphabet. What successful activity makes a good doctor? Obviously, knowledge of how to treat the sick. "But bad when they go ill" – who, then, might become a bad doctor? Obviously the person who in the first place *is* a doctor, and secondly is a good doctor. This person could become a bad doctor, whereas we who have no medical knowledge couldn't possibly, by practising badly, become either doctors or carpenters or anything of the kind. And if you can't become a doctor at all by practising badly, then obviously you can't become a bad doctor either. The same goes for the good man. It could happen that he becomes bad as a result of age, hardship, illness or some other mischance – doing badly only ever amounts to loss of knowledge.[71] The bad man, on the other hand, can't possibly become bad, because he is always bad. For him to become bad, he must first become good. So this part of the poem too is making the point that to be a good man who goes on being good is not possible, though to *become* a good man – or indeed a bad man, this same person – is possible. And "they remain best for the longest time whom the gods love".

---

[71] The introduction of knowledge as what distinguishes the good from the bad person is highly characteristic of the Platonic Socrates. There is no trace of this concern in what Simonides actually wrote.

'So, everything he says is directed against Pittacus, as the part of the poem which follows makes even clearer. He says:

> I will not cast my life's portion away
> In hopeless quest for what can never be –
> A man who's blameless among those who reap
> The broad earth's harvest. Should I find one,
> I'll bring you word.

So strongly, throughout the whole poem, does he challenge Pittacus' d saying:

> All those who do no shameful action willingly
> I praise and love. Against necessity
> Not even gods can fight.

This too is directed at the same saying. Simonides is not such an ignoramus as to say he praises those who do no wrong willingly, as if there were people who do do wrong willingly. For my part, I'm pretty much of the opinion that no wise person thinks anyone in the world goes wrong e willingly, or performs disgraceful or evil actions willingly.[72] They are well aware that all those who do disgraceful and evil things do them involuntarily. In this example Simonides is not saying he praises those who do no wrong willingly. No, he applies this word "willingly" to himself.[73] He thought a fine, upstanding person could often force himself to be a friend to someone, and praise them – the kind of thing which often happens to 346 a man who finds himself completely at odds with his mother or father, or his country, or whatever. When this kind of thing happens to wicked people, they almost seem to enjoy it, making a great parade of their criticisms, and accusing their parents or their country of wickedness, so that they can neglect them without people blaming them or reproaching them for their neglect. And this makes them go further than they need in their criticisms, deliberately adding gratuitous enmities to the enmities b

---

[72] The thesis that nobody who has knowledge goes wrong willingly will be given extended philosophical defence in the long argument beginning at 353c. Initially it will be worked out in terms of success or failure in the hedonistic calculus. But from 358b onwards it will be agreed that when someone gets that wrong they will be doing something shameful or disgraceful.

[73] The Greek technically permits Socrates' reading – indeed without distorting the shape of the sentence. But it is clearly not what Simonides meant to say. Once more Socrates introduces his own characteristic philosophical preoccupations (this time his conviction that error is due only to ignorance), again in anticipation of subsequent argument (here 358b–d in particular).

they can't avoid. Whereas good people practise concealment, forcing their tongues to praise. If they've been wronged by their parents or their country and are angry with them, they calm down and are reconciled, and even force themselves to love and praise their own. I imagine Simonides often thought he himself had sung the praises of a tyrant or somebody like that, not willingly but under compulsion. This is what he is saying to

c Pittacus too: "Speaking for myself, Pittacus, I am not finding fault with you because I like finding fault. Enough, for me:

> A man who is not bad, not wholly useless,
> A sound and healthy man, one who well knows
> Justice, the city's profit, I will not
> Blame him

(having no appetite for blame):

> The tribe of fools is numberless –

anyone who does enjoy finding fault would have his hands full with them.

> All things are fair wherein no foul is mixed."

d He says this not in the sense that everything is white in which no black is mixed – that would be absurd, for a number of reasons – but in the sense that he himself accepts something intermediate, without finding fault with it. "I am not looking," he says, "for a man who is blameless among those who reap the broad earth's harvest – though should I find one, I'll bring you word. No, if that is what I am after, I shall praise no-one. Enough for me if someone is half-way to being good, if he does nothing wicked, since 'all I praise and love'" – and at this point he uses the Mytilenaean

e dialect,[74] to show that it is Pittacus to whom he addresses the words "all willingly I praise and love" ("willingly" has to be taken with "I praise and love") – "who do no shameful action; though there are people I praise

347 and love against my will. In your case, Pittacus, if what you said were even half-way reasonable or true, I would never be finding fault with it. As it is – well, what you say is utterly false, and on matters of the greatest importance, and it passes for true, and that is why I find fault with you."

'That, Prodicus and Protagoras,' I said, 'is what I think Simonides meant when he wrote that poem.'

---

[74] The form of the verb for 'praise' is indeed Aeolic, the dialect of the poets Alcaeus and Sappho, who worked on the island of Lesbos. But it appears also in Hesiod, who lived on the mainland (*Works and Days* 683). The idea that Simonides selects it to flag to Pittacus that he is being addressed at this point is another piece of perverse ingenuity on Socrates' part.

And Hippias said: 'That is very good, Socrates. I think your explanation of the poem is excellent too. And I do actually have an excellent b theory about it myself as well. I could give you all a presentation, if you like.'

'Yes, we would, Hippias,' said Alcibiades. 'Not at this precise moment, though. The right thing now, as Protagoras and Socrates agreed between the two of them, is for Socrates to answer any further questions Protagoras wants to ask, or if he wants to answer Socrates, for Socrates to ask the questions.'

And I said: 'For my part, I'm happy to leave it to Protagoras, whichever he prefers. If he is willing, why don't we forget about songs and epics and go back to the questions I asked you originally, Protagoras – I'd really like c to complete the enquiry with you. Conversations about poetry, if you ask me, are very like the drinking parties of inferior, commonplace people, whose lack of education makes them incapable of entertaining themselves when they spend time together over the wine. They can't make do with their own voices and their own conversation, so they bid up the price of girls who play the pipe, and hire, at great expense, a voice which is not d their own, that of the reed pipe – and that is the voice they rely on in their gatherings. Where the drinkers are gentlemen, and educated, you won't see girls playing the reed pipe, or dancing, or playing the harp. You'll see a group of people who are quite capable of entertaining themselves in their gatherings without any of that childish nonsense, who rely on their own voices, taking turns to speak and listen in an orderly way, no matter how much wine they may drink.[75] It's the same with gatherings like e this. If they're made up of men such as most of us claim to be, they have no need of outside voices, least of all poets. It isn't possible to ask poets questions about the things they say, and when they are brought into the conversation, people for the most part can't agree what they mean, as they're discussing something they can't settle by questioning. The people I'm talking about have no time for gatherings of that kind; they form their 348 own self-sufficient and self-reliant gathering, putting one another to the test in the course of their own arguments. These are the kind of people I think you and I should rather be following. Let's put our poets back on their shelves and make our own conversation with one another, relying

---

[75] These remarks read like a commentary on the passage in the *Symposium* where the girl playing the reed pipe is dismissed and the company left free to entertain each other with speeches (*Symp.* 176e).

on our own resources, putting ourselves and the truth to the test. If you want to go on asking questions, then I'm quite ready to take the stand and provide the answers. Or if you like, you be the one to take the stand, so we can round off the discussion we broke off half-way.'

b   Well, as I was saying this, and a few other things along the same lines, and Protagoras was not making it at all clear what he was going to do, Alcibiades looked at Callias: 'Do you still think, Callias,' he asked, 'that Protagoras is in the right – refusing to make it clear whether he is going to give an account of himself or not. I don't think he is. No, let him either take part in the discussion, or say that he refuses to take part, so that we can know where we stand as far as he's concerned, and so that Socrates can have a discussion with somebody else – or anybody with anybody, if they feel like it.'

c   Protagoras was embarrassed, I thought, by these remarks of Alcibiades, as also by the entreaties of Callias and pretty well everybody else there. He was coaxed back into the discussion, pretty much against his will, telling me to ask my questions, and saying he would answer.

And I said: 'Please don't think, Protagoras, that my aim in discussing with you is anything other than to enquire into things which I myself have always had difficulty with. I think there's a lot in what Homer says:

d   Where two together go, one will be first
                     To see.[76]

It somehow makes all of us, human as we are, better able to cope with any action or speech or thought. But "if it be one alone that sees", the first thing he does is go round looking for someone to show it to and confirm it with, until he does find someone. That's certainly how it is with me – and the reason I'd like to have a discussion with you more than anyone else is because I think you would be the best at investigating the

e   questions a civilised person is likely to want to look into – in particular questions about goodness. Who better, after all? You don't just regard yourself as a fine, upstanding person yourself – plenty of civilised people are that, but yet have no ability to make others civilised – no, you are both a good person yourself and able to make others good. Such confidence do you have in yourself that where others keep quiet about their art, you

349   have had yourself openly proclaimed throughout Greece. You describe yourself as a sophist, you advertise yourself as a teacher of culture and

---

[76] A popular quotation from *Iliad* 10.224 (from the night mission undertaken by Odysseus and Diomedes), also found at *Symposium* 174d.

human goodness, and are the first to feel entitled to charge a fee for this. Wasn't I bound to appeal to you, ask you questions, and make you a partner in the enquiry? Of course I was.

'What I want to do now is go back to the beginning, to the original questions I asked about these things, with you reminding me of some, and jointly enquiring into others.[77] The question, I think, was this: wisdom, prudence, courage, justice, holiness – are these five names for one single thing, or is there, for each of these names, a separate underlying entity or object, each with its own function, and none of them like any of the others? What you said was that they were not names for one single thing, but that each of these names applies to a separate thing, that all these things are parts of human goodness – not as the parts of a piece of gold, which are like one another and like the whole of which they are parts, but as the parts of a face, which are unlike the whole of which they are parts, and unlike one another, having each its own function. Now, if you are still of the same opinion as you were then, please say so. If you have changed your mind, then make the change clear. I'm not going to hold it against you if you now say something different. It wouldn't surprise me if you were testing me out in what you said then.'

'My position, Socrates,' he said, 'is this. These things are all parts of human goodness. Four of them are pretty similar to one another, but courage is something quite different from all the others. Here is how you can be sure I am right: you will find plenty of people who are extremely unjust, unholy, undisciplined and ignorant, who are yet outstandingly courageous.'

'Hang on,' I said. 'It's worth examining what you say. Do you call courageous people daring? Or something else?'

'Yes, daring,' he said. 'Ready to face things which most people are afraid to face.'

'Very well, and do you maintain that human goodness is something admirable? Is it in the belief that it is something admirable that you offer yourself as its teacher?'

'Yes, something very admirable indeed – unless I have taken leave of my senses.'

'And is it partly shameful and partly admirable? Or wholly admirable?'

'Wholly admirable, surely – as admirable as can be.'

---

[77] Socrates refers to the discussion between him and Protagoras at 329c–330b.

350   'Do you know which people are daring when it comes to diving into wells?'[78]

'Yes. Divers.'

'Because they know what they are doing? Or for some other reason?'

'Because they know what they are doing.'

'And which people are daring when they fight on horseback? Horsemen, or people who are not horsemen?'

'Horsemen.'

'And skirmishing? Is it light infantry, or people who are not light infantry?'

'Light infantry. And the same with everything else,' he said, 'if that is what you are after. Those with knowledge are more daring than those who do not know; and more daring themselves after learning something than they were before learning it.'

b   'And have you ever,' I asked, 'seen people without knowledge of all these activities, who were still daring in the way they approached each of them?'

'I have indeed,' he said. 'Only too daring.'

'And are these daring people also courageous?'

'Courage would be something to be ashamed of,' he said, 'if they were. No, these people are mad.'

'And how,' I asked, 'do you describe the courageous? Didn't you say they were the daring?'

'Yes, and I still say it,' he said.

c   'So these ones,' I said, 'the ones who are daring in this way – aren't they clearly mad, not courageous? The others, by contrast – the wisest ones – aren't they also most daring? And if most daring, then also most courageous? On this argument wouldn't wisdom be courage?'

'No, Socrates,' he said. 'Your recollection of the things I said and the answers I gave is at fault. The question I was asked by you was whether the courageous were daring, and I agreed they were. Whether the daring were also courageous – that was a question I was not asked. If you had asked me that question, I would have said "Not all of them". You have
d   nowhere shown that I was wrong to agree to what I did agree to, which was that the courageous are daring. Secondly, you point out that people

---

[78] Jars of wine and oil would be stored in wells during the summer, doubtless to keep them cool (Aristophanes, *Assemblywomen* 1002–4, *Wealth* 810): hence perhaps the need for divers to retrieve them. Thucydides confirms that people became expert at it (4.26.8).

with knowledge are more daring than they were without knowledge and
than other people without knowledge, and on the strength of that you
conclude that courage and wisdom are the same thing. Why not go on,
using this line of argument, to conclude that strength is wisdom? You
could proceed by asking me, first, if the strong are powerful.[79] I would   e
say yes. Next, if those who know how to wrestle are more powerful than
those who do not know how to wrestle, and more powerful themselves
after learning than they were before learning. I would say yes. Once I had
agreed those things, there would be nothing to stop you using this same
method of proof to say that, according to what I had agreed, wisdom was
strength. But I nowhere agree, in this example either, that the powerful
are strong – only that the strong are powerful. Power and strength are
not the same thing, I would say: one of them, power, can come from   351
knowledge, but also from madness or rage, whereas strength comes from
nature and the proper development of the body. And the same, I would
say, in the first example. Daring and courage are not the same thing,
which is how it comes about that the courageous are daring, whereas the
daring are not all courageous. And that is because daring can come from
people's expertise, but also from rage or madness – just like power –   b
while courage comes from nature and the proper development of the
soul.'[80]

'And do some people have a good life and others a bad life, would you
say, Protagoras?'[81]

He said they did.

'And do you think a person would have a good life if he lived in pain
and distress?'

He said they would not.

'How about pleasantly? Suppose he came to the end of his life having
lived it pleasantly, don't you think in doing so he would have had a good
life?'

[79] 'powerful', 'power' here translate *dunatoi, dunamis*, rendered 'able', 'ability' by some trans-
lators. But we need something as easily confused with strength as daring is with courage.
[80] Protagoras again displays impressive logical ability in the powerful objection he develops
against Socrates' argument.
[81] Socrates' apparently anodyne and inconsequential question about the good life introduces the hugely complex argument – the longest sustained single sequence of dialectical questioning in the whole of Plato – which he will pursue until he secures the answer
about knowledge and courage that he wants at 360e. He will use the equation of good with
pleasure as a premise for arguing that knowledge of what is good cannot be overpowered
by pleasure.

'Yes, I do,' he said.

'In which case, living pleasantly is good, and unpleasantly bad.'

c 'Yes, if the things which give him pleasure in his life are admirable,' he said.

'Really, Protagoras? You're surely not accepting the common view, and calling some pleasant things bad and painful things good? What I mean is, in so far as they are pleasant, ignoring any other consequences which may follow from them, aren't they as far as that goes good? And the converse – in just the same way – aren't painful things, in so far as they are painful, bad?'

'Well, Socrates,' he said, 'that is a simple enough question. But I am

d not sure I can give such a simple answer – that pleasant things are all good and painful things all bad. I think a safer answer for me, with a view not just to my answer now but also to the whole of the rest of my life,[82] is to say there are some pleasant things which are not good, and then again some painful things which are not bad, some which are bad, and a third group which is not either of these – things which are neither bad nor good.'

'And do you describe as pleasant,' I asked, 'things which have some

e pleasure in them or which produce pleasure?'

'Exactly,' he said.

'What I'm saying is, in so far as they are pleasant, aren't they good? I'm asking whether pleasure itself is not a good thing.'

'Let us, as you are so fond of saying, Socrates, look into it,' he said. 'If we think the proposition, once investigated, is reasonable, and it is apparent that pleasant and good are the same thing, then we shall accept it. If not, that will be the point at which we shall challenge it.'

'Do you want to lead our enquiry?' I asked. 'Or am I to lead it?'

'You should by rights,' he said, 'since you are the prime mover in the argument.'

352 'Very well,' I said. 'I wonder if we can make things clearer like this. Imagine you were assessing a person's health or one of their bodily functions from their appearance. After looking at their face and what you could see of their arms, you might say: "Now, bare your chest and back, and show them to me, if you'd be so good, so I can make a more

[82] The safety Protagoras presumably has in mind is the need for a travelling sophist who wants to maintain a successful position to avoid being perceived as holding immoral views (recall his stress on the need for caution at 316d, and compare his similar hesitation at 333b–d).

thorough examination." I want to do the same kind of thing in this enquiry. Observing that your position on the good and the pleasant is
as you describe, what I want to ask you is something like this: "Now,
Protagoras, be good enough to lay bare another part of your mind for me. b
What is your position on knowledge? Is that another area where you
share the commonly held view? Or have you a different view? What most
people think about knowledge, roughly speaking, is that it is not something strong, not something which directs or rules. They don't regard
it as anything of that kind at all. They think that while a person may
well have knowledge within him, he is ruled not by knowledge, but by
something else – now anger, now pleasure, now pain, sometimes sexual
appetite, often fear. They regard knowledge simply as some kind of slave, c
dragged this way and that by all the other things. Is that how you too
regard it, or do you regard knowledge as a fine thing, capable of ruling a
person? If someone can tell good from evil, do you think he will never be
overpowered by anything which will make him act differently from the
way knowledge tells him to act? Do you think understanding is all the
help a person needs?" '

'That is what I think, Socrates,' he said. 'What is more, I of all people
should be embarrassed not to maintain that of all things human wisdom d
and knowledge are the most powerful.'[83]

'Well spoken,' I said. 'And truly too. But do you realise the greater part
of humanity does not believe us? They say lots of people know what is
best, but refuse to do it – though they could – and do something else instead. Whenever I've asked anybody just what the reason for this is, they e
say people who act like this do so because they are overcome by pleasure
or pain, or overpowered by one of the things I mentioned just now.'

'People say a lot of things which are incorrect, in my view, Socrates,'
he said.

'Come on then, help me try and persuade people, teach them what this
thing that happens to them really is – this thing they call being overcome
by pleasure, so that in consequence they don't act for the best, despite 353
knowing what the best is. Imagine us saying to them: "Look, you haven't
got it right, you people. What you say is false." They might perhaps ask
us: "All right, then, Protagoras and Socrates, if this thing that happens

[83] Again Protagoras answers in terms of the response appropriate for someone in his position
(i.e. a prominent teacher).

to us is not being overcome by pleasure, what exactly is it? What do you say it is? Tell us." '

'But Socrates, why should we examine the opinion of the majority – people who say the first thing that comes into their heads?'

b   'I think it has some bearing,' I said, 'on our attempt to discover just how courage is related to the other parts of goodness. So if you think we should stick to what we decided just now – that I should lead on in whatever direction I think will best make things clear – then follow. If you don't want to, then I'll call it a day, if you like.'

'No, you are right,' he said. 'Carry on as you have begun.'

c   'To resume, then,' I said, 'suppose they asked us: "All right, what do you say it is, this thing we called being overcome by pleasures?"[84] What I would say to them is this: "Listen, and Protagoras and I will try and tell you. You people say, don't you, that what happens to you in these situations is this – it's generally a question of being overpowered by things like eating, drinking or sex – which are pleasant – realising they are bad, but doing them anyway?" They would agree. So the next thing we'd ask them, you and I, would be: "In what way do you say they are bad? Is it

d   because each of them gives this pleasure – is pleasant – here and now, or because it causes illness at some later time, and brings poverty and all those kinds of things? Or would they still be bad even if they bring none of those things later, if all they do is give enjoyment, simply because in one way or another they do give enjoyment?" Do we think the only answer they could possibly give, Protagoras, is that they are not bad by virtue of the actual pleasure they produce, there and then, but because of

e   the things which come later, disease and so on?'

'My own view,' said Protagoras, 'is that most people would give that answer.'

' "So is it by causing disease that they cause pain, and by causing poverty that they cause pain?" They would say yes, I think.'

Protagoras agreed.

---

[84] 353c In response to this request that Socrates and Protagoras say what they think, Socrates will proceed by extracting *from the majority themselves* concessions – including eventually the equation of pleasure with good and pain with bad (355b) – which leave *them* agreeing that 'being overcome by pleasure' cannot be the right way to describe the phenomenon they have in mind. But this procedure is probably to be understood as Socrates' way of converting them to accepting what he claims himself to be the truth as he sees it. All parties are represented as accepting the truth of the equation by the end of the argument (see note on 358a below).

' "Well then, you people, is it clear to you, as Protagoras and I are saying, that the only reason these things are bad is because they bring us pain in the end, and deprive us of other pleasures?" Would they agree?'   354

We both thought they would.

'Then again, suppose we asked them the opposite question: "You people who also say that painful things are good, don't you mean things like exercise and military service and medical treatment by cautery or surgery or drugs or starvation – that these things are good, but painful?" Would they say yes?'

He agreed they would.

' "And is the reason you call them good because they cause the most   b acute pain and agony here and now, or because the result of them, at some later time, is health, bodily wellbeing, the safety of cities, rule over others, and wealth?" They would say yes, I imagine.'

He agreed they would.

' "Is there any other reason why these things are good, other than that they result in pleasure and the relief or prevention of pain? When you call them good, do you have any other end result you can point to, apart from   c pleasures and pains?" I think they would say no.'

'Yes, I think they would say no, too,' said Protagoras.'

' "And do you pursue pleasure in the belief that it is a good thing, and avoid pain in the belief that it is a bad thing?" '

He agreed they did.

' "In which case, the thing you regard as bad is pain, and the thing you regard as good is pleasure, since even enjoyment itself you say is bad in the situation where it deprives you of pleasures greater than the ones it brings, or where it produces pains greater than its own intrinsic pleasures. If there's some other reason why you call enjoyment itself bad,   d some other end result you can point to, you'd be able to tell us what it is. But you're not going to be able to." '

'No, I don't think they will be able to either,' said Protagoras.

' "Then again, isn't it just the same with the actual feeling of pain? Don't you call the actual feeling of pain good on the occasions when it either frees you from pains greater than its own intrinsic pains, or produces pleasures greater than the pains? If there's some other end result you can point to when you call the actual feeling of pain good, apart from the one I'm talking   e about, you can tell us what it is. But you're not going to be able to." '

'True,' said Protagoras.

' "Suppose then," ' I said, ' "you people were to ask me in my turn why on earth I keep going on about this, and from so many angles. 'Forgive me,' I would say. 'For one thing, it's not easy to demonstrate exactly what this thing you call being overcome by pleasure *is*; but also, it's precisely on this point that all the proofs depend. Though even now it's still open to you to take back what you've said, if you can find any way of identifying the good other than as pleasure, or identifying the bad other than as pain. Or is it enough for you to live your lives pleasantly, without pain? If it is enough, if you can't find any way of identifying good and bad which doesn't come down to this in the end, then hear what follows. If this is how things are, then what I say to you is that it is absurd for you to maintain that a person can often recognise what is bad, see that it *is* bad, and still do it anyway – though he could perfectly well not do it – because he is led on and distracted by pleasures. Or again, you say the person recognises what is good, and refuses to do it because of the pleasures of the moment, being overcome by them.'"

' "The absurdity of all this will become plain if we stop using all these different names – pleasant, painful, good, bad – and since it has become clear that there are two things, let's also call them by two names, good and bad in the first instance, and then after that pleasant and painful.[85] On that basis, we will then say the person recognises what is bad, sees it *is* bad, and yet does it anyway. If someone asks us why, we shall say 'because he was overcome – '? 'By what?' he will ask us. It won't any longer be open to us to say 'by pleasure', now that it has changed its name to the good instead of pleasure. Are we to answer him saying 'the person was overcome' ' – by what?' he will say. 'By the good, as god is our witness,' we shall say. Unless the person questioning us is extremely well brought-up, he'll laugh at us and say: 'What you're talking about is an absurdity, if somebody does what is bad, knowing it is bad, when he could perfectly well not do it, because he is overcome by what is good. Assuming that what is good is not a match for what is bad?' he will ask. 'Or that it is a match?' 'That it is not a match,' will obviously be our reply. 'Otherwise the person who we say succumbed to pleasures wouldn't have gone wrong.' 'What is it,' he will perhaps ask, 'that makes what is good not a match for what is bad, or what is bad for what is good? Isn't it simply where one is larger and the other smaller, or one more and the other less?' We shall have no alternative but to agree. 'In which case it's clear,' he will

---

[85] Does Socrates mean without qualification that the truth of hedonism has become clear? Or that hedonism clearly follows from the theses to which the majority have by now assented?

say, 'that by being overcome you mean taking greater evils in preference to lesser goods.'[86] So much for that."

' "Now, change the names for these same things back to pleasant and painful, and let's say a person does – what we then called bad but now we are to call painful, knowing that it is painful, but overcome by what is pleasant, assuming – obviously – that it is not a match for what is painful. And when we're talking about pleasure in relation to pain, what is 'not being a match for' other than a greater or lesser quantity of one compared with the other? That is to say, being greater and smaller than one another, or more and fewer, or more and less intense. Suppose someone says: 'But there's a great difference, Socrates, between immediate pleasure and pleasure or pain at some later time.' My reply would be: 'Surely not a difference in anything other than pleasure and pain? There's nothing else it can be. It's like being good at weighing things. You put the pleasant things together, and the painful things together, add nearness and distance to the balance as well, and say which is more. If you weigh pleasures against pleasures, you must always take the greater and more numerous. If pains against pains, then the fewer and smaller. And pleasures against pains? Well, if the painful things are outweighed by the pleasant things – whether near by distant or distant by near – then the course of action to be followed is the one with the pleasures. If the pleasures are outweighed by the pains, it should not be followed. Well, you people," I would say, "isn't that how things are?" I don't see how they could object.'

Protagoras agreed too.

' "And that being so, answer me this," I shall say. "Do things the same size appear to you, just looking at them, larger from close up and smaller from a distance, or not?" They will say they do. "And the same with things which are equally thick or equally numerous? And sounds – if they are the same – are they louder from close to, and quieter from further away?" '

'They would say they were.'

' "Now, suppose our wellbeing lay simply in doing and taking things with large dimensions, and avoiding and not doing things with small, what would our lives clearly depend on? The science of measurement, or the power of appearance? Wasn't it appearance that caused us to go astray, leading us a merry dance as we kept taking the same things differently

---

[86] It remains puzzling, of course, what could explain a person's ever doing something described in these terms. Socrates defers his answer until 357c–e – he needs first to introduce the idea of a science of measurement.

and changing our minds in our actions and choices of large and small? Wouldn't the science of measurement, by contrast, have nullified the effect of appearance? By making clear to us what was true, wouldn't it have caused our soul to remain calm and stand by what was true? Wouldn't this have saved our lives?" Would the people agree, when confronted by this argument, that the science of measurement would be our salvation? Or would they say it was something else?'

'No, they would say it was the science of measurement,' he agreed.

'"What about odd and even? Suppose our lives depended on that choice – when it was right to choose more and when less, as we compared one thing with itself or with another, close to or far off. What would our lives depend on then? Wouldn't it be knowledge – some kind of measurement, surely, since that is the science of too much and too little? And since it's the measurement of odd and even, wouldn't it have to be the study of numbers?" Would the people agree with us, or not?'

Protagoras thought they would agree.

'"Well then, you people, since it's become clear to us that our lives in fact depend on a correct choice of pleasure and pain – more and less, greater and smaller, further off and nearer – for a start, isn't this clearly measurement, since it is an examination of their excess or deficiency or equality with one another?"'

'It must be.'

'"And given that it is measurement, it is necessarily a science and a branch of knowledge, I take it."'

'Yes, they will agree with that.'

'"Very well. Now, the question, *what* science and branch of knowledge, is one we can leave for another time. The fact that it *is* knowledge is enough for the proof demanded by your question to Protagoras and me. You asked it, if you remember, when we were agreeing with one another that nothing was more powerful than knowledge, and that in any context it was always the master – of pleasure and all the other things. What you said was that pleasure is often the master even of the person who knows; and when we didn't agree with you, you went on to ask us: 'Protagoras and Socrates, if this thing that happens to people is not being overcome by pleasure, what exactly is it? What do *you* say it is? Tell us.' Now, if at that point we had told you, straight out, that it was ignorance, you would have laughed at us. But if you laugh at us now, you will be laughing at yourselves as well, since you have yourselves agreed it is lack of knowledge that causes people to make wrong choices about pleasures and

pains – good things and bad things, in other words. And not just knowledge, but the knowledge which you have also agreed, earlier on, to be
measurement. And wrong action without knowledge, as you yourselves   e
are no doubt aware, is the result of ignorance. So that is what letting
pleasure get the better of you is – it is ignorance on the grand scale,
and Protagoras here, together with Prodicus and Hippias, says he has
the remedy for it. The trouble with you is you don't think the answer is
ignorance, and so you neither go yourselves, nor send your children, to
the people who teach these things, these sophists here, because you don't
think it is something which can be taught. Instead you count the pennies,
spend nothing on these sophists, with disastrous consequences both for
yourselves and your cities."

'Well, as far as the majority view goes, that's the answer we would have   358
given. And now, Hippias and Prodicus – since I want you to be partners
in the discussion – I want to ask you, with Protagoras, whether you think
what I say is true or false.'[87]

There was exceedingly strong agreement that what had been said was
true.

'In which case,' I said, 'you agree that good is what is pleasant and
bad what is painful. With apologies to Prodicus here and his distinctions between terms – call it pleasant, or enjoyable, or delightful, or
whatever name (and of whatever origin) you care to give things of
this sort, Prodicus – be a good fellow and answer in the spirit of my   b
question.'

Prodicus laughed and said he agreed – as did the others.

'And what about my next question, gentlemen?' I asked. 'Aren't all
actions which are directed towards the end of living painlessly and pleasantly fine? And isn't a fine deed good and beneficial?'[88]

They agreed it was.

'In which case,' I said, 'if good is what is pleasant, then nobody who
either knows or thinks there is something better than what he is doing –
and that it is possible – will then continue to do what he is doing, when   c

[87] The results of the argument with the majority about knowledge and pleasure will now be
exploited in Socrates' final proof that courage must be a form of knowledge. From his next
remark it transpires that his question here means: 'Is the philosophical position I have
been working out – particularly the hedonism fundamental to it – true?' 'Say' therefore
amounts to something close to 'assert'.

[88] Talk of what is 'fine' (*kalon*), or as we might say 'morally admirable', here re-enters the
discussion for the first time since Protagoras insisted on a crucial qualification (now effectively abandoned) at 351c. See note on 345d.

it is possible to do something better. Not getting the better of himself is, quite simply, ignorance, and getting the better of himself is, quite simply, wisdom.'

They all agreed.

'And this ignorance, what do you call that? Isn't it having a false opinion, being mistaken, about things of great importance?'

They all agreed with this as well.

'In that case,' I said, 'surely no-one of his own accord goes anywhere near what is bad or what he thinks is bad? A willingness to go anywhere near what you think is bad in preference to what is good is not in human d nature, it seems. Compelled to choose between two evils, no-one will choose the greater if it is possible to choose the smaller.'

All this was generally agreed.

'Next,' I said, 'is there something you call fear or panic? And do you mean by it what I mean? That's a question for you, Prodicus. What I mean is some sort of expectation of evil, whichever you call it – fear or panic.'

Protagoras and Hippias thought this was fear and panic, while Prodicus e thought it was fear, but not panic.

'Well, it's not important, Prodicus,' I said. 'The point is this. If what has gone before is true, will anybody in the world be prepared to go any-where near what he fears, if he's free to choose what he doesn't fear in-stead? Or is that impossible, given what has been agreed? It has been agreed, after all, that what a person fears, that he thinks is bad; and that nobody of his own accord goes anywhere near it or chooses it.'

359   This too was accepted by everybody.

'On that basis, Prodicus and Hippias,' I said, 'let Protagoras here appear before us to defend the correctness of the first answer he gave. Not the very first answer, when he said there were five parts of human goodness, and that no part was like any other part, but that each had its own specific function. I don't mean that answer, but the one he gave a bit later. What he said later was that four of the parts were pretty similar to b one another, but that one of them, courage, was something quite different from the others, as I would know, he said, from the following proof: "You will find people, Socrates, who are extremely unholy, unjust, undiscip-lined and ignorant, and yet extremely courageous. That tells you courage is very different from the other parts of human goodness." I was quite astonished by that answer at the time – and still more so after I had gone c into it with you – so I asked him whether he would describe courageous people as daring. "Yes. Ready to face things," he said. Do you remember giving that answer, Protagoras?'

He said he did.

'Come then, tell us,' I said, 'what do you say the courageous are ready to face? Not the things cowards are ready to face?'

'No.'

'Something else, then?'

'Yes,' he said.

'Do cowards make for what people feel confident about, while the courageous make for what is to be feared?'[89]

'So it is said, Socrates,' he replied, 'by people in general.'

'True enough,' I said, 'but that's not what I'm asking. I'm asking you. What do *you* say the courageous are ready to face? What is to be feared – d thinking that it is to be feared – or what is not to be feared?'

'It can't be what is to be feared,' he said. 'Your arguments just now have proved that to be impossible.'

'True again,' I said. 'So if that proof was correct, nobody goes anywhere near what he believes is to be feared, since not getting the better of himself was shown to be ignorance.'

He agreed.

'Whereas what people feel confident about – well, everybody makes for that, cowardly and courageous alike.'

'But, Socrates,' he said, 'what cowards make for is the exact opposite e of what the courageous make for. For example, the courageous are willing to go to war, which cowards refuse to do.'

'Going to war being a fine thing?' I asked. 'Or something to be ashamed of?'

'A fine thing,' he said.

'And if fine, then also good, we agreed earlier, since we agreed that all fine actions were good.'

'That is true – and as far as I am concerned, what I have always thought.'[90]

'Quite right too,' I said. 'But which group do you say refuse to go to 360 war, despite its being fine and good?'

'Cowards,' he said.

[89] 'What people feel confident about' is *tharralea*, the same word – applied to prospects they face – as has just been translated as 'daring' (*tharraleoi*) when applied to persons.

[90] Perhaps there is an element of desperation in Protagoras's wish to find in what he is now agreeing to something that he can still represent as a belief he has always held.

'And if fine and good,' I said, 'then also pleasant?'

'That is certainly what has been agreed,' he said.

'And do the cowards act with knowledge when they refuse to go any-where near what is finer and better and pleasanter?'

'If we say yes to that, it is goodbye to what we have agreed so far.'

'What about the courageous person? He makes for what is finer and better and pleasanter, doesn't he?'

'I have to agree,' he said.

b   'As a general rule, then, are the fears felt by the courageous, when they do feel fear, nothing to be ashamed of, and is their daring, when they are daring, also nothing to be ashamed of?'

'Yes, that is true,' he said.

'And if it's nothing to be ashamed of, isn't it fine?'

He agreed.

'And if fine, then also good?'

'Yes.'

'Those who are cowardly, daring or insane, by contrast – do they have fears they should be ashamed of, and a daring they should be ashamed of?'

He agreed.

'And is this daring, which is bad and which they should be ashamed of, the result of anything other than folly and ignorance?'

'No, that is how it is.'

c   'Next question – this thing which makes cowards cowardly, do you call it cowardice or courage?'

'Well, personally, I would call it cowardice,' he said

'And wasn't it made clear that it is their ignorance of what is to be feared which makes them cowardly?'

'Absolutely.'

'In which case, it is this ignorance which makes them cowardly?'

He agreed.

'And has the thing which makes them cowardly been agreed by you to be cowardice?'

He accepted that.

'So would cowardice be ignorance of what is to be feared and what is not to be feared?'

He nodded.

'But surely,' I said, 'courage is the opposite of cowardice.'

He said it was.

'And is wisdom about what is to be feared and what is not to be feared   d
the opposite of ignorance of those things?'

Another nod.

'And ignorance of them is cowardice?'

Pause, then a very reluctant nod.

'In which case, is wisdom about what is to be feared and what is not to
be feared courage, since it is the opposite of ignorance of these things?'

He said nothing. This time he could not even bring himself to nod.

So I said: 'What's up, Protagoras? Aren't you going to say yes or no in
reply to my question?'

'You can finish it yourself,' he said.

'I will,' I said, 'when I've just asked you one more question. Do you   e
still think, as you did at the beginning, that there are some people who are
very ignorant, but very courageous?'

'You are determined not to come off second best, it seems, Socrates.
Determined that I should be the one answering. Very well, I will do you a
favour and say that on what has been agreed I think it is impossible.'

'My only reason for asking all these questions,' I said, 'is because
I want to examine what exactly the position is with regard to human
goodness, and what this thing, goodness, itself is. I'm quite sure that
if that were made clear, the question you and I have been discussing   361
would become completely straightforward. We've spun out this great
long discussion, the two of us – with me saying that goodness is not
something that can be taught, and you saying that it is something that
can be taught. After this latest outcome, I can imagine our discussion
taking on a life of its own, accusing us and laughing at us. What it would
say, if it could speak, is: "Socrates and Protagoras, you are a laughing
stock. One of you starts off by saying that goodness is not something
that can be taught, and is now set on contradicting himself by trying to
demonstrate that all things are knowledge – justice and prudence and   b
courage – in a way which would mean goodness is something which
clearly *can* be taught. If goodness were something other than knowledge, as Protagoras was trying to maintain, then clearly it couldn't be
taught. As it is, if the whole thing is going to turn out to be knowledge –
as you are set on it being, Socrates – then it will be extraordinary if
it cannot be taught. And then you've got Protagoras, who first of all
assumes that it can be taught, and now looks set on maintaining the opposite, that it is clearly pretty well anything *but* knowledge – in which   c
case it could not be taught."

'Speaking for myself, Protagoras, when I see the whole subject in this state of confusion, all topsy-turvy, I feel a strong desire to see it all sorted out. Now that we've finished this investigation, I'd like us to move on to human goodness, find out what it really is, and *then* ask our question about it – whether or not it is something which can be taught. We don't want our old friend Epimetheus to pull the wool over our eyes in our enquiry,

d just as he short-changed us in his distribution of gifts, according to you. In the story, in fact, I had more time for Prometheus than Epimetheus. I take Prometheus as my model, and it is forethought for my entire life which makes me busy myself with all this.[91] If you were interested, as I said originally, I'd very much like to carry out an enquiry into it jointly with you.'

'For my part, Socrates,' said Protagoras, 'I am full of admiration for

e your enthusiasm, and the thoroughness of your arguments. Indeed – regarding myself in general as not a bad sort, the last person to resent another's success – I have actually spoken about you to a number of people, and told them that of all the people I meet, you are the one I have by far the most time for – certainly among people your age. It would be no surprise to me, I declare, if you joined the ranks of men famous for their wisdom. As for today's questions, we will come back to them, when you feel like it, and examine them thoroughly. Now, though, it is time to turn to something else.'

362 'Yes,' I said. 'If you think so, that's certainly what we should do. As for me, it's way past the time I said I had to be somewhere. I only stayed as a favour to the excellent Callias.'

That ended the conversation, and we left.

[91] As noted above (on 320c), Prometheus's name means 'forethought'.

Appendix

Simonides' poem reconstructed

Truly becoming good is hard for a man,
Standing four-square with hands and feet and mind,
Fashioned beyond reproach.
  (*Missing lines*)

It strikes a wrong note,
That saying of Pittacus – though wise the man
Who spoke it – 'Being good,' he said, 'is hard.'
Only a god can have this privilege.
He cannot but be bad, a man, when once
Helpless disaster brings him down.
For any man is good when things go well,
But bad when they go ill.
Best for the longest time are they – whom the gods love.

I will not cast my life's portion away
In hopeless quest for what can never be –
A man who's blameless among those who reap
The broad earth's harvest.
Should I find one,
I'll bring you word.
All those who do no shameful action willingly
I praise and love.
Against necessity not even gods can fight.

(*Missing lines*)
Enough, for me,
A man who is not bad, not wholly useless,
A sound and healthy man, one who well knows
Justice, the city's profit, I will not
Blame him.
The tribe of fools is numberless –
All things are fair wherein no foul is mixed.

Index

Abdera 143
  admirable (*see also* fine) 189, 192
Aeschines of Sphettos xx, 119
Agathon xxiii–xxiv, 2, 120–1, 149, 150
aidôs (respect) 159
Alcibiades xxiii–xxiv, 55–6, 86, 104, 137, 156
  in *Protagoras* 143, 150, 151, 175, 187, 188
agora 7, 117–18
amnesty
  in post-war Athens 129
Amphion 60, 88
Anaxagoras 8, 27, 31
Antiphon 57
Anytus xi
Archelaus viii, 39–40, 41, 52, 53, 111
Archytas 90
Arginusae, battle of xxxiv, 43, 116, 127
argument 161, 172, 183
Aristides 112
aristocracy
  Athenian elite xxv, xxvii, xxix, 150, 165, 181
  in Athenian political system xx, 123
Aristophanes xxiii–xxiv, xxv, 82, 100, 103, 114, 118, 139, 142, 144, 149, 150, 151
arithmetic 13, 154
arithmêtikê (the study of numbers) 13
Artemisium, battle of xxxiii, 124, 125
arts and sciences 8, 8–16, 92–3, 122, 159
Aspasia xix–xxiii, 119
  funeral speech in *Menexenus* 116, 119–36
  teacher of Socrates 119

assembly 14, 55, 83, 155
astronomy 13, 138, 150, 154
Athens, Athenians (*see also* democracy, demos) xi, xii–xiii, xvii, xix–xxii, xxvi–xxvii, xxxiii–xxxv, 1–2, 16, 40–1, 43, 63, 98–104, 116, 120–36, 155–6, 159, 164, 176
  autochthony 116, 121, 121–2, 131
  history 123, 123–31
  political system 122, 122–3
aulos (reed pipe) 154

barbarians, *see* Persia
beauty 30
being and becoming 179
body 29–31, 44, 49, 51, 52, 109–10, 148–9, 162, 191
boulesthai (will) 32
bravery, *see* courage
businessmen 14

Callias xxiii–xxiv, xxv, 137
  in *Protagoras* 145, 150, 153, 174, 176, 204
Callicles vii, xiii, xiv, xv–xvii, xxvii, xxxii, 1, 7, 22, 44, 55–114
Ceos 139, 180
Chaerephon 1–2, 7–9, 22, 55
choice
  and the good xxx–xxxi
  between goods 196–7
  between evils 200
  of lives xxvi, 59–61, 80–1
Cicero 133

Cimon xxxiii, 84, 99, 101, 104
cities
    conditions for existence 159, 163
    foundation 158
    government 155
citizens, citizenship xxvii, xxx, 83–4,
        98–103, 122–3, 155, 159, 160, 164,
        176
civilisation xii
classification of sciences and skills 28–31,
        80, 81, 97
comedy viii, xxiii–xxvi, 144
common opinion (*see also* popular opinion)
        192, 193
community 90
confidence 201
Conon xxxv, 130, 131
consolation and encouragement (*see also*
        funeral oration, Pericles)
    to families of war dead 132–6
convention 57, 64, 176
conventional views 41, 44, 56, 57, 67
conversation (*see also* discussion) 173–7,
        187
conviction 17
cookery 27, 27–31, 81, 103, 107
Corinthian War xx, xxxv, 116
council 14, 43, 117
    chamber 117
courage
    at Sparta 181
    Callicles' view (and Socratic critique)
        xvi, 67, 68, 72, 75, 76–8
    exhortation to children of Athenian war
        dead 132–4
    in *Protagoras* xxviii, xxxi, 166, 189–91,
        194, 200, 203
    of Athenians in battle 120, 124, 125, 126,
        127, 128, 131
cowardice xvi, xxxi, 76–78, 132–3, 162,
        201–3
Crete 181, 182
Critias xxxiv, 138
    in *Protagoras* 151, 175
    on Sparta 138
    perhaps author of *Sisyphus*, 138

daring 189–91, 201, 202
Darius xxxiii, 58, 124
death of Socrates xviii, 3, 60, 92, 107–10
Delian League xxxiii, xxxiv, 60

democracy
    and power xvii
    and rhetoric xix
    as political system 122
    Athenian xxvi–xxviii, xx–xxi, 2, 86,
        117, 122
    in the *Protagoras* xii
demonstration, rhetorical and sophistic
        (*see also* display) viii–ix, x, xvi, 7,
        9, 10, 156
dêmos (popular assembly) viii, xvii
demos, Athenian 55–6, 96–7
Demos, son of Pyrilampes 1, 55,
        97
desire xv–xvi, 41, 67 84, 86, 90, 179
dikaiosunê (justice) 159, 167
dikê (justice) 159
discipline (*see also* moderation, prudence,
        vestraint, self-control)
    restrain 86–7
    self-restraint 127, 162
discoveries 156
discussion (*see also* conversation,
        philosophy, questions) xvi–xvii, 7,
        9, 188, 199
disease 50–2, 53, 95, 194
disgraceful (*see also* fine) 44–6, 49–50,
        201–2
display (*see also* demonstration) 165
dockyards xii–xiii, 18, 38, 98, 103–5,
        104–5
doctor 8, 19, 22–3, 24–7, 29–30, 84, 98–9,
        106, 107, 145, 148–9, 184
Dodds, E.R. xiii, 54, 62, 69
dokein (pleases) 32
drinking parties 13, 187
dunamis (power) 191

education 39, 177, 187
    Athenian 122
    Callicles' 62
    city's responsibility 134, 134–5
    for women 182
    Menexenus's 117
    philosophical 59
    rhetorical 40
    sophistic 104–6, 146–9, 153–5,
        164
Egypt xxxiii, xxxiv, 95, 124, 126
empeiria (skill based on experience) 27
enquiry 189, 192

enslavement
  and Persian empire 124
  by conventional justice 57, 68
  by rhetoric 14
  by self-control 67
  in non-democratic systems 123
  of Greeks 129
epideixis (demonstration, display,
    exhibition) 165
Epimetheus xxvii, 157–8, 204
  etymology 156
equality 57–8, 64, 90, 123, 175, 176
Eryximachus xxiii, 150
Eupolis xxv, 137
Euripides 59, 60, 69, 107, 122
evil, greatest 49–53, 90–4
exhibition piece 179
experience 27, 59, 81, 156
expertise vii, xii, 80, 155

fear 193, 200, 201, 202–3
fine 44–5, 57, 199–203
  and just 47–8, 51
folly 169, 169–71, 202
  foolish 76, 76–8, 89
Four Hundred, regime of xxxiv, 1, 40
frankness 26, 61, 68
freedom
  Athens as champion 123, 125, 126, 128,
    129, 131
  Callicles' view xiv, xv, 61, 68, 103
  Gorgias's view 14
friendship
  admits disagreement, not quarrelling 175
  and community 90
  and philosophy 61–2, 79, 80
  as social bond 159
  based on kinship 129
  Hippias's view 176
  how forfeited 132
  with demos 96–7
  with tyrant 93–4
funeral oration (*see also* consolation
    Pericles) xiii, xix–xxiii, xlii, 117,
    117–19
  celebrates deeds 123–31
  encourages and consoles 131
  three functions 120

geometry 12–13, 30, 89–90, 90, 154
gods 90, 108, 109, 121, 156, 158

good
  absolute or relative 46, 172–3
  ancestry and noble birth 120–1
  and fine 44–6
  and pleasure xv–xvi, 30, 71–81, 88–9,
    192–3, 195–6, 199
  and punishment 48–53
  best as object of science (*see also*
    wellbeing) 30, 81–2, 107
  human 14, 41
  life (*see also* happiness) vii, xviii, 37,
    134, 191
  object of wanting xiii–xiv, 30–6, 38
  Socrates' view 21, 22
  teaching children 161
  truth as 87
  upbringing and education 120
goodness, human (*see also* virtue) xii, xxiii,
    xxvi, 89, 96, 123, 133
  all share 160
  in our mutual interest 163
  in Simonides' poem 177, 177–81
  its nature 161, 203, 204
  parts of xxvii–xxviii, 140–1, 166–7, 189,
    194, 200
  question of teachability 140, 155, 155–6,
    160–1, 164, 203
  question of transmissibility by fathers to
    sons 156, 161–4
  teaching of 161–3, 164
Gorgias viii, xxxi, 2
  contribution and treatment in *Gorgias*
    7–27, 56, 61, 75, 80, 81, 87, 88, 91,
    103, 113
  view of rhetoric xiii, 18
  use of proportionality 30
  writings and profession x–xi, 118
gratification (*see also* sycophancy) xiii, 27
Great King (*see also* King's Peace, Persia)
    xxi, xxxiv–xxxv, 39, 111, 116, 126,
    128, 130, 131
Greek
  Lesbian dialect 180, 186
  teachers 164

Hades xxv, 69, 108–12
Handel, G.F. 162
happiness xv–xvi, 37, 38–40, 41–3, 51–3,
    67–71, 89–90, 90, 113, 133
harbours xii, 18, 19, 38, 104
harmony 162, 171

health 34, 35, 36, 72, 85
hedonism
  in *Gorgias* xvi, xli, 71–81, 75, 76, 80
  in *Protagoras* xliii, xxix, 141, 185, 192,
    194, 196, 199
Hesiod 34, 152, 156, 158, 179, 186
Hippias 138
  in *Protagoras* ix, xxiii, xxv, xxx,
    149, 150, 153, 154, 165, 175, 176,
    187, 199, 200
Hippocrates of Cos 145
Hippocrates, son of Apollodorus 138
  in *Protagoras* vii–viii, xxiv, xxvii, 140,
    144–54, 165
Hippocratic medical corpus 21, 27
holiness 89, 161, 162, 166–9, 167, 171
Homer ix, 10, 143, 150, 152, 178, 188
  Iliad 60, 109, 112, 177, 178, 188
  Odyssey xxv, 93, 101, 112, 150, 151
hosion (holy) 168
household management 154
human nature
  Protagoras's views 157–60, 172–3,
    191, 200
hunger 70, 74–5, 86

ignorance 185, 198–9, 201, 202–3
indiscipline (*see also* lack of restraint) 86,
  89–90
intellectualism xxix–xxxi, 140
  Socratic paradox that no-one sins
    willingly 93, 140, 185
Ionian revolt xxxiii, 124
Isocrates 2, 28
Italy 69

judgment (*see also* wisdom) 154
jury 14, 16, 107
justice (*see also* wrongdoing)
  administration of 29, 29–30, 50–1
  and courts 16–17
  and happiness 37, 41–2
  and rhetoric 24–6, 91
  Archytas's treatment 91
  as good xiii
  as equality 57–8, 64
  as psychic order 85–6
  as virtue 161, 163, 203
  as virtue part 166–9, 171
  Callicles' view xv, xli, 57–8, 63–7, 68
  common view 64

contract theory 57
cosmic 90
  in *Gorgias* myth of judgment 109–13
  in moral education 161
  in two lives xiii, xviii
  precondition for city life 159–60
  Socrates on committing injustice xviii,
    xvii–xviii, 3, 36–7, 37, 38–55, 56,
    91–4
  terms for 159
  treatment in *Protagoras* xxvii, xxviii

King's Peace (*see also* Great King Persia,
  xix, xxii, xxxv, 131
kingship
  at Athens 122
kithara ix, 82, 119, 146, 162
knack, *see* skill
knowledge xxvii, xxviii–xxxi, 41, 61, 72,
  75, 158
  and courage 190–1, 203
  and Gorgianic rhetoric 17, 22–6
  and moral goodness 133, 184
  and the idea of willing 36
  nourishes the soul 148
  political 158–9
  power of 140, 191, 193, 198
  Prodicus's 180
  of sophists 147, 148
kolakeia (flattery, sycophancy) 28

lack of restraint (*see also* indiscipline)
  68–70
large gatherings 16, 19–20, 22, 83
law 57, 123
  in education 162
  in soul 85
lawcourts 16, 40, 60, 107
lawgivers 162
leaky jars 69–70
Lechaeum, battle of xxii, 131
legislating 29–30
logistikē (study of ratios, arithmetic,
  calculation) 12
'long walls' xii–xiii, xxii, xxxiii, xxxiv–
  xxxv, 19, 129, 130–1
luxury 68
Lysias xx–xxi, 2, 118–19, 122, 132, 133

majority view 171–2, 194
  examined by Socrates 199

man, 'real' 57, 59, 81, 96
'many', the xxvi, xxix–xxx, 43, 57, 63–4, 65
masses 122
Marathon, battle of xiii, xx, xxxiii, 101, 116, 124, 131, 174
means vs end distinction xiv
measurement 197
medicine 11, 27, 29–31, 51, 81
    drugs 33
Melos 63
Menexenus 115, 117
    in *Menexenus* 117–20
Mill, J.S. xxvi
Miltiades xxxiii, 84, 99, 101
moderation (*see also* discipline, prudence, restraint, self-control) 67–70
Musaeus 152
music 154, 162
    teacher 119, 146, 152, 162–3
mystery cults 69, 75, 150, 152
    violations of 137, 138
myth (*see also* story)
    of last judgment (in *Gorgias*) xlii, 90, 109–13
    of water carriers (in *Gorgias*) 69–70
    of origins of civilisation (in *Protagoras*) xii, 140, 156–9

nature
    Callicles' idea xvi, 57–8, 63–5
    focus of science 81
    Hippias's treatment 176
Nemea River, battle of xxxv, 118, 131
Nicias 40
Nietzsche, F. xv, xl, 58
Noble Lie 121
nomos (convention, law) 57, 176
numbers 12–13, 16, 198

ochlos (large gathering, crowd) 18
oligarchy 123
opposites 45, 73, 160, 169–71, 201, 202–3
oratory (*see also* rhetoric)
    contests in xi
    in practice xiii
orators (*see also* politicians) 118–19, 165
order
    in city 159
    in soul 88–9

ordered life 70, 84–5
    world order 90
Orpheus 152
Orphics 109
ostracism 101, 112

pain (*see also* pleasure) 45–6, 74–9, 191, 194–6, 197
Parthenon xxxiv
Pausanias xxiii, xxiv, 151
Peloponnesian War viii, xix, xxi, xxxiv, 104, 116, 117, 165
    war against Greeks 126–8
performance culture x–xi, xxxi
Pericles xii, xvii, xxxi, xxxiv, 19, 41, 84, 99–101, 100, 104, 119, 137
    as orator 165
    funeral speech xix–xxi, xxxiv, 117, 120
    inability to transmit wisdom to sons 156
    final words of funeral speech 136
    offers encouragement and consolation 131, 132
    on the Athenian political system 122
    on the city's responsibilities 135
    words vs deeds contrast 120
Persia (*see also* Great King. King's Peace) xiii, xx, xxi–xxii, xxxiii–xxxv, 58, 116, 124, 128, 129–31
persuasion 14–24, 69
Phaedrus xxiii, 150
Pherecrates 82, 164
Philochorus 131
philosophos (lover of wisdom) 143
philosophy xxiii
    and life (*see also* choice of lives) xiii, xviii, xxvi, xxxii, 3, 59, 62–3
    and Menexenus's education 117
    art of discussion (*see also* discussion) 4, 20–1, 21, 26, 41, 43, 47, 87–8, 88
    at Sparta 181, 181–2
    Callicles' view 59–61, 113
    in *Gorgias* myth of judgment 112
    Socrates' passion 55–6
phronimos (having understanding) 65, 72
phusis (nature) 57
physical fitness 11, 103, 105–6, 146
    expert 14, 20, 25, 29–30, 84, 148, 152, 162
    training 11, 181, 182

piety xxvii
Pindar ix, 58, 63, 176
Piraeus xxi, xxxiii, 19, 95, 130
    as base of democratic party, 403–4
    BC 129
Pittacus ix, 178–9, 180, 182–6
Plataea, battle of xxxiii, 124, 125, 130
Plato
    related to Charmides 150
    related to Critias 138
Platonic writings
    authenticity xix
    dating and development viii, xix, xxii,
        xxiii, xxiv, xxxviii
    form vii
    references to:
        Alcibiades 152
        Apology x, xviii, 43, 132, 133–5,
            137, 139
        Crito xvii, xviii, 54, 65, 132
        Euthydemus 119
        Gorgias vii–viii, x, x–xii, xxiii,
            xxxi–xxxii, xl–xlii, 118, 119,
            129–30, 150, 176
        Hippias Major viii, x, xi, 138
        Hippias Minor 138
        Laches xxiii, 65, 152
        Lysis 115, 120
        Menexenus xiii, xix–xxiii, xxxi, xlii
        Meno ix, xi, xxiii, 14, 105, 139
        Phaedo xix, 115
        Protagoras ix, vii–viii, xi, xii,
            xxiii–xxxi, xlii–v, xliv, 18, 21,
            62, 82, 100, 106, 110
        Republic xi, xix, xxxii, 13, 54, 57,
            121, 179
        Statesman 65
        Symposium xxiii–xxv, 121, 143, 149,
            150, 151, 167, 187, 188
        Theaetetus 59
    tone vii–viii
pleasure (*see also* pain)
    absolute vs relative 46
    and desire 67–8
    and fine 44–5, 48, 202
    and good xvi, xxiii, xxix–xxxi, 30–1,
        70–83, 83, 191–2, 194–6, 199
    and rhetoric xix, 27–8, 97, 107–8
    Aspasia provides 119
    being overcome by 193–4, 194, 196,
        198–9

comparison between 197–8
    defined 192
    measurement 198
    Prodicus on 175
    whatever you please (vs will) xiv, xv, 32,
        32–6, 36, 38
pleonexia (getting as much as you can)
    90
poets, critique of viii, 177
poetry 83, 123, 140, 152, 162, 177–87
    teachers 119
politicians (or orators) xiii–xv, xvii, 5, 13,
    31–5, 43, 52, 59, 83–4, 97
politics xiii–xiv, xviii, xvi–xviii, xix, xxvi,
    xxvii, 5, 98–108
    art of 155
    as science 29–30, 107, 114
Polus vii, 2
    in *Gorgias* xiii–xv, xvii–xviii, xxxi,
        8–9, 10, 25–55, 56–7, 61, 71, 80,
        91, 92, 93, 94, 105, 107, 111, 113
ponêria (bad condition) 49
popular opinion xxvi, xxx, 57, 68
power (*see also* knowledge, rhetoric)
    and Protagoras's teaching, 191
    Callicles' view 63–7, 96–7
    distinguished from strength 191
    Polus's view 32–6, 37–8
    its nature debated xiii–xvi, xli, 4, 32–6,
        92–4
    of appearance 197
    realities xiii–xviii
powers
    of animals 157
Prodicus viii, 139
    Choice of Heracles xi, 165
    in *Protagoras* xxiii, xxiv, xxv, xxx, 149,
        151, 153, 157, 165, 175–6, 178–81,
        186, 199, 200
Prometheus xxvii, 110, 156, 204
    etymology 156, 204
proof 43, 46, 92, 159, 161, 183, 198, 201
Protagoras viii–xii, xxv–xxxi, 139
    educational manifesto 105, 106, 155,
        188
    fees policy 164
    in *Protagoras* 144–204
    man the measure xi, 139
prudence xxvii, xxviii, 159–60, 161, 166,
    169, 203
public works 98, 155

punishment 38, 41, 47–55, 90, 109–13,
140, 160, 161
Pythagoreans 90, 109

questions (*see also* discussion) 165–6,
166, 167

rational explanation 30, 81, 156
ratios 12–13, 31
reed pipe 81–2, 154, 159, 163, 163–4,
187
refutation 183
religion and justice
distinctively human practices 121,
158, 168
resemblance 169
respect 159, 166
restraint 128
rhetoric (*see also* oratory)
as Gorgias's profession 9–31
as science 83–6, 101, 113
Callicles' on Socrates' ineptitude 60
compared with helmsmanship and
engineering 95–6
distinction of Antiphon of Rhamnus
119
distinguished from discussion
174
Gorgianic conception and practice
2, 118
historical development of xxxix–xl,
in Aristophanes 118
in structure of *Gorgias* 4, 80
Platonic view xxiii
poetry as 83
Polus's view 2
power of xii, xiii, 7, 15, 18, 19–20, 24
Socrates as student of 115
Socrates distinguishes from sophistry
x, 30, 105
Socratic critique xvii–xviii, xix, xxxi
Socratic paradox of use and uselessness
49, 53–5, 91
rule
over others 14, 58, 65, 68, 195
over self 67

sages
of early Greece 182
their sayings 182
their wisdom 182

Salamis, battle of 116, 124, 125, 130
Sardis, sack of 124
savages 164
schoolteachers 146, 162
science 12–13, 27–31, 69–81, 97
of measurement 197–8, 199
sculptors 145
servility, and rhetoric xiii, xvii
self-control 88–91, 90, 134
shipbuilding xii
Sicily 69, 90, 103, 125
Sicilian expedition xxi, xxxiv, 40, 116,
127, 128, 137
Simonides 140, 152, 177–86
evidence for his poem 178
reconstruction 205
skill, practise-based 27–31, 28, 81
Solon ix, 18
sôma (body) 69
sophia (wisdom) xxix, xxvi, 58–61, 169
Sophists vii–xii, xxv–xxxi, xxxix
antiquity of art 152
as traders 148
at Sparta 181–2
caution 192
charging of fees viii–ix, xi, xiii, xxix,
xxx, 105–6, 145, 145–6, 189
competitiveness 180
critique of poetry 177
defined x, 30, 104, 105–6, 146–55
display performances 165
etymology of *sophistês* 147
method viii, xxx
self-advertisement by Protagoras 153,
188
sôphrosunê (self-control, restraint,
prudence) 90, 159, 169
soul xviii, 29–31, 49, 53, 69, 109–10,
110–11
care of 51, 81, 84, 148–9
development and education 162, 191
mind, personality 49
need for sincere approval not false
praise 175
order in 85–7, 89
Sparta xix, xxiv, xxi–xxii, xxxiii–xxxv, 100,
125–31, 179, 181–2
story (*see also* myth) 156, 161
sycophancy (*see also* gratification) xix,
xvii, xviii, 4, 5, 27, 28, 28–31, 32,
55, 81, 83–4, 97, 106, 108, 113

teaching 16, 17, 23–4
  Athens as educator of Greece 125
  teachability of virtue xxvii
  vs nature or chance 160
technê (art, science) 8, 18, 27
testing 168, 172, 188
Themistocles xii, xvii, xxxiii, 19, 38, 84,
  99, 101, 104
thirst 71, 86
Thirty Tyrants xx, xxxiv–xxxv, 2, 122,
  129
  oligarchic party at Eleusis 128, 129
Thrasybulus 2
Thucydides xix, xxi, 2, 14, 63, 117, 119,
  122, 126, 127, 128, 132, 133, 135,
  136
tragedy 83
  as civic occasion 135
tribê (knack) 27
truth 40, 41, 42, 42–3, 52, 53, 57, 59, 61,
  61–2, 87, 90, 92, 109, 110, 111,
  159, 182, 183, 186, 188, 194, 199
tyrants xiii–xv, xvii, 32–5, 37, 37–8, 41,
  52, 93–4, 111
  Athenian empire as tyranny xxi, 42–3,
  127

understanding 65–7, 68, 76

virtue (*see also* goodness) x, xi, xv–xvi,
  xxiii, xxvii
  Callicles' view 68
  gender neutral 39
  Gorgias's definition 14, 15
  Gorgias's refusal to teach 24

traditional conception 90
true 114

want, rational (*see also* will) xiii–xiv, 32, 36
wellbeing 29, 197
will xiv–xv, 32, 32–6, 34, 35, 36, 93, 185
wisdom (*see also* sages)
  and courage 190–1
  and goodness 133, 134
  and philosophical discussion 61–2
  anonymous wise persons 61–2, 69, 77–8
  archaic ix
  as getting the better of oneself 200
  as qualification for ruling 123
  Callicles' xvi, 61
  folly its opposite 169–71
  importance 166
  named wise persons: Hippias 176;
    Pericles 144, 156; Pittacus 178;
    Protagoras 143, 144, 176
  of sophists vii, ix, x, xxvi–xxviii, xxix,
    176
  political xii
  Socrates' promise of 204
  Socrates' view attacked 61
  Spartan 181
witnesses 40–1, 43
wretchedness, *see* evil, happiness
wrongdoing (*see also* justice) 171
  and being wronged xvii–xviii

Xenophon xxii, 131, 165
Xerxes 58

Zethus 59, 60, 61, 65, 88

CAMBRIDGE TEXTS IN THE
HISTORY OF POLITICAL THOUGHT

Titles published in the series thus far

Aquinas *Political Writings* (edited by R.W. Dyson)
    978 0 521 37595 5 paperback
Aristotle *The Politics* and *The Constitution of Athens* (edited by Stephen Everson)
    978 0 521 48400 8 paperback
Arnold *Culture and Anarchy and other writings* (edited by Stefan Collini)
    978 0 521 37796 6 paperback
Astell *Political Writings* (edited by Patricia Springborg)
    978 0 521 42845 3 paperback
Augustine *The City of God against the Pagans* (edited by R. W. Dyson)
    978 0 521 46843 5 paperback
Augustine *Political Writings* (edited by E. M. Atkins and R. J. Dodaro)
    978 0 521 44697 6 paperback
Austin *The Province of Jurisprudence Determined* (edited by Wilfrid E. Rumble)
    978 0 521 44756 0 paperback
Bacon *The History of the Reign of King Henry VII* (edited by Brian Vickers)
    978 0 521 58663 4 paperback
Bagehot *The English Constitution* (edited by Paul Smith)
    978 0 521 46942 5 paperback
Bakunin *Statism and Anarchy* (edited by Marshall Shatz)
    978 0 521 36973 2 paperback
Baxter *Holy Commonwealth* (edited by William Lamont)
    978 0 521 40580 5 paperback
Bayle *Political Writings* (edited by Sally L. Jenkinson)
    978 0 521 47677 5 paperback
Beccaria *On Crimes and Punishments and other writings* (edited by Richard Bellamy)
    978 0 521 47982 0 paperback
Bentham *Fragment on Government* (introduction by Ross Harrison)
    978 0 521 35929 0 paperback
Bernstein *The Preconditions of Socialism* (edited by Henry Tudor)
    978 0 521 39808 4 paperback
Bodin *On Sovereignty* (edited by Julian H. Franklin)
    978 0 521 34992 5 paperback
Bolingbroke *Political Writings* (edited by David Armitage)
    978 0 521 58697 9 paperback
Bossuet *Politics Drawn from the Very Words of Holy Scripture* (edited by Patrick Riley)
    978 0 521 36807 0 paperback
The British Idealists (edited by David Boucher)
    978 0 521 45951 8 paperback

Burke *Pre-Revolutionary Writings* (edited by Ian Harris)
    978 0 521 36800 1 paperback
Cavendish *Political Writings* (edited by Susan James)
    978 0 521 63350 5 paperback
Christine De Pizan *The Book of the Body Politic* (edited by Kate Langdon
    Forhan)
    978 0 521 42259 8 paperback
Cicero *On Duties* (edited by M. T. Griffin and E. M. Atkins)
    978 0 521 34835 5 paperback
Cicero *On the Commonwealth* and *On the Laws* (edited by James E. G. Zetzel)
    978 0 521 45959 4 paperback
Comte *Early Political Writings* (edited by H. S. Jones)
    978 0 521 46923 4 paperback
Conciliarism and Papalism (edited by J. H. Burns and Thomas M. Izbicki)
    978 0 521 47674 4 paperback
Constant *Political Writings* (edited by Biancamaria Fontana)
    978 0 521 31632 3 paperback
Dante *Monarchy* (edited by Prue Shaw)
    978 0 521 56781 7 paperback
Diderot *Political Writings* (edited by John Hope Mason and Robert Wokler)
    978 0 521 36911 4 paperback
The Dutch Revolt (edited by Martin van Gelderen)
    978 0 521 39809 1 paperback
Early Greek Political Thought from Homer to the Sophists (edited by Michael
    Gagarin and Paul Woodruff)
    978 0 521 43768 4 paperback
The Early Political Writings of the German Romantics (edited by Frederick
    C. Beiser)
    978 0 521 44951 9 paperback
Emerson *Political Writings* (edited by Kenneth S Sacks)
    978 0 521 71002 2 paperback
The English Levellers (edited by Andrew Sharp)
    978 0 521 62511 1 paperback
Erasmus *The Education of a Christian Prince* (edited by Lisa Jardine)
    978 0 521 58811 9 paperback
Fenelon *Telemachus* (edited by Patrick Riley)
    978 0 521 45662 3 paperback
Ferguson *An Essay on the History of Civil Society* (edited by Fania
    Oz-Salzberger)
    978 0 521 44736 2 paperback
Fichte *Addresses to the German Nation* (edited by Gregory Moore)
    978 0 521 44873 4 paperback
Filmer *Patriarcha and Other Writings* (edited by Johann P. Sommerville)
    978 0 521 39903 6 paperback

Fletcher *Political Works* (edited by John Robertson)

978 0 521 43994 7 paperback

Sir John Fortescue *On the Laws and Governance of England* (edited by Shelley Lockwood)

978 0 521 58996 3 paperback

Fourier *The Theory of the Four Movements* (edited by Gareth Stedman Jones and Ian Patterson)

978 0 521 35693 0 paperback

Franklin *The Autobiography and Other Writings on Politics, Economics, and Virtue* (edited by Alan Houston)

978 0 521 54265 4 paperback

Gramsci *Pre-Prison Writings* (edited by Richard Bellamy)

978 0 521 42307 6 paperback

Guicciardini *Dialogue on the Government of Florence* (edited by Alison Brown)

978 0 521 45623 4 paperback

Hamilton, Madison, and Jay (writing as 'Publius') *The Federalist* with *The Letters* of 'Brutus' (edited by Terence Ball)

978 0 521 00121 2 paperback

Harrington *A Commonwealth of Oceana* and *A System of Politics* (edited by J. G. A. Pocock)

978 0 521 42329 8 paperback

Hegel *Elements of the Philosophy of Right* (edited by Allen W. Wood and H. B. Nisbet)

978 0 521 34888 1 paperback

Hegel *Political Writings* (edited by Laurence Dickey and H. B. Nisbet)

978 0 521 45979 4 paperback

Hess *The Holy History of Mankind and Other Writings* (edited by Shlomo Avineri)

978 0 521 38756 9 paperback

Hobbes *On the Citizen* (edited by Michael Silverthorne and Richard Tuck)

978 0 521 43780 6 paperback

Hobbes *Leviathan* (edited by Richard Tuck)

978 0 521 56797 8 paperback

Hobhouse *Liberalism and Other Writings* (edited by James Meadowcroft)

978 0 521 43726 4 paperback

Hooker *Of the Laws of Ecclesiastical Polity* (edited by A. S. McGrade)

978 0 521 37908 3 paperback

Hume *Political Essays* (edited by Knud Haakonssen)

978 0 521 46639 4 paperback

King James VI and I *Political Writings* (edited by Johann P. Sommerville)

978 0 521 44729 4 paperback

Jefferson *Political Writings* (edited by Joyce Appleby and Terence Ball)

978 0 521 64841 7 paperback

John of Salisbury *Policraticus* (edited by Cary Nederman)

978 0 521 36701 1 paperback

Kant *Political Writings* (edited by H. S. Reiss and H. B. Nisbet)
978 0 521 39837 4 paperback
Knox *On Rebellion* (edited by Roger A. Mason)
978 0 521 39988 3 paperback
Kropotkin *The Conquest of Bread and other writings* (edited by Marshall Shatz)
978 0 521 45990 7 paperback
Lawson *Politica sacra et civilis* (edited by Conal Condren)
978 0 521 54341 5 paperback
Leibniz *Political Writings* (edited by Patrick Riley)
978 0 521 35899 6 paperback
The Levellers (edited by Andrew Sharp)
978 0 521 62511 4 paperback
Locke *Political Essays* (edited by Mark Goldie)
978 0 521 47861 8 paperback
Locke *Two Treatises of Government* (edited by Peter Laslett)
978 0 521 35730 2 paperback
Loyseau *A Treatise of Orders and Plain Dignities* (edited by Howell A. Lloyd)
978 0 521 45624 1 paperback
Luther and Calvin on Secular Authority (edited by Harro Höpfl)
978 0 521 34986 4 paperback
Machiavelli *The Prince* (edited by Quentin Skinner and Russell Price)
978 0 521 34993 2 paperback
de Maistre *Considerations on France* (edited by Isaiah Berlin and Richard Lebrun)
978 0 521 46628 8 paperback
Maitland *State, Trust and Corporation* (edited by David Runciman and Magnus Ryan)
978 0 521 526302 paperback
Malthus *An Essay on the Principle of Population* (edited by Donald Winch)
978 0 521 42972 6 paperback
Marsilius of Padua *Defensor minor* and *De translatione Imperii* (edited by Cary Nederman)
978 0 521 40846 6 paperback
Marsilius of Padua *The Defender of the Peace* (edited and translated by Annabel Brett)
978 0 521 78911 0 paperback
Marx *Early Political Writings* (edited by Joseph O'Malley)
978 0 521 34994 9 paperback
Marx *Later Political Writings* (edited by Terrell Carver)
978 0 521 36739 4 paperback
James Mill *Political Writings* (edited by Terence Ball)
978 0 521 38748 4 paperback
J. S. Mill *On Liberty*, with *The Subjection of Women* and *Chapters on Socialism* (edited by Stefan Collini)
978 0 521 37917 5 paperback

Milton *Political Writings* (edited by Martin Dzelzainis)
978 0 521 34866 9 paperback
Montesquieu *The Spirit of the Laws* (edited by Anne M. Cohler, Basia Carolyn
Miller and Harold Samuel Stone)
978 0 521 36974 9 paperback
More *Utopia* (edited by George M. Logan and Robert M. Adams)
978 0 521 52540 4 paperback
Morris *News from Nowhere* (edited by Krishan Kumar)
978 0 521 42233 8 paperback
Nicholas of Cusa *The Catholic Concordance* (edited by Paul E. Sigmund)
978 0 521 56773 2 paperback
Nietzsche *On the Genealogy of Morality* (edited by Keith Ansell-Pearson)
978 0 521 69163 5 paperback
Paine *Political Writings* (edited by Bruce Kuklick)
978 0 521 66799 9 paperback
Plato *Gorgias, Menexenus, Protagoras* (edited by Malcolm Schofield and Tom
Griffith)
978 0 521 54600 3 paperback
Plato *The Republic* (edited by G. R. F. Ferrari and Tom Griffith)
978 0 521 48443 5 paperback
Plato *Statesman* (edited by Julia Annas and Robin Waterfield)
978 0 521 44778 2 paperback
Price *Political Writings* (edited by D. O. Thomas)
978 0 521 40969 8 paperback
Priestley *Political Writings* (edited by Peter Miller)
978 0 521 42561 2 paperback
Proudhon *What is Property?* (edited by Donald R. Kelley and Bonnie G. Smith)
978 0 521 40556 0 paperback
Pufendorf *On the Duty of Man and Citizen according to Natural Law* (edited by
James Tully)
978 0 521 35980 1 paperback
The Radical Reformation (edited by Michael G. Baylor)
978 0 521 37948 9 paperback
Rousseau *The Discourses and other early political writings* (edited by Victor
Gourevitch)
978 0 521 42445 5 paperback
Rousseau *The Social Contract and other later political writings* (edited by Victor
Gourevitch)
978 0 521 42446 2 paperback
Seneca *Moral and Political Essays* (edited by John Cooper and John Procope)
978 0 521 34818 8 paperback
Sidney *Court Maxims* (edited by Hans W. Blom, Eco Haitsma Mulier and
Ronald Janse)
978 0 521 46736 0 paperback

Sorel *Reflections on Violence* (edited by Jeremy Jennings)
  978 0 521 55910 2 paperback
Spencer *Political Writings* (edited by John Offer)
  978 0 521 43740 0 paperback
Stirner *The Ego and Its Own* (edited by David Leopold)
  978 0 521 45647 0 paperback
Thoreau *Political Writings* (edited by Nancy Rosenblum)
  978 0 521 47675 1 paperback
Tonnies *Community and Civil Society* (edited by Jose Harris and Margaret
  Hollis)
  978 0 521 56782 4 paperback
Utopias of the British Enlightenment (edited by Gregory Claeys)
  978 0 521 45590 9 paperback
Vico *The First New Science* (edited by Leon Pompa)
  978 0 521 38726 2 paperback
Vitoria *Political Writings* (edited by Anthony Pagden and Jeremy Lawrance)
  978 0 521 36714 1 paperback
Voltaire *Political Writings* (edited by David Williams)
  978 0 521 43727 1 paperback
Weber *Political Writings* (edited by Peter Lassman and Ronald Speirs)
  978 0 521 39719 3 paperback
William of Ockham *A Short Discourse on Tyrannical Government* (edited by
  A. S. McGrade and John Kilcullen)
  978 0 521 35803 3 paperback
William of Ockham *A Letter to the Friars Minor and other writings* (edited by
  A. S. McGrade and John Kilcullen)
  978 0 521 35804 0 paperback
Wollstonecraft *A Vindication of the Rights of Men* and *A Vindication of the Rights
  of Woman* (edited by Sylvana Tomaselli)
  978 0 521 43633 5 paperback

CPSIA information can be obtained
at www.ICGtesting.com
Printed in the USA
LVOW03s2110051217
558747LV00013B/254/P